What Makes a Resilient Mind?

Discover the 5-Star Framework
to
Activate your Psychological Immune System.

★

Dom de Lima

Tiny Brain
www.tinybrain.co.uk
ISBN: 978-1-0687851-1-5
First Edition: 2024
Published in The United Kingdom

Disclaimer: The content of this book is based on the author's personal experience and thorough research and is intended for educational purposes only. It should not be construed as a substitute for clinical advice. Readers are encouraged to consult a qualified mental health professional for specific psychological concerns or conditions.

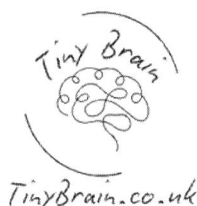

TinyBrain.co.uk

Dedication

To all those who strive for growth and resilience.

Acknowledgments

To my husband,
for standing by me every step of the way.

Foreword

It was in 2021, during a small study on happiness, that I first encountered the concept of the psychological immune system. Inspired by this discovery, I decided to start writing a book that would explore the resilience that lies within all of us. Investigating what makes people thrive—rather than what makes them ill—became a passion that persisted even as my next academic pursuit led me into the field of mental illness, focusing on its psychological and neurobiological roots. But back to 2021—just as the world began to recover from one of the most terrifying, sweeping, and unexpected events in recent history: the COVID-19 pandemic.

As the pandemic unfolded, we were all unprepared for the isolation, losses, and unthinkable challenges that affected every one of us. Whether to a greater or lesser extent, every person on the planet was touched by it. Confined at home with my husband, I, too, was affected by the virus, and to this day, I live with a form of long COVID. While it no longer impairs my daily life, it did for nearly two years. During that time, the world felt heavy, and the future uncertain.

Then one day, as we were driving back from the supermarket, I experienced a shift in perspective. The world was beginning to reopen, and the taste of freedom was palpable. I looked at the train station and saw a wave of people emerging—wearing masks, sanitizing their hands, cautiously navigating a world that was starting to feel familiar again. Nearby, others patiently queued outside a mini-market. In that moment, something clicked. Suddenly, all I could see were people reopening their businesses, some restarting their lives from scratch, others healing from unimaginable losses, and many battling the lingering effects of the virus. These people became superheroes in my eyes. They were bouncing back, often without even realising it—as if resilience was woven into their very nature, as if this is what we are meant to do.

Helen Keller once said, "Although the world is full of suffering, it is also full of the overcoming of it." Writing this book has deepened my appreciation for the innate resourcefulness that exists within all of us. So many people are drawing on these inner resources without even knowing they're there, achieving remarkable outcomes. Imagine what could happen if they knew—if they realised that they already have what it takes to overcome the most unimaginable challenges.

In many ways, the process of writing this book mirrored the very resilience it seeks to highlight. Three years later, this book is finally complete—a testament to the inner strength and resourcefulness we all possess. As you read through its pages, I invite you to see yourself as I'd see you: a person with a deep well of resilience, ready to be fully recognised and harnessed. We all possess this extraordinary capacity—it's just a matter of recognising it and making it a deliberate part of our lives.

Contents

Part 3
Factors that Impact the
Psychological Immune System

Part 4
Strengthening Your
Psychological Immune System

Part 5
Fine Tuning the
Psychological Immune System

Introduction

★

When exploring the academic literature on resilience, you'll find that pinpointing exactly when interest in the concept began varies depending on which researcher you consult. Take Atkinson and co-writers, for example, who trace the roots of interest in resilience back to the early 20th century, citing the remarkable story of polar explorer Ernest Shackleton and his crew during their Antarctic expedition. When their ship became trapped in ice and eventually sank, Shackleton led his men through a two-year ordeal of survival against all odds. Despite the extreme conditions and immense challenges, every member of the crew returned home alive, making Shackleton a lasting symbol of resilience.

While many had overcome great hardships long before, Atkinson highlights Shackleton's achievement because it became celebrated in management training as a powerful example of resilience under extreme, prolonged adversity. What's more, at one point, Shackleton became a role model for psychologists studying resilience. His optimism and unwavering faith were seen as key components of what it meant to be truly resilient.

However, as with many psychological concepts, the understanding of resilience continues to evolve. Some psychologists describe it as a capacity that exists on a continuum, ranging from "less optimal resilience" to "optimal resilience." This perspective aligns with the core message of this book. In the pages ahead, you'll discover that resilience is an ability we all possess, enabling us to overcome life's adversities. This ability stems from a system that defends our minds against both minor and major challenges: the psychological immune system (PIS). It follows that, the better this system functions, the more resilient we feel in the face of life's stresses.

You see, much like our bodies have a biological system to defend us from threats like the flu, our minds have a psychological immune system to protect us from stress, low mood, life's losses, and more. Although, just as our biological defences require regular maintenance to fend off diseases or help us recover when we can't fully avoid them, our psychological immune system also needs consistent care. But here's the thing, prior to writing this book, I asked family members, friends, colleagues, neighbours, just about everyone "What steps do you take to look after your body?" Prompt answers varied, from "Oh, I'm not eating well right now, but I'm going to start a diet soon," to "I stopped smoking." But when I asked, "What steps do you take to look after your mind?" most people were unsure how to respond. Those who did respond were often mindfulness practitioners, offering answers like "I meditate daily."

In today's fast-paced and often overwhelming world, the need to actively care for our minds has never been more critical. As a graduate psychologist with extensive studies in counselling and a Masters degree focused on the neuropsychology of mental health, I've always believed in the importance of taking mental wellbeing seriously, not just as a response to psychological distress, but as a proactive measure to prevent it. My background in these areas has provided me with a deep understanding of the psychological processes that protect and strengthen our minds. This understanding led me to create the 5-Star Framework, a practical approach designed to help you nurture your psychological immune system and build resilience.

The 5-Star Framework centres around "The Daily 5-Star PIS Goal," which serves as a guide to help you proactively care for your mind, or more specifically, the system that protects it: your Psychological Immune System. This Framework encourages you to aim for excellence (your own "5 stars") each and every day.

How is this done? By incorporating simple, small steps into your routine that suit your lifestyle and individuality. These steps are intended to help you build the confidence to take control of your mental wellbeing and steadily move toward the 'optimal resilience' end of the spectrum we discussed earlier.

In the pages to come, you'll discover a wide range of activities, behaviours, and even moments of non-action that can help you boost your psychological defences. While practices like daily meditation are powerful tools, there are many more actions you can take, big and small, that collectively contribute to a greater outcome: a resilient mind. You may be surprised to find that some of these actions are already part of your daily routine. Make no mistake: just as individual stars come together to form a brilliant constellation, these practices collectively strengthen your Psychological Immune System.

The aim of this book is to provide you with the knowledge and motivation to be intentional about caring for your mind. Just as Shackleton navigated the challenges of his voyage with optimism and faith, you too can face life's minor and major adversities with confidence, strength, and resilience. Through practical guidance and actionable steps, this book will help you build the resilience needed to navigate your own journey.

How to read this book?

What Makes a Resilient Mind? has been thoughtfully structured into five parts, each building upon the last to provide a comprehensive understanding of how to activate or strengthen your Psychological Immune System and cultivate resilience.

In Part 1, you'll be introduced to the basics of the PIS, gaining a foundational understanding of its function and importance. Note that you'll first be introduced to the 5-Star Framework in Chapter 3. Part 2 delves into the factors that influence the PIS, highlighting the elements within your control that can enhance your mental defences. In Part 3, we examine the challenges and stressors that can impact the PIS, along with strategies for overcoming them. Part 4 focuses on strengthening the PIS through inner resources and key practices that foster resilience. Lastly, Part 5 dives into the 5-Star Framework itself, explaining the rationale behind it and how to integrate this daily approach into your life for sustained psychological health.

This book is designed to be read in sequence, as each part builds on the insights of the previous one. However, you are free to explore the sections in the order that interests you most. If you're particularly curious about the 5-Star Framework, you can jump straight to Part 5 and then return to Part 1 afterward. The choice is yours.

To get the most out of it, I encourage you to engage actively with the material. Throughout the chapters, you'll find reflection questions, exercises, and daily practices designed to help you apply what you've learned. It'll be helpful to set aside a simple notepad or any other means to jot down your thoughts and answers. This doesn't need to be anything fancy or pricey, just a place to capture your reflections as you go. By the time you reach the end of the book, you'll have a record of your progress, which will be invaluable when we revisit some of the key insights. You'll be able to see just how much you've grown and changed along the way.

Remember, the 5-Star Framework is designed to be flexible and adaptable to your unique needs, lifestyle, and goals. Whether you're an early riser or a night owl, a busy professional or someone with more free time, you can tailor this approach to fit seamlessly into your life. It's all about finding what works best for you. This approach gives you the opportunity to awaken your creativity, enhance your sense of competence, and demonstrate your commitment to your own mind.

Take your time with the content. There's no rush! Allow yourself to absorb and apply the insights gradually. Building resilience is a journey, not a race, and each step forward is a step toward a stronger, more resilient you.

Finally, don't hesitate to revisit sections as needed. Resilience-building is a continuous process, and sometimes the lessons we learn take on new meaning when we revisit them. The more you engage with the material, the deeper your understanding and the greater your progress.

Have a good journey!

Part 1

The Basics of the
Psychological Immune System

Look well into thyself, there is a source of strength which will aways spring up if you will always look. – Marcus Aurelius

Chapter 1

The Psychological Immune System: Protection & Healing

★

Have you ever thought about the need to protect your mind, just as you do your body? What if our mental processes needed healing just like our physical selves? You might wonder, protection and healing from what? The answer is straightforward, life's challenges and hardships.

Right from the moment we arrive in this world, we're up against a myriad of biological challenges. From pesky microorganisms ready to make us ill to potentially deadly threats, our bodies are in a constant battle, despite our defences being naturally limited at first. But it's not just our physical health that's under siege, newborns also navigate a complex neuropsychological landscape. Imagine the struggle to recognise and bond with parents or primary caregivers, a vital emotional connection. And communication? It's mostly limited to crying, whether they're hungry, tired, or just need a comforting hug. Plus, the world itself can be an overwhelming place for a baby. Bright lights, loud noises, and fluctuating temperatures bombard their delicate senses, which aren't fully equipped to filter out these stimuli yet. Indeed, from the very start, the world is a tough place to navigate.

However, time and again, humans have proved to be even tougher. Largely thanks to the mechanisms of our psychological immune system - which from now on we'll call the PIS - we are endowed with an extraordinary ability to naturally regulate distressing emotions and bounce back from negative experiences. This is quite similar to how the biological immune system promotes the recovery of our physical health when confronted with harmful biological entities.

On that note, it's important to recognise that the PIS serves two primary functions: to protect and heal our mental health. Psychologists point to the endurance displayed by the majority of people as evidence for its existence. Typically, individuals encounter impactful life events, yet they continue to function, to experience positive emotions, and even derive personal growth from adversities. Indeed, among those struck by misfortune, only a minority develop psychological disorders or become incapacitated by it. For example, research conducted in the US shows that although approximately 90% of the U.S. population experience a traumatic event in their lifetime, a remarkable 93 out of 100 people overcome these adversities without developing mental disorders such as Post Traumatic Stress Disorder (PTSD). This demonstrates the incredible resilience most individuals possess in the face of trauma. Inspirational stories of those who have endured the most horrific and heartbreaking circumstances are plentiful. Both collectively and individually women and men have made it through distress, loss and grief.

Black communities provide a profound example of enduring and overcoming hardship. Around the world, Black people have faced profound hardships and systemic racism, from the legacies of slavery in the Americas to colonial exploitation and discrimination in Africa, Europe, and beyond. Despite such challenges, they have shown remarkable resilience, notably shaping the cultural, political, and economic landscapes of their societies. The global struggle against racism, including movements like the Civil

Rights Movement in the United States and anti-apartheid efforts in South Africa, exemplify their perseverance and strength.

As for an individual example of psychological strength, consider Lizzie Velasquez. Born with a rare syndrome that prevents her from accumulating body fat and caused blindness in one eye, Lizzie faced severe bullying growing up. Instead of succumbing to victimization, she turned her challenges into a platform for advocacy and inspiration through public speaking and authorship. Her TEDx talk, 'How do you define yourself?' highlights her journey towards self-acceptance and her fight against bullying, making her an impactful example in discussions of resilience.

Beyond resilience

I want to highlight that the functions of the PIS contribute to qualities that go beyond resilience, although resilience undoubtedly serves as one of its fundamental components. Resilience refers to the ability to endure and bounce back from adversities. Consider a time when you faced a significant challenge: you may have emerged in one piece, yet you still feel somewhat dazed by the experience. This demonstrates resilience at work, a key indicator that your PIS is functioning well.

However, the PIS also facilitates true healing, which psychologists consider a step further than resilience. This process, known as *recovery*, involves returning to psychological states akin to those experienced before the negative event occurred. It's helpful to think of resilience and the PIS as part of a two-way process: the more resilient you are, the more robust your PIS becomes, which in turn enhances your capacity for recovery. This is similar to how the biological immune system functions; the healthier you are, the more effectively your immune defences operate, leading to even greater health. Remember, like the biological immune system, the PIS operates based on many interconnected components (which is why true healing occurs), some of these are: resilience, self-aware-ness, self-esteem, self-control, acceptance, and humour.

A full illustration of the PIS in action is the inspiring story of the surfer Bethany Hamilton. Hamilton survived a shark attack during which her left arm was bitten off, yet eventually returned to surfing after her physical recovery. In her wisdom, she confessed to having learnt that "Life is a lot like surfing. When you get caught in the impact zone, you need to get right back up because you never know what's over the next wave." Hamilton's ability to over-come such a life-altering event and regain not just competence, but wisdom and excellence in her sport demonstrates the profound strength and adaptive capabilities of the human mind.

Innate & automatic

So, think of the PIS as an innate, automatic mental response that operates without conscious effort. It helps us adapt to emotional distress through mechanisms like humour, often without our awareness. Certainly, several thinkers have acknowledged the value of humour in shifting perspectives. Immanuel Kant, in his work *Critique of Judgment,* saw humour as a play of thoughts, where the mind is briefly taken out of its usual patterns and led into a differ-ent direction. After him, Freud noted that humour often involves a surprising shift in perspective that offers a way of gaining mastery over a situation by making light of it.

Such rationale explains why, whenever I'm confronted with news that a loved one has died, I begin to giggle. When I was 16 years old, on a typical school day, I was summoned to the head-master's office only to be told that my grandmother had passed away, and I could go home. I was very close to her and loved her dearly. Yet, upon receiving the news, I started to giggle. While I don't recall the exact thought or memory that triggered my gig-gling, this response was likely activated by my PIS. A response that helped me navigate the situation with calm when I returned home.

This personal account illustrates how the PIS operates automatically and preventively, shielding one from the full impact of negative experiences. Now, I encourage you to take a minute or two to reflect and understand how the PIS functions in your life. By identifying and thinking through a situation where your emotions were fairly stable despite potentially overwhelming circumstances. An occasion when you, perhaps, even surprised yourself with how composed you were.

Pause & reflection

Can you recall a time when you reacted to a stressful event with unexpected humour or indifference? What might have been going on in your mind that led to that reaction? Think about an instance where you felt surprisingly calm during or after a significant life challenge. How do you think your PIS contributed to this calmness?

It's completely normal if you can't recall a specific instance where you responded to stress or trauma with unexpected humour or indifference, or if it's been a long time since you felt truly calm and composed during challenging times. Much like our biological immune system, our psychological immunity can also become depleted. When worn out, it leaves us more vulnerable not only to major life events but also to ordinary daily stressors.

Similar to how we take steps to maintain our physical health and boost our biological immunity, such as taking supplements and avoiding contact with those who have the flu, we need to similarly nurture and protect our psychological immunity. Yet, many of us have never stopped to consider actively safeguarding our mental health throughout our lives. Often, we only think about our psychological wellbeing when already overwhelmed by stress, sadness, or desperation. This oversight is partly due to the values promoted by our culture. For example, there is no doubt physical health is emphasised and promoted, but predominantly as a means to achieve beauty, rather than for health itself. This focus can undermine a more balanced approach where both mind and body are equally cared for. Indeed, while practices like physical exercise and healthy diets undeniably benefit mental health, their positive impact can be diminished if pursued with goals that may adversely affect our psychological state, such as adhering to rigid beauty standards or seeking social influence.

Surf the waves

So, if you feel that your ability to cope has weakened, this does not reflect a failure on your part. Instead, it highlights a natural fluctuation in your psychological defences, which can be influenced by numerous factors, including physical health, stress levels, and current life experiences. Just as we can take supplements to boost our biological immunity and temporarily avoid a friend to not catch their flu, we can also take proactive steps to strengthen our mental capacities against daily stressors and life adversities. Likewise, we can learn the importance of avoiding situations that jeopardize our psychological health. In this context, avoidance does not refer to neglecting significant, unresolved issues. Instead, it means strategically circumventing difficulties by finding alternative solutions that prevent unnecessary psychological stress.

Our psychological immunity, like our biological counterpart, can be activated and strengthened. It's true that just as some of us are more prone to infections or allergic reactions, some of us are more emotionally or psychologically vulnerable, perhaps due to personal history or genetic traits like chronic anxiety. However, this does not mean that enhancing your psychological strength is out of reach. On the contrary, these scenarios often present the greatest opportunities for growth, as they offer ample scope for exploration and self-discovery.

Research shows that everyone, even those facing substantial psychological challenges, has a strong potential for improvement. For example, studies in the *Journal of Consulting and Clinical Psychology* demonstrate that proactive strategies like those used in Cognitive Behavioural Therapy (CBT) can dramatically improve mental health in people with major depression. CBT is proactive and effective because it tackles harmful thoughts and behaviours early on, preventing them from escalating into more serious problems. For instance, a person might learn to identify automatic negative thoughts and challenge them with evidence-based reasoning, gradually replacing them with more balanced and positive thoughts. Such as when Lucy, who struggled with feelings of worthlessness, learned to counter her negative self-talk with factual affirmations about her achievements and strengths.

Similarly, mindfulness techniques, which nurture self-awareness, have helped individuals under severe stress not only reduce their stress levels but also enhance their overall lifestyle. For example, practices such as mindful breathing enable individuals to focus on the present moment, reducing the impact of stressors and fostering a sense of inner peace and balance. These successes highlight how practical steps can make a significant difference, especially for those who might be more vulnerable initially, offering them real chances for growth and transformation. Additionally, taking steps to improve psychological wellbeing has been shown to benefit even those who are generally considered healthy, underscoring the widespread advantages of actively caring for our mental health.

Note that the goal of this book is not merely to explore concepts of mental resilience, but to equip you with practical advice and information necessary to strengthen and rebuild your psychological defences. It aims to awaken the innate responses that underlie psychological recovery and enhance your capacity to rise above difficulties through inner strength. By fortifying your PIS, you'll be better prepared to navigate both major challenges and the everyday pressures of life. Just as the ocean, life is unpredictable and uncontrollable. While Hamilton reflects on the literal waves,

Professor Jon Kabat-Zinn encourages resilience in a metaphorical way that resonates with this book. He suggests that "We shouldn't try to stop the waves, but rather learn to surf them." This book aims at helping you to do that, surf the waves of life with strength and confidence.

That which does not kill us makes us stronger.
- Friedrich Nietzsche

Chapter 2

Mind & Matter:
Phycological & Biological Defences

★

So far, we've explored the basics of the PIS, compared our biological and psychological defences, and I've even shared a personal story to show how the PIS works quietly behind the scenes. In this chapter, we're going to dive a bit deeper into how our bodies' and minds' defence systems work to keep us safe and sound. We'll look at what these systems have in common and what makes them unique, all with the goal of making this journey easy to follow.

Let's start with our biological immune system, the body's highly sophisticated defence network that protects us from all sorts of invisible threats. Biological immunity is essentially the body's ability to recognise and defend itself against pathogens like bacteria, viruses, and toxins. This system is made up of different parts, like white blood cells, antibodies, and even our microbiome, all working together to keep us healthy.

When pathogens enter our body, the immune system jumps into action. It starts by identifying the intruders and signalling immune cells to respond. These cells produce antibodies that latch onto the pathogens, marking them for destruction. You've probably heard these terms during the COVID-19 pandemic.

This whole process is like a castle defending itself, the guards (immune cells) spot the enemy (pathogens), use their intelligence (antibodies) to mount a defence, and make sure the castle stays secure. Note that, from the attack onwards, the castle will stay secure not just by defending itself, but by remembering the attack (pathogens), learning from it and preparing for the future.

Invisible shield

Let's now turn our attention to the equally crucial but abstract realm of psychological immunity. This system defend us from emotional and cognitive threats, where 'cognition' refers to the mental processes involved in obtaining knowledge and understanding, by way of thought, experience, and the senses.

Consider the process of learning to drive a car. Cognition plays a key role here as it involves multiple mental processes. Initially, through reading and listening, you acquire knowledge about driving rules and techniques. As you sit behind the wheel, your senses become engaged: you see the road, hear traffic, and feel the car's responses. Through repeated driving experiences, you integrate these sensory inputs with the rules you've learned, allowing you to make quick decisions and act appropriately to changing traffic conditions.

This integration of thought, experience, and sensory information not only exemplifies how cognition enables us to navigate complex tasks like driving, but also prepares us to handle life's daily stresses and unexpected challenges. Via similar cognitive processes, we learn to manage emotional reactions and build psychological defences in the face of adversity.

Psychological defence mechanisms are the mind's frontline warriors. These are unconscious processes that protect our mental health by managing and mitigating distressing thoughts and emotions. For example, as mentioned earlier, humour instantly enables a change in perspective, allowing you to gain mastery over a situation by making light of it. Similarly, rationalisation allows us to soften the blow of harsh truths by creating acceptable explanations for unsettling events.

Imagine your proposal for a major project at work was rejected. Initially, you might feel shocked and disappointed, but then, without even realising it, you naturally start to see the situation from a different perspective. You tell yourself, *Maybe the project criteria weren't clear enough*, or *Perhaps the boss was having a bad day and judged more harshly than usual.* This spontaneous shift in thinking is an example of rationalisation, a defence mechanism where you automatically create acceptable reasons for such unsettling outcomes.

By reframing the event in this way, you soften the blow of the harsh reality, making it easier to cope with the disappointment and maintain your self-esteem and mental stability. This process can be compared to an invisible shield that absorbs and deflects psychological impacts, ensuring that we remain functional and capable of recovery. This is an indication that your PIS is functioning well, working behind the scenes to help you adapt and maintain balance.

However, there are times when our psychological defences become depleted impairing helpful responses like rationalisation. Later in the book we'll explore how to intentionally use techniques such as 'mental restructuring' to activate the PIS and awaken our inner resources.

Neuroplasticity

Just as our bodies remember pathogens, our minds learn from emotional scars. This learning allows the PIS to evolve over time, handling future challenges more proficiently. At the core of this adaptation and evolution is a process called neuroplasticity.

Each time we face a stressful event or an emotional challenge, our brain goes to work, processing the experience and its outcomes. This involves the strengthening of certain connections that help in coping strategies and the weakening of others that might have been less effective, akin to building new bridges and abandoning old ones.

For example, stress at work used to cause David to panic, impairing his decision-making. Now, he uses a grounding technique, focusing on his senses to stay present. During tense meetings, he presses his feet into the floor to anchor himself. This simple change has notably improved his ability to handle stress effectively. As David continues to use this grounding technique, his old reactions are fading away, replaced by new, more effective habits (new neural connections). Similar to when outdated bridges become obsolete as new ones are built.

This enhancement and trimming of neural pathways enable the PIS to become more efficient and resilient, preparing us to handle similar and new challenges more efficiently in the future. This learning process is similar to turning pain into a playbook for emotional resilience. Friedrich Nietzsche famously captured this concept when he said, "That which does not kill us makes us stronger." Just like a character in a novel who emerges wiser and more resilient after facing great adversity, our PIS is reinforced each time we encounter and overcome emotional trials.

Take, for example, Harry Potter, who throughout his series of magical adventures, repeatedly faces daunting challenges and loss. With each hardship, Harry not only survives but grows stronger, more empathetic, and more adept at facing the next challenge. Similarly, our PIS integrates these experiences, continually updating its strategies to better protect our mental health.

Adaptation & resilience

It's crucial to recognise that not everyone is able to overcome difficulties as seamlessly as fictional characters like Harry Potter or as we might idealise in narratives of resilience. Real-life experiences can vary widely, and for some, the scars left by trauma might not lead to apparent strength or immediate recovery. Factors such as the severity of the trauma, the presence of supportive relationships, and individual psychological characteristics play significant roles in determining how effectively one can bounce back.

This disparity highlights the importance of understanding mental strength not just as a personal trait but also as a complex interplay of environmental, biological, and social factors. We will explore these themes in greater depth in upcoming chapters, delving into the nuances of resilience and offering insights into how we can better support ourselves and those who struggle to 'bounce back.' Acknowledging these challenges is essential in fostering more supportive and compassionate interpersonal relationships at home, in the work place and society as a whole.

Rewiring the brain through thought

Still, to illustrate the brain's remarkable capacity for adaptation and resilience, consider an academic review of studies on the effects of Cognitive Behavioural Therapy (CBT) on brain function and structure in pain management. Using advanced neuroimaging techniques like MRI, the study observed changes in the brain following CBT sessions. Results showed significant alterations in areas of the prefrontal cortex (PFC), a region involved in thought processes and emotional regulation (more about the PFC in Chapter 3).

These changes were associated with improved pain management and altered perceptions of pain. In essence, the study demonstrates how a shift in mindset can lead to significant changes in the brain, fostering resilience and better coping mechanisms during challenging times.

Psychological vs. biological defences

This leads us into further examination of our PIS and how it differs from our biological counterpart. The biological immune system operates through tangible elements like cells and antibodies, which we can observe and measure objectively. In contrast, the psychological immune system functions through more abstract processes, emotional and cognitive responses that are not as easily quantified. While a blood test can reveal the presence of antibodies fighting an infection, there is no straightforward test for measuring the strength of our psychological defences.

However, psychologists and researchers use different tools to measure these abstract mental experiences. These tools, often in the form of interviews or questionnaires, are called 'psychometric scales' and help assess levels of happiness, depression, and other mental states. They provide real-world evidence that confirm how effective CBT and mindfulness strategies are in improving, for example, wellbeing and quality of life.

Even though we as individuals may not have access to these professional measurement tools, we can still gauge our psychological wellbeing by becoming more attuned to our own subjective experiences. Paying closer attention to our emotions, behaviours, and thoughts allows us to monitor our mental health informally. Adopting simple practices, like David's grounding technique or maintaining a written or audio journal can greatly enhance self-awareness. By regularly documenting our feelings and reactions, we create a personal record that can help us identify patterns, recognise triggers, and measure changes over time, thus playing an active role in managing and enhancing our psychological health.

Keep in mind, this isn't a task you'll need to maintain indefinitely. Much like learning to drive a car, the initial effort required to register and reflect on your emotions is part of the learning process. Over time, this practice will become second nature. You'll find that awareness of your emotional states and triggers will increasingly come automatically, allowing you to intuitively manage your responses and sustain calm without conscious effort.

Pause & reflection

As we look deeper into understanding our PIS, I invite you to pause and reflect: How attuned are you to your inner self? Are you aware of both the limitations and strengths of your psychological mechanisms? It's common to underestimate our resilience, often because our attention naturally gravitates towards negative experiences, as they impact us more profoundly and are more memorable as a result.

This is why it's important to recognise that you might be stronger and more resilient than you realise. In case you feel less connected to the inner workings of your mind, there's no need to fret. Throughout history, simple yet powerful techniques have been employed to enhance self-awareness and emotional regulation—the ability to manage and respond to your emotional experiences in a healthy way. These methods, now validated by scientific research, are readily accessible and can significantly aid in our journey towards a resilient mind.

If you're like my brother, who might roll his eyes at the mention of mindfulness or meditation, I respect your opinion. Yet, I encourage you to be open and not dismiss the smaller, more manageable practices that can still make a substantial difference in grounding you. Consider the simple act of taking deep breaths while stuck in traffic or before an important call. This small pause can be a profound tool for engaging with your current reality and getting you out of your head, curbing brooding or anxious thoughts. Please note that taking deep breaths is more than just a relaxation technique. It's a powerful tool for enhancing mental clarity and physical wellbeing. When you breathe deeply, you increase the supply of oxygen to your brain, promoting a state of calmness and activating the parasympathetic nervous system. This 'rest and digest' state helps counter the stress-induced 'fight or flight' reaction triggered by the sympathetic nervous system. Regular deep breathing can reduce stress and decrease anxiety, ultimately leading to improved mental focus and heightened self-awareness.

Self-awareness is the cornerstone of emotional regulation and self-control. It paves the way for mental resilience and ultimately, self-mastery. In a recent psychological study, researchers explored the relationship between self-awareness and social media usage among university students. Their findings revealed an expected, but still interesting link: individuals with higher levels of self-awareness demonstrated greater self-control, leading to reduced reliance on something as spellbinding as social media.

This highlights the powerful impact of self-awareness on moderating behaviour. By becoming more aware of our emotional responses and learning to manage them consciously, we equip ourselves with the tools to face both life's ordinary and major challenges more effectively.

Now that you've been introduced to the PIS, your mental guardian, and learned how it compares and contrasts with your old acquaintance, the biological immune system, it's time to leave the familiar behind (after all, this is not a book on immunology!). Next, we'll look a little further into the inner workings of the PIS. We'll explore the neurological and biological underpinnings of this invisible armour, uncovering how it protects and strengthens your psychological defences.

Prepare to get personal with the architecture of resilience and the brick and mortar that enable us to face life's challenges head-on. In the next chapter we'll also meet the 5-Star Framework, your practical guide to activating the PIS and building resilience.

Bridges are perhaps the most invisible form of infrastructure, yet they connect worlds, both physical and metaphorical. – Karl Popper

Chapter 3

The Architecture of the Psychological Immune System

★

Let's begin with a refresher on what the PIS encompasses. This system represents our mind's ability to handle and recover from psychological stressors. It involves a complex network of emotional and cognitive processes that help us maintain mental stability in the face of challenges. From adjusting our mood after a disappointing event to shifting our perspective towards a more positive outlook, the PIS plays a crucial role in how we interpret and respond to the world around us.

Here, we will explore the intricate workings of this system by examining the neurological and biological underpinnings that facilitate resilience and recovery, what I like to call the brick and mortar of our psychological immunity. We'll also briefly explore how specific brain structures collaborate to protect and heal our mental states.

Just as our bodies are composed of parts and subparts responsible for various functions, our brain is similarly organised. The brain's functioning is not as straightforward as once thought. Historically, it was believed that specific areas of the brain were solely responsible for particular functions. For example, it was once thought that Broca's area, located in the frontal lobe of the left hemisphere, was exclusively responsible for speech production. Modern neuroscience, however, has revealed a more complex picture. Broca's area is not only involved in speech production but also plays a crucial role in language comprehension and other aspects of language processing. Recent studies, particularly those using functional MRI (fMRI) and other neuroimaging techniques, have shown that this region is active during various language tasks, not just speech production. These findings illustrate that the functions of brain areas like Broca's area are more diverse and intertwined than previously understood.

You see the point. The brain is highly interconnected, making it impossible to attribute any single function to one narrowly defined area. So, while certain brain structures are indeed more active during specific tasks, such as the left hemisphere during language-related activities, the rest of the brain continues to work in concert.

The city that never sleeps

Consider the brain as a sort of city, a comparison neuroscientist David Eagleman often uses. In this city, while certain areas might be more active during specific mental processes, the rest of the city never truly shuts down. This illustrates the continuous activity throughout the brain, even when it appears that only one part is actively engaged. In fact, our brains are incredibly active even during sleep and rest, continuously processing information and maintaining our mental health. This dynamic interplay ensures that our PIS can operate efficiently, seamlessly adapting to and managing mental stressors.

To better understand how our brain manages mental health, it's crucial to familiarise ourselves with key areas involved in emotional regulation and stress response. This is similar to knowing the main sites of a city. In our simplified context, there are three principal sites: the amygdala, the hippocampus, and the prefrontal cortex. Each of these has a main function and specific location within the brain, working together in complex ways to maintain our psychological wellbeing.

The amygdala is located deep within the temporal lobe, it's part of the limbic system, a group of structures underneath the cerebral cortex. It's like the brain's alarm system, primarily responsible for processing emotions, especially fear and anxiety. From an evolutionary perspective, the amygdala is one of the oldest parts of our brain, indicating its fundamental role in survival mechanisms such as the fight-or-flight response.

The hippocampus is located deep within the brain's medial temporal lobe and it is crucial for memory formation and linking emotions to those memories. It also plays a role in how we respond to stress, helping to regulate the body's stress response in coordination with the amygdala and prefrontal cortex.

The prefrontal cortex (PFC) is situated at the front of the brain, just behind the forehead, the prefrontal cortex is involved in complex cognitive functions, personality expression, decision making, and moderating social behaviour. It's like the brain's executive – a function in charge of other functions, handling planning and regulating emotions through connections with other brain areas, including the amygdala. This region is relatively newer evolutionarily, highlighting its role in the advanced aspects of cognition and emotional management.

Essential pathways

Just as bridges connect different points across a city, facilitating smooth traffic flow, the amygdala, prefrontal cortex, and hippocampus form vital pathways within our brain to manage our emotional and cognitive functions. However, when these neural 'bridges' are damaged or 'burnt', much like physical bridges that become old and worn out, the communication between these brain regions becomes less efficient. This disruption can lead to significant mental health disturbances.

Imagine the amygdala as a city area that alerts us to potential threats and emotional responses. Normally, the prefrontal cortex, acting as the executive, regulates these responses by providing rational assessment and control. However, if the 'bridge' connecting them is compromised, this emotional regulation fails, leading to exaggerated stress responses or prolonged fear states that are disproportionate to the actual threat. For instance, suppose you have a disagreement with your partner. A well-regulated brain might process the emotional upset, come to terms with the disagreement, and return to calm. By contrast, if the communication between the amygdala and the prefrontal cortex is compromised, the amygdala might continue to amplify feelings of anger and distress long after the argument has ended.

The result? You might find yourself unable to sleep, ruminating over the disagreement, and feeling upset for hours or even days, even though the actual conflict, a simple argument, has been resolved. This prolonged emotional response is disproportionate to the initial trigger, but because the brain's 'control system' isn't communicating properly, the intense emotions do not subside as they should.

Similarly, the hippocampus plays a critical role in both forming and retrieving memories and in regulating stress responses. For it to function properly, it must maintain robust communication with other brain regions. Again here, when the neural pathways "bridges" within the brain, are compromised, it can disrupt memory processing. This disruption is evident in conditions such as PTSD, where traumatic memories are often recalled without the usual regulation by a healthy neural network. Understanding PTSD requires insight into the complex interactions among the prefrontal cortex, hippocampus, and amygdala. Research indicates that abnormalities in the function, structure, and biochemical processes of these areas are closely linked to the manifestation of this stress response disorder.

Messengers

Lastly, in our bustling brain city, not only are the bridges (neuronal pathways) crucial for connectivity, but the messages that travel across these bridges are equally important. These messages are carried by special messengers known as neurotransmitters. Imagine serotonin as the city's streetlights and mood-enhancing billboards, keeping our city well-lit and promoting a sense of wellbeing. When the city faces a threat or needs to be on high alert, norepinephrine, the emergency alert system, springs into action, preparing the city's resources to respond swiftly. To maintain peace and order, the city relies on GABA, akin to strict zoning laws and noise control measures that prevent chaos and ensure calm. And at the heart of the city's progress and innovation is dopamine, the reward and recognition program, driving motivation and pleasure through its rewarding signals. Together, these neurotransmitters ensure that the brain city operates smoothly, balancing alertness (norepinephrine), calmness (GABA), mood regulation (serotonin), and motivation (dopamine).

Investing in maintenance

These scenarios underline the importance of maintaining robust neural pathways and ensuring open, solid communication lines between these crucial brain regions. Just as a city invests in maintaining its bridges to ensure smooth transit and connectivity, so too must we consider practices that restore and reinforce these neural connections within the brain, thus improving mental health outcomes.

As we've explored how vital the 'bridges' within our brain are for maintaining mental health, think of your own 'city's infrastructure'. Now, it's worth asking yourself a couple of important questions:

First, are you investing in maintaining your brain's bridges? Consider your daily habits and behaviours. Are they helping to strengthen these critical connections within your brain? Regular mental exercises are crucial for strengthening the brain's 'mental bridges.' My husband keeps his bridges in top shape by tackling puzzles. He's particularly adept at the Rubik's cube, so much so that I suspect he might secretly be a cube-solving robot!

Second, what improvements could you make to maximise the return on your investment? Reflect on changes or additional activities you could integrate into your routine that might serve as upgrades to your brain's infrastructure. As you'll see in upcoming chapters, wider social interactions, physical activity and mindful meditation are like diversifying your portfolio, they help fortify these neural pathways even further.

Reflecting on these questions isn't just an exercise in thought, it's about deliberately participating in the upkeep and enhancement of your mental health. Just like city planners, the choices you make today determine the efficiency and resilience of your 'mental city' tomorrow. We will look deeper into these strategies in the chapters to come, but there's no need to delay starting with the effective techniques we've discussed so far (i.e. journalling).

Emotional continuum

Note that, while we have discussed key brain areas and the concept of burnt or damaged 'brain bridges' in the context of serious mental health disturbances like PTSD, it's important to recognise that mental disturbances are not simply present or absent. Instead, they exist along a continuum. The more these neural 'bridges' are compromised, the more communication between different brain parts is hindered. PTSD represents one extreme on the stress response continuum, indicative of severely damaged bridges, but there are many stages within this continuum. This is where the 5-Star Framework can play a vital role. By engaging in daily proactive steps, we can help maintain and repair these neural connections, strengthening our psychological defences and building resilience.

Importantly, understanding our current position on this psychological continuum requires analysing our reactions to the world around us. Are we overreacting to relatively minor situations? Not everyone on this continuum will develop PTSD, a condition that affects only a minority. Yet the potential to become overly reactive and respond disproportionately to life's challenges is a reality for all of us. Such behaviour can alienate others and significantly impair personal and social functioning. Early recognition of these signs can lead to actions that strengthen our mental 'bridges' and bolster our defences. Incorporating the Daily 5-Star PIS Goal into our day-to-day routine is an effective way to reinforce these mental 'bridges,' helping to balance our reactions and enhance overall mental health.

Activate your PIS

At the heart of this book lies a fundamental message: the importance of maintaining mental health. More than that, I want to emphasise that caring for your psychological wellbeing should be as routine and deliberate as caring for your physical health. Just as you might pause to consider whether to indulge in an extra cookie with your blood sugar levels in mind, I urge you to consider the health of your PIS in your daily life choices.

This chapter provides an overview of the practical aspects of the Five-Star Framework, giving you a sense of what it entails. For a deeper dive into the theories and the scientific foundations that underpin the 5-Star Framework, feel free to skip ahead to Part 5 of the book and return here afterward.

The 5-Star Framework

The 5-Star Framework is a practical approach I designed to help you boost your PIS through simple, daily proactive steps: the Daily 5-Star PIS Goal. Each day, aim at achieving a 5-Star PIS by engaging in five actions (stars) that contribute to activating your psychological defences and mental wellbeing.

The 5-Star Framework is designed to be practical and encouraging. Psychological resilience is a destination you can reach via various roads, pathways, and bridges. Like so, there are many possibilities for you to accumulate your daily 5 stars. For example, in the first three chapters of this book, we've already discussed several strategies that count as stars. These include: developing a sense of humour by not taking yourself too seriously, engaging in self-discovery by asking questions like, 'How attuned am I to my inner self?', and adopting grounding techniques, such as pressing your feet on the floor during moments of distress. Other strategies are starting a written or audio journal to increase self-awareness by identifying triggers and tracking emotional changes, solving puzzles like the Rubik's Cube to enhance focus, and taking regular deep-breath breaks to activate your 'rest and digest' response.

Also, keep in mind, every day you pick up this book and read at least one page, you earn a star for taking a proactive step toward bettering yourself. Remember, when it comes to your mental wellbeing, every positive action counts (as a star!). This includes actions you already take every day, like walking the dog, chatting with a friend, taking a short break to stretch, and mindfully enjoying a cup of tea.

Intention matters

You might be wondering, *How can activities I'm already doing activate my PIS and help build a resilient mind, if I still feel like I need improvement?*

The key lies in how you perceive these activities. Did you know that simply changing how you think about your daily actions can lead to real health benefits? In a study led by psychologist Alia Crum, 84 female hotel room attendants were divided into two groups. Group 1 was informed that their daily work, cleaning rooms, was a form of good exercise that met doctors' recommendations for an active lifestyle. They were even given examples of how their work counted as exercise. Group 2 wasn't given any information. Four weeks later, although neither group changed their actual behaviour, participants in Group 1 displayed real physiological changes. They lost weight, showed reduced blood pressure, and even lower body fat and BMI.

This indicates that when you bring intention to your daily actions, it can lead to measurable positive outcomes. Even without changing what you've been doing! Indeed, Crum's study showed that participants who simply changed how they *viewed* their daily work saw tangible improvements in their health. Suggesting that by not just going through the motions, but by recognizing the benefits of what you're already doing, you can experience meaningful shifts in your health. So, why not take a quick break now to stretch or roll your shoulders? It's a simple action, but seeing it as a boost for your mental wellness can make all the difference.

Remarkably, these kinds of benefits are not just seen in physical health, they can significantly impact our psychological wellbeing too. Think about how you perceive the stresses in your life: do you see them as damaging to your health, or as challenges to be conquered? In another study, Alia Crum explored how simply changing our perception of stress can transform its effects on mental health. Participants who were encouraged to see stress as a helpful response to life's challenges, rather than a harmful one, experienced better emotional outcomes and felt more capable of managing stressful situations. This demonstrates that, just like recognising daily activities as beneficial exercise can improve physical health, viewing everyday actions as valuable for your mental well-being follows the same principle.

Interestingly, this idea isn't new. The Stoic philosopher Epictetus once said, "It's not what happens to you, but how you react to it that matters." Modern scientific research now supports what Stoics have known for millennia: how we perceive and approach life's events fundamentally shape our experience of them and their outcome. Hence, next time you engage in a routine task, like talking to a friend or tackling a challenging project, try to see it as a step toward activating your PIS.

In this way, the 5-Star Framework provides you with a structured approach to do just that. It offers a clear path to direct your goals and intentions, encouraging you to adopt new, simple steps for activating your psychological defences while also recognising and embracing the beneficial actions you already take as important steps in building a healthier, more resilient mind.

Earning your first stars

With that in mind, challenge yourself each day to take five simple yet meaningful steps that strengthen your psychological defences and build a more resilient mind. As we continue this journey, we'll gradually work on this goal, deepening your understanding of it and your practice over time. Feel free to track your 5 stars on your phone or any device you prefer. However, I encourage you to start by writing them down. Writing engages more cognitive processes, aids memory retention, and allows for deeper reflection and understanding. Plus, the writing can be as casual as you like.

To give you a practical example, here's how I accumulated my 5 stars yesterday:

Star 1: I had a healthy breakfast.
Star 2: I apologised for overreacting.
Star 3: I socialised with family.

Star 4: I engaged in self-reflection.
Star 5: I had an early night.

As I carried out each of these actions, I did so with the conscious awareness that I was strengthening my psychological defences. This is similar to eating a bowl of salad or drinking fresh juice while fully appreciating how beneficial it is for your physical health.

★

Now it's your turn to put these concepts into action. Grab a journal or a simple notepad and start tracking your first steps toward a Daily 5-Star PIS Goal. Remember, these seemingly simple actions have a powerful cumulative effect, each one contributing to a more resilient mind. Just as individual stars form bright constellations, your daily efforts will collectively shine.

In the next two chapters, we'll delve into how our psychological immune system develops across the lifespan, laying the groundwork for deeper understanding. Then, in Part 2 of the book, we'll return with more practical steps and exercises to further activate your PIS.

I suppose it is true that most psychiatric disturbances can be regarded as disorders of attachment. - Jonh Bowlby

Chapter 4

The Psychological Immune system : Infancy & Adolescence

★

Our psychological defences, like the biological ones, begin its development early in life. This initial phase is crucial, as it lays the foundation for the structure and function of the PIS and emotional resilience, shaping the stress management capabilities we carry into adulthood. Here, we'll investigate the earliest stages of this development: from infancy through adolescence, examining how interactions with caregivers, early social experiences, and the first academic challenges contribute to the formation of a resilient mind. Understanding these early influences provides crucial insights into the ways we can support and enhance wellbeing from the very beginning.

This is where Attachment Theory, developed by psychiatrist John Bowlby in the late 1950s, comes into play, revolutionising our understanding of early emotional development. Bowlby suggested that the bonds formed between infants and their primary caregivers are essential for the child's survival and development. These early interactions establish the foundation for all future emotional and social behaviours.

In the beginning

From the moment a newborn enters the world, they face a series of neuropsychological challenges, as discussed in Chapter 1. One of the first and most significant is bonding, or forming an attachment to their caregivers (i.e. mother or father figures). The nature of this bond, whether secure or insecure, hinges significantly on how caregivers respond to the infant's needs. A secure attachment develops when caregivers consistently provide comfort, support, and meet the child's needs, creating a sense of safety and trust. Securely attached children tend to grow up with a stronger ability to cope with the world around them, displaying resilience, confidence, and healthier relationships.

Let's consider my sister-in-law and her interactions with my nephew when he was just 10 months old and came to visit us for a couple of weeks. Whenever my nephew cried, whether from hunger or discomfort, his mum would respond promptly by picking him up, soothing him with gentle words, and addressing his needs. This consistent and nurturing response reassured my nephew, teaching him that his environment was safe and his needs would be met. Each time his mum responded to his cues, he learned to trust her and, by extension, his surroundings. This development of trust laid the foundation for a secure attachment.

Now, five years later, my nephew has grown into a child who perhaps feels a tad too confident! He eagerly explores his world, forms relationships easily at school and on the playground, and manages stress effectively. One day, when I was visiting, his parents were deep in conversation about work, but he couldn't resist jumping in. First, dad delivered the usual line, "Please, do not interrupt. Wait until I finish!"; but my nephew interrupted again. Then, mum followed with her own version. Instead of feeling down about it, he pulled off a smooth escape plan by turning to me and saying, "Hey aunt, want to play?" My nephew has a smart way of coping with being told off. His life experiences have unconsciously instilled in him a deep sense of safety and love, which in turn secure his confidence and resilience.

Conversely, inconsistent, or neglectful responses can lead to insecure attachments, marking the beginning of potential emotional and interpersonal difficulties. Now, imagine a mother named Anne and her baby daughter, Rose. When Rose cries for attention Anne sometimes delays responding, burdened by her own inner struggles. Occasionally, Anne hears Rose cry but waits to see if Rose will 'settle down' on her own. Over time, these inconsistent and neglectful responses teach Rose that her environment may not always be reliable for meeting her needs. This uncertainty may lead to the development of an insecure attachment. As Rose grows, she may become anxious about exploring her surroundings or hesitant to form relationships, fearing that her needs might not be acknowledged or valued. This insecurity affects psychological defences and can manifest as difficulty in managing stress as well as reluctance in social interactions, setting a challenging course for emotional and interpersonal development.

Notice how this phase of infancy, where caregivers' responsiveness to cries, feeding cues, and emotional displays shapes an infant's view of the world. See, this is when infants learn whether the world is a safe and predictable place or a more uncertain and threatening environment. This learning lays the foundation of their PIS, influencing how they will emotionally and socially engage with others and the world throughout life.

However, it's important to note that even if you experienced an unstable childhood that may have led to developing insecure attachments, this does not mean you are forever doomed to be psychologically vulnerable. Our brains are remarkably adaptable, and with the right support, it's entirely possible to rebuild and restore our mindsets and views of the world. The right mode of therapy, approaches and positive relationship-building can all contribute to reshaping our perspectives. Remember, our past influences us, but it does not have to define us.

Beyond the nest

With the foundation of either secure or insecure attachments formed during infancy, as illustrated by the interactions between my sister-in-law and nephew or Anne and Rose, we now turn to the subsequent stages of development. As children grow into early and middle childhood, the initial patterns established by their attachments begin to interact more intricately with expanding social environments and family dynamics. During these years, children continue to rely on their primary caregivers while increasingly engaging with the wider world, including friends, teachers, and community members. Each interaction acts as a mini-test and development opportunity for their psychological resilience, shaping their ability to navigate diverse social landscapes.

Friends provide a platform for emotional expression and mutual support, offering a sense of belonging and validation. Teachers and school settings introduce structured challenges and rewards, promoting problem-solving skills and the ability to cope with success and failure in a safe environment. Community involvement, such as participating in sports or cultural activities, broadens a child's experience and introduces diverse social norms and expectations. Each of these interactions contributes to the child's growing ability to adapt to different social situations, manage a range of emotions, and confidently navigate the complexities of interpersonal relationships. Collectively, these experiences fortify the child's PIS, equipping them with the tools necessary to face life's varied challenges.

Essentially, skills and coping mechanisms that develop from early interactions are influenced by subsequent social experiences. These can either reinforce positive behaviours or exacerbate initial insecurities. A valid concern is overprotective parenting, where parents may shield their children from minor adversities, potentially stunting their emotional growth. Highlighting the drawbacks of this approach, psychologist Jonathan Haidt argues that such parenting prevents children from facing essential life challenges, thereby impairing their psychological defences. He advises, "Prepare the child for the road, not the road for the child," linking excessive sheltering to increasing rates of depression and anxiety among youth.

Noteworthy, nowadays, social media adds complexities to the emotional landscape of children and adolescents. While it expands their social networks, it also fosters cyberbullying and harmful social comparisons. For example, the anonymity and distance of online interactions can embolden some to engage in severe cyberbullying, relentlessly following individuals and infiltrating their personal spaces, exacerbating feelings of insecurity and vulnerability. Further, the curated images and narratives on social platforms present idealised versions of life, setting unrealistic standards that young people feel pressured to meet, potentially leading to low self-esteem.

Still, expanding social experiences are vital for developing key life skills, preparing children to manage stress, overcome challenges, and build resilience. For example, successfully navigating social and academic realms boosts self-esteem and teaches recovery from setbacks. However, consistent difficulties in these areas may lead to increased anxiety and more severe mental health issues. Recognising and acknowledging these developmental challenges is essential for nurturing a strong PIS that equips children to face future struggles.

Admittedly, the journey to develop a child's psychological resilience is complex and varied. Children often encounter mixed environments: they might excel in the structured setting of school, enjoying academic achievements and peer interactions, yet face less supportive family dynamics at home. These contrasting experiences can counterbalance each other, with positive school experiences mitigating home challenges. As children mature, their social support network widens to include peers, providing essential emotional support and resilience during the turbulent teenage years.

A work in progress

As we've seen with our bridge analogy, the construction of pathways in the brain, particularly those connecting key regions like the prefrontal cortex (PFC), hippocampus, and amygdala, is crucial for the development of the PIS. During adolescence years, these bridges are far from complete. In fact, the brain continues its construction well into the mid-20s. This ongoing development means that the foundational neural pathways are not yet solidified, leading to characteristic teenage behaviours such as impulsivity, insecurity, and a tendency to overthink.

The implications of this extended period of brain development are profound. The still-maturing connections can make teenagers particularly vulnerable to emotional swings and risky behaviours, which are often driven by an underdeveloped PFC, the brain's centre for decision-making and impulse control. Moreover, adolescence is a delicate time recognised by psychologists as a critical period for the onset of psychological disorders, including depression and psychosis. Just as in infancy, the social environment during these years plays a significant role in shaping an individual's mental health. Positive interactions and supportive relationships can help stabilize the ongoing construction of neural pathways, while negative experiences can exacerbate vulnerabilities, potentially leading to a frail PIS and long-term psychological issues.

Thus, when dealing with challenges with a teenager at home, let's remember that they're a work in progress. With our love and support, they can grow into stable, well-centred adults. The key is to make them feel they can trust us. Aiming at a Daily 5-Star PIS will enable us to stay patient and consistent, and aware that our efforts will make a lasting difference. Understanding that the brain is still 'under construction' during adolescence explain as much of the typical teenage behaviour that can often seem puzzling as it underscores the importance of a nurturing and stable environment that can support the healthy completion of these critical brain development years.

Crucially, it's important to recognise that the adolescent years are a period of both vulnerability and opportunity. This phase of life is marked by the ongoing construction of critical neural 'bridges,' making the brain particularly susceptible to negative influences like drugs and alcohol. Because these neural structures are still forming, substance use can severely disrupt the development of essential pathways, leading to potential long-term cognitive and emotional harm.

However, the very malleability of the adolescent brain also presents a unique chance to build a strong foundation for lifelong resilience. Engaging in positive practices, such as regular physical activity, can significantly influence this developmental stage. Physical exercise not only boosts mood and energy but also helps regulate stress and anxiety, reinforcing healthy neural pathways and promoting overall wellbeing. Developing artistic skills such as drawing or painting offers a creative outlet that can enhance emotional expression and coping mechanisms. Moreover, maintaining a balanced diet and ensuring ample sleep each night is crucial for supporting the brain's development and overall psychological defences. So, why not invite your children to join you in the Daily 5-Star PIS Goal? It can be a fun and rewarding way to bring your family even closer together, strengthening not just individual resilience, but also the emotional unity that your family represents.

Overall, by embracing healthy habits, young individuals can significantly influence the function and structure of their psychological defences. These proactive steps help ensure that as the brain matures, it does so with robust pathways that promote long-term emotional and mental stability. In the following chapter, we will explore how these pathways continue to evolve and strengthen throughout adulthood and into the later years of life.

Age is not 'lost youth' but a new stage of opportunity
& strength. — Betty Friedan

Chapter 5

The Psychological Immune System : Adulthood & Senior Years

★

As we transition from adolescence into adulthood, the PIS faces new challenges and opportunities for growth. Adulthood encompasses a wide range of life stages, from young adulthood, through midlife, and into old age; each marked by distinct developmental milestones, psychosocial challenges, and the eventual reflection on mortality. During adult years, we work to establish our careers, form romantic relationships, start families, and eventually prepare for retirement. Each stage brings its own set of demands, requiring us to continually adapt and refine our coping strategies.

Aging, a natural progression of life, involves more than just the physical signs of getting older. It also includes changes in roles and responsibilities, shifts in social dynamics, and often a revaluation of life goals and achievements. As we age, our cognitive functions and emotional resilience are tested in different ways, influenced by both our earlier life experiences and our current environment. So, let's explore how the PIS develops and transforms during adulthood. Let's look at how early foundations in resilience continue to serve us, or conversely, how we need to develop new strategies to handle the unique challenges of this life phase. By understanding these transitions, we can better prepare to maintain and enhance our PIS function and resilience as we age.

Solid foundations

As we enter adulthood, the neural pathways or 'bridges' within our brains, which have been forming throughout childhood and adolescence, become more solidified. This solidification process means that the strategies for managing stress and emotional responses are now more deeply ingrained, providing us with a stable basis for handling the complexities of adult life. However, if these pathways have been cemented around insecurity and anxiety, they can pose challenges when, as adults, we face the increased demands of self-reliance and responsibilities associated with work, partnerships, and parenting.

For those of us whose early experiences led to the development of insecure attachment, the transition into adulthood can exacerbate stress, making it difficult to adapt to new roles that require confidence and a stable emotional base. Adults with an insecure attachment style often face challenges when it comes to managing financial responsibilities, for example. They may either procrastinate on financial decisions until they become crises, or exhibit impulsive spending behaviours, reflecting their instability and lack of confidence. In contrast, those with a secure attachment style typically handle their finances with more confidence and prudence. They set long-term goals, budget carefully, and are well-prepared for unexpected expenses, showcasing their stability and trust in their ability to manage life's practical challenges, reflecting a well-functioning PIS.

Differences between these two attachment styles extend into their relationship commitments as well. Insecurely attached adults might struggle with commitment, oscillating between dependency and a high degree of turbulence in relationships. Their fears of abandonment or intimacy can hinder the development of healthy, long-term partnerships. On the other hand, adults who have a secure attachment foundation tend to foster relationships characterized by trust, openness, and mutual respect. They communicate effectively and manage conflicts constructively, which is indicative of their strong relational skills and healthy PIS function.

Parenting also reflects one's attachment style markedly. Parents with insecure attachments may find it difficult to provide consistent emotional support, often vacillating between being overly intrusive and somewhat disengaged. This inconsistency can perpetuate a cycle of insecure attachment with their own children. Affecting, in turn, their children's development of psychological defences and resilience. Conversely, securely attached adults are likely to be more responsive and attentive parents. They meet their children's needs effectively and create a nurturing environment that promotes the development of secure attachments, contributing positively to their children's emotional and social growth.

While it may seem that attachment styles are being given undue emphasis, their role in shaping personality and subsequent psychological traits throughout life cannot be overstated. John Bowlby, the founder of Attachment Theory, observed that the nature of bonding between an infant and their primary caregiver has a profound impact on the individual's mental development. Indeed, Bowlby noted that some individuals might never develop in a well-rounded manner if their early attachment experiences are flawed. This is because the foundational years are critical in shaping core personality traits such as extraversion, openness, conscientiousness, agreeableness, and, last but not least, emotional stability.

A fascinating study published in the *Self and Identity* Journal involved 170 participants from the Minnesota Longitudinal Study of Risk and Adaptation, which followed them for 30 years. Researchers assessed the participants' early attachment styles when they were just 12 and 18 months old. Then, at age 32, researchers measured participants' levels of extraversion, openness, conscientiousness, agreeableness and emotional stability.

The study found that children who were securely attached early in life were more likely to display higher levels of agreeableness and conscientiousness and higher levels of emotional stability as adults. In contrast, children with insecure attachment styles tended to display lower agreeableness and conscientiousness and poor emotional stability. This research provides evidence of how early childhood experiences can shape key aspects of our adult psychological traits.

Traits that influence our paths in profound ways. For instance, they can lead to a life rich with fulfilling relationships and personal satisfaction or, conversely, to ongoing struggles with interpersonal dynamics and self-awareness.

Understanding the pivotal role of early attachment thus provides crucial insights into the full trajectory of an individual's psychological development. It underscores the importance of nurturing and stable early relationships as foundational to developing a healthy personality and, by extension, a robust PIS. This strong foundation is essential not just for a fulfilling life, but also for enduring resilience, enabling individuals to manage stress effectively, maintain positive relationships, and navigate life's challenges with confidence.

Not set in stone

On the bright side, as the brain's capacity for neuroplasticity persists into adulthood, traits stemming from insecure attachment styles can be ameliorated through the activation of the PIS guided by therapy and life approaches like the 5-Star Framework, which foster the cultivation of life skills and positive relationship experiences. I mentioned this previously. By engaging in activities that foster personal growth and forming healthy connections with others, individuals can reshape ingrained neural pathways, similar to building new bridges and abandoning old ones. This process leads to more secure and productive patterns of interaction with others, oneself and the world, ensuring a smoother journey through life's varied landscapes. However, acknowledgment and acceptance of oneself are crucial stepping stones for transformation and healing, allowing for continuous personal evolution throughout adulthood. As Carl Rogers observed, "The curious paradox is that when I accept myself just as I am, then I can change."

Old age

What are you doing today to ensure a healthy and resilient mind in your old age? As we enter old age, our PIS undergoes yet further changes, influenced by decades of life experiences and biological aging processes. Although, this stage of life is often marked by a paradoxical blend of challenges and psychological advantages. On one hand, older adults may face decline in physical health, the loss of loved ones, and changes in social roles, which can all pose serious challenges to their mental health. On the other hand, there is substantial evidence suggesting that levels of wellbeing actually increase with age. Older adults often report feeling less self-conscious, and they tend to overthink less, perhaps due to a shift in perspective that prioritizes meaningful experiences over less important concerns.

One theory that explains this increase in wellbeing is the Socioemotional Selectivity Theory, which suggests that as we age, we become more selective about our social networks. This definitely indicates that my husband and I are approaching our senior years, as we've become quite picky about who we spend our time with! What about you, are you selective about who you spend your time with? By focusing on the relationships that matter most, we enhance our emotional health. This selectivity helps older adults maintain a stronger, more supportive social environment and bolsters their PIS. Additionally, many seniors develop refined coping strategies that emphasise acceptance, wisdom, and prioritise meaningful engagement over confrontation or avoidance.

Therefore, the capacity to adapt and maintain psychological resilience in old age greatly depends on the integrity of our PIS, which has been shaped throughout our lifetime. Those who have nurtured their mental health in earlier years generally find themselves better equipped to handle the challenges of aging. Another excellent reason to adopt the Daily 5-Star PIS Goal straight-away. Also, it's important to note that while the decline in certain cognitive functions is inevitable, the capacity for emotional growth and resilience remains intact, if not strengthened, in old age. This underscores the importance of development and adaption across one's life, ensuring that old age can be a time of calm and continued personal growth, rather than decline.

Openness & adaptation

While increased wellbeing is a notable advantage of aging, it is essential to address the challenges many of us are likely to face, particularly loneliness and, possibly, social isolation. A substantial number of elderly individuals live alone, often due to the loss of a partner or because they are geographically distant from family members. In some cases, the lack of a caring family exacerbates this isolation. These factors can lead to various physical and mental health issues. In this context, the PIS's role becomes even more critical. A strong PIS can help individuals cope with these challenges through mechanisms such as acceptance, which we'll discuss in depth in Chapter 17.

Openness and adaptation also play a crucial role here. Embracing technology, for example, can mitigate feelings of isolation by keeping older adults connected with their families and friends, regardless of physical distances. Social media platforms, video calls, and other communication tools can provide vital social interactions that might otherwise be missing. Moreover, online communities and forums can offer support as well as a sense of belonging, helping seniors to maintain an active social life.

Therefore, it's vital for us to develop and maintain robust psychological defences to be able to adapt to the social, physical, and cognitive changes of aging and to empower ourselves in managing emotional and social challenges.

Also, for many seniors, cultivating a healthy relationship with the concept of mortality and embracing the latter stages of life can considerably enhance PIS function. A touching study performed in nursing homes found that older persons who viewed death as a natural and inevitable part of life tended to experience less fear and worry about dying. These individuals often expressed a sense of readiness and peace about the end of life, which contributed to their psychological comfort and quality of life in their remaining years.

Renewal

At the neurobiological level, a particularly encouraging aspect of aging is the continuation of neurogenesis, the process of generating new neurons, well into later decades of life, challenging common myths about inevitable cognitive decline.

A detailed study by neuroscientists, published in the journal *Nature*, found that even as we age, our brains continue to produce neurons. The researchers discovered this by examining brain tissue from donors, revealing that new neurons can form in the hippocampus—the part of the brain important for memory formation, as we discussed previously—even well into a person's 90's. Think of this as replacing old bricks on a bridge with new ones. Just as a bridge requires ongoing maintenance and occasional replacement of worn-out materials to remain sturdy and functional, our brain pathways benefit from the addition of new neurons. This process of neurogenesis ensures that critical neural 'bridges' do not weaken over time but are continually reinforced.

By actively nurturing our psychological health, we effectively 'lay down new bricks,' ensuring that our mental 'bridges' remain robust. This ongoing renewal is crucial as it allows us to continue learning, maintain cognitive flexibility and resilience, essential for adapting to new challenges and changes, well into our senior years. You can see how proactively engaging in practices that activate the PIS can help prevent cognitive decline and support emotional stability. By facilitating the renewal of neurons, these practices enable us to navigate the later stages of life with confidence and vitality.

As we conclude our exploration of the PIS across different life stages, I'm reminded of my grandmother, a woman of simple pleasures and serene tenacity. She faced life's challenges with a calm demeanour, never seeking recognition or praise for her resolution. In her final years, marked by the loss of her husband, dear friends, and even her beloved dog, she found solace in the tranquillity of her garden. There, she cultivated a sense of peace that sustained her through moments of solitude. She lacked formal education and material wealth, but possessed wisdom, kindness and good humour, a testament to the power of her inner strength and stability.

As she peacefully passed away in her sleep, she left behind an example of grace and humility, a reminder that true resilience lies not in grand gestures or dramatic displays, but in the quiet strength of the human spirit.

Part 1
Takeaways
★

Well done for concluding the first part of this book. This shows your ongoing commitment to strengthening your PIS and boosting your mental health. As you prepare to move on to the next stage of our exploration into the workings of our psychological defences, let's recap what you've covered throughout the past five chapters.

In Part 1 of *What Makes a Resilient Mind?*, I introduced you to your invisible mental armour: the PIS. An automatic, spontaneous mechanism within us which provides us with an incredible ability to endure life's adversities and bounce back from negative experiences, much like our biological immune system helps us recover from infections. I additionally highlighted that, similar to our biological immune system, the capacity of our PIS to protect us from life's hardships or daily challenges can fluctuate, especially when we are overworked or facing difficulties. In times when our PIS functioning is less than desirable, we might lose our sense of humour and rationalise things in ways that bring us down instead of helping us move forward. Our breathing often becomes shallow and agitated, further signalling stress cues to our brain, making us more alert and wary of those around us and the situations we encounter. Although, I also discussed that by being proactive and deliberate in looking after your mental health, just as you do with your physical health, you can replenish your psychological defences.

Next, we toured the brain and made stops at the main sites of our emotional landscape. We learned that the amygdala and the hippocampus are older brain sites responsible for processing fear, forming memories, and regulating emotions. We also visited the prefrontal cortex (PFC), a more modern and advanced site where functions that manage other functions, such as emotion regulation, goal-directed behaviour, and attention maintenance, occur. Hopefully, this helped you appreciate how intentionally calming yourself, developing self-awareness, adopting grounding strategies in moments of distress, and setting goals (like aiming for a daily 5-Star PIS) are crucial for your mental and emotional stability. The more you adopt such practices, the more efficiently our prefrontal cortex (PFC) functions, and in turn, the more self-aware you'll become.

During our tour we also encountered neurotransmitters or, in our analogy, the 'city messengers' that travel across bridges ensuring that the brain city operates smoothly, balancing alertness (norepinephrine), calmness (GABA), mood regulation (serotonin), and motivation (dopamine). I highlighted the importance of neural pathways, or the "bridges" that connect brain sites, in ensuring smooth information flow without congestion. An instance of a disagreement with a partner illustrated this point. It indicated that if your "brain's bridge network" is open and information flows efficiently, you can process the emotional upset, come to terms with the disagreement, and return to life with minimal lingering annoyance, or even a valuable lesson learned.

Learning lessons either from minor or major life events is crucial as they help us navigate through life's phases with openness and flexibility, embracing each phase's unique psychological challenges and advantages. To provide a comprehensive introduction to the PIS, I further discussed how it develops across the lifespan. We explored how the quality of the bond we form with our caregivers during our early years is crucial in shaping our perceptions and responses to the world. This bond influences whether we see the world and others as reliable and trustworthy or as unreliable and ambiguous. A view which, in turn, elicits corresponding behaviours like uncertainty and insecurity, which can potentially accompany us our entire lives, if not acknowledged and addressed.

Crucially, we also explored the brain's extraordinary capacity to adapt, learn, and renew itself well into our senior years. This capacity offers numerous opportunities for transformation, self-development, and personal growth, irrespective of the quality of care we received as infants. As discussed in Chapter 5, the key to transformation lies in first acknowledging and accepting who we are, and then embracing change. Reaching our senior years with greater psychological stability depends on how proactive we remain in maintaining our mental health now. Remember, even the most vulnerable among us have great capacities for healing and recovery. With the right support and attitude, we can all become the best versions of ourselves.

Lastly, to encourage you to strive for the best version of yourself as one of your life's goals, in Part 1, I introduced you to the Daily 5-Star PIS Goal, an actionable Framework that you can easily incorporate into your daily routine.

Here are a few reasons why this Framework can be particularly effective for you. (As a side note, the in-depth explanation of the theories and rationale underlying the 5-Star Framework is provided in Part 5 of the book. Feel free to jump ahead if you wish, or continue here for a comprehensive summary of Part 5).

1.It's clear and straightforward: A 5-star system is easy to remember and provides a concrete goal to aim for each day without feeling overwhelmed.

2. Encourages consistency: Having a daily target helps build consistent habits. By aiming for five positive actions each day, you're likely to develop routines that support your PIS over time.

3. Flexibility and personalisation: The 5-Star Framework is flexible and allows you to choose activities that best suit your needs and preferences, making it more likely you'll stick with it.

4. Holistic approach: Including a variety of activities (e.g., deep breathing breaks, grounding practices, healthy meals) ensures a well-rounded attitude towards mental health by encouraging you to take care of different aspects of your wellbeing.

5. Positive reinforcement: Completing five positive actions each day provides a sense of achievement, reinforcing the importance of self-care and self-reliance.

Take a moment to reflect on how these strategies have already started to make a difference in your life. Celebrate the progress you've made and the commitment you've shown to enhancing your PIS.

Looking ahead: Building a PIS constellation

In the second part of our journey, we'll investigate some factors that influence our psychological defences. Our investigation will offer new ways for you to earn stars every day through actions that enhance your mental wellbeing. Keep in mind, each star you accumulate is a step towards creating your own constellation, a symbol of your continuous effort and progress in building a resilient mind.

Imagine each positive action you take as a star in the sky. Individually, each star is undoubtedly important, but together, they form a brilliant constellation, reflecting your dedication and growth. By focusing on daily actions, you'll gradually see the empowering, interconnected pattern of your efforts.

As you embark on this quest, remember that every small action counts. Whether it's taking a moment for deep breathing, engaging in a meaningful conversation, or simply enjoying a healthy meal, each star you earn contributes to your mental resilience. Let's aim to create a constellation that shines brightly, embodying the strength of your dedication.

Part 2

Factors that Influence the Psychological Immune System

Genetics loads the gun, environment pulls the trigger.
— Francis Collins

Chapter 6

Nature & Nurture: Factors that Influence the Psychological Immune System

★

Having explored how the PIS develops throughout different life stages, we now turn our attention to the external and further internal factors that influence its function. Genetic predispositions and environmental influences, such as socio-cultural values, play crucial roles in shaping this system. For example, while genetic factors may predispose individuals to varying levels of psychological resilience, elements like social expectations can exacerbate mental health challenges. In this section, we will examine how genetic factors influence—but do not fully determine—the workings of the PIS, particularly in how they affect an individual's ability to cope with stress and adversity. To make this exploration engaging, we will focus on anxiety, a common issue that affects us all to varying degrees.

Anxiety is a normal part of the human experience. Who hasn't felt anxious once, twice, or even a hundred times before? While anxiety can be highly unsettling, it isn't entirely detrimental. It's speculated that it may have served an evolutionary purpose by enhancing preparedness and alertness, and today, it can motivate us to take action. For instance, the nervousness you feel before an important job interview can compel you to prepare thoroughly, ensuring you are well-equipped to answer tough questions and make a good impression. However, anxiety becomes problematic when it is disproportionate to any actual danger, causes significant distress, physical symptoms, or perpetuates itself in a vicious cycle. This is evident in Penny's case, where her worries and fearful thoughts intensify her anxiety, gradually wearing down her PIS and leaving her less able to cope with everyday challenges.

Speaking of Penny, her experience underscores that anxiety can be chronic, as seen in generalised anxiety disorder (GAD), which is more like a persistent trait. Those with GAD often live on edge, feeling anxious from seemingly trivial triggers. Penny, for example, recently felt extremely uncomfortable while queueing in a supermarket because a nearby couple was giggling and speaking in a foreign language. When I asked her what made her uneasy, she was convinced they were laughing at her.

Anxiety manifests in various forms and clinical descriptions, typically categorised into general anxiety, panic, phobia, and sometimes, obsessive-compulsive disorder (OCD). Anxiety can also be transient and situation-specific, like an episodic state rather than a trait. For our present discussion, I'll focus on generalized anxiety and its episodic counterpart. As in Dina's example, who (understandably) experiences anxiety during specific events like upcoming presentations or family crises, but does not endure a constant underlying sense of dread.

At this point, you might realise how Penny's and Dina's experiences with anxiety can be largely explained by the function and structure of their PIS. You're aware that the way their parents responded to their needs as toddlers laid the foundations for how they perceive and respond to the world now as adults, and potentially into their senior years.

Although, you might wonder: Is it possible that Penny had responsive, loving parents and still grew up to be insecure and anxious? Certainly. Some babies, despite receiving sensitive and caring responses from their parents, are hard to soothe and continue to respond with irritation or distress. While parental responsiveness is crucial, genetic factors also play a significant role in shaping our reactions to the world. A fascinating study conducted by the National Institute of Mental Health (NIMH) shows that some babies are naturally more anxious and nervous due to their genetic makeup, even with loving, responsive parents. The researchers found that infants with a temperament known as 'behavioural inhibition' - characterised by cautious, fearful, and avoidant behaviours - are likely to grow into adults displaying introverted and anxiety-prone personalities. This groundbreaking study highlights that, while parental support is essential, genetics significantly influence a child's emotional development and how they respond to their environment, no matter how nurturing their environment may be.

Indeed, John Bowlby, whose Attachment Theory we discussed previously, faced criticism for placing too much responsibility on the mother. Critics argued that he overlooked other factors that could influence attachment styles. Indeed, while maternal sensitivity and responsiveness are crucial, they are not the only determinants of a child's attachment style. Along with genetic predispositions, broader family dynamics, such as the number of siblings or sibling rivalries, and social conditions like poverty can significantly impact how a child develops attachments. Random events, such as a sudden family move or the loss of a close family member, can also profoundly influence attachment styles by disrupting the child's sense of security and routine.

Genetic threads of anxiety

Now, let's take a closer look at the role of genetics. How exactly do genetic factors influence the PIS, particularly in the context of anxiety? This exploration will help us understand the complex interplay between our inherited traits and our environmental experiences.

Before we go any further, it's important to clarify that there is no single "anxiety gene" or "resilience gene", for that matter. While a genetic predisposition to anxiety undoubtedly exists, the nature and extent of genetic contributions to anxiety are complex and not fully understood. Research shows that about 30% to 40% of the reasons why people might experience anxiety disorders can be traced back to their genes. Now, you might wonder, if there isn't a specific anxiety gene, what contributes to this heritability?

Recent advances in genetic research show that anxiety isn't caused by just one gene; instead, it involves several genes that work together and are influenced by our surroundings and life experiences. Imagine each gene as a player on a football team. No single player is solely responsible for the game's outcome, much like no single gene dictates anxiety. Rather, it's the combination of players, their interactions, their strategies, and how they respond to the playing field conditions that determine the team's success. Similarly, multiple genes work together with environmental influences to shape our psychological traits.

The science behind anxiety

To better grasp how genetics play a role in anxiety, researchers often study twins. Identical twins share all of their genes, whereas fraternal twins share about half. By comparing these twins, scientists have observed that identical twins often exhibit anxiety traits more frequently than fraternal twins, suggesting a strong genetic influence on anxiety. Researchers also look at animals specifically bred to display high anxiety. For example, some rodents are bred to react more fearfully to light or loud noises, which mimics how some people with anxiety might react to everyday situations. These studies help us understand the genetic basis behind behaviours typical of anxiety, such as heightened alertness or avoidance of social interactions.

If you're curious about whether disorders such as GAD run in families, consider the case of Penny. Look at whether multiple first-degree relatives, like Penny's parents or siblings, have been diagnosed with similar conditions. This was indeed the case for Penny's brothers, suggesting a genetic link in her family. Additionally, observing how family members respond to treatments can offer clues about genetic influences. For instance, Penny and her older brother both responded similarly to specific medications, indicating shared genetic factors affecting their reactions to these treatments.

The consistency of anxiety traits over time can also point to a genetic component. Penny, for example, has displayed anxiety-related behaviours and personality traits consistently throughout her life, regardless of the specific situations or environmental changes she has faced. This kind of enduring pattern suggests genetic influences on the development of brain structures and functions that regulate anxiety (i.e. the amygdala), as well as on the production and regulation of neurotransmitters involved in stress responses. Such consistency in anxiety traits is often a clear indicator of underlying genetic factors.

In Dina's case, who does not have an anxiety disorder, those genetic threads of anxiety, representing 30% to 40%, still play a significant role in shaping how she handles stress and uncertainty. That is because our genes, which we inherit from our parents, are like a set of instructions that influence our personality and our reactions to various situations. Some people might possess genes that combine in a way that predisposes them to worry more, while others might have genes that combine in a way that make them naturally more laid-back. So, even though Dina doesn't struggle with chronic anxiety, her genetic makeup still influences how she copes with life's challenges.

Nature & nurture

It is time to consider this: if your genes only account for 30% to 40% of how you respond to stressful situations and life challenges, what about the remaining 60% to 70%? We will return to this shortly, but for the time being, contemplate how fascinating it is that our biology and genetic makeup play a considerable but not exclusive role in shaping our perception and responses to the world, or of who we are. As the outdated nature vs. nurture debate questions.

This, once again, brings me to Penny, who feels overwhelmed by her anxiety, which is a common way many people experience their symptoms. However, feeling "preyed on", as she often puts it, by anxiety can be an unhelpful perspective, it positions the anxiety as an external force with control over her, which makes her feel helpless or stuck. It would be beneficial for Penny to work on shifting her perspective. For instance, instead of viewing anxiety as something preying on her, she could see it as a signal or a part of herself that needs attention and care. This perspective shift has the potential to empower her, echoing Alice Walker's insight: "The most common way people give up their power is by thinking they don't have any." With this newfound empowerment, Penny could be motivated to explore various coping techniques and approaches to manage her symptoms. For example, adopting the 5-Star Framework could help her recognise that despite living with chronic anxiety, she can still take charge and make decisions to enhance her wellbeing. Breathing exercises, diving into a great novel, and limiting caffeine intake could all count towards building her constellation of positive actions. This effective strategy could help Penny improve her mental health by creating a consistent and holistic routine that supports her PIS.

Returning to our earlier discussion, while genetics account for about 30% to 40% of our responses to the world, the remaining 60% to 70% is influenced by a variety of environmental and psychological factors. Our life experiences profoundly shape how we see and interact with the world. Both positive and negative experiences influence our beliefs, behaviours, and emotional responses. The people around us, our cultural context, and our social interactions also influence how we respond to the world. Supportive relationships can enhance our resilience, whereas toxic environments may increase our vulnerability to stress. Note that our coping strategies and behaviours are also shaped through observation and experience. These learned behaviours can either help us manage stress and adversity more effectively or contribute to more problematic responses. Hence the importance of seeking environments that foster development and relationships that promote personal growth.

Furthermore, our cognitive processes, that is how we think about and interpret the events in our lives, greatly affect our emotional and behavioural responses. Cognitive biases, mindset, and individual perceptions are critical in shaping our reactions. Additionally, the values we cultivate and the goals we pursue considerably influence how we perceive and respond to life's events. Often, some of us become consumed with keeping up with others, maintaining a certain image, or pursuing status and admiration. This relentless chase can distract us from what truly matters: nurturing habits that promote personal growth and development. When our goals align more with external validation rather than internal fulfilment, we may find ourselves more vulnerable to stress and less equipped to handle life's challenges. By focusing on values that foster self-improvement and genuine wellbeing, we can build a more resilient and fulfilling life - something we'll discuss at length in Chapter 15.

Pause & reflect

Since you have more control over your environment, attitudes, and behaviours than your genes — and these factors can influence your genes positively or negatively, affecting your psychological defences — what steps will you take to improve them? Have you ever realised that you don't need to succumb to genetic traits or those aspects that run in your family? Have you ever realised that you are, in fact, a product of both your biology and your environment?

Understanding and addressing this interplay provides powerful ways to improve our responses to the world, enhancing our overall mental health and wellbeing. Keep in mind that our environment interacts with our genetic predispositions in complex ways, shaping our unique personal experiences and reactions. This interaction shows that the 'nature vs. nurture' debate is not as clear-cut as once thought. We are not solely the product of nature (our genes) or nurture (our culture and environment); rather, we are the result of intricate interactions between both. Recognising this complexity opens up numerous possibilities for change and improvement.

Let's take this opportunity to reflect on some aspects of your life. Consider the following questions to better understand how your environment influences your PIS.

1. What aspects of your current environment feel like they drain your energy rather than replenish it? Consider whether these aspects are within your control to change, and think about steps you might take to reduce their impact on your life.

2. Who are the people in your life that support your growth, and who are those that may hinder it? Reflect on how you can spend more time with supportive individuals and less with those who negatively affect your psychological defences.

3. Are your daily activities aligned with your long-term goals for building a resilient mind? Identify one small habit you could start

or one detrimental habit you could stop that would bring you closer to these goals.

If you are struggling with answering these questions, don't worry, this is exactly what we will be focusing on in the upcoming chapter.

Everything can be taken from a man but one thing; the last of the
human freedoms: to choose one's attitude in any given set of
circumstances, to choose one's own way. – Viktor Frankl

Chapter 7

Harnessing Control: Enhancing Resilience Through Daily Choices

★

With all the demands of life—family responsibilities, work, financial obligations, and social interactions—it's often hard to find a
moment to pause and reflect on the aspects of our day-to-day that
we can control and that are crucial for our wellbeing. These aspects, if neglected, can slowly erode our PIS. Conversely, they can
be key to maintaining and enhancing our psychological defences.
So, congratulations on taking the time to read this book. Your proactive approach to caring for your mental health is commendable,
showing that you're in charge and have a strong commitment to
yourself and those around you. Give yourself a star!

Now that we've set the stage, we are about to explore important aspects that invite you to reflect on the many possibilities
available to boost your inner strength and, by extension, live a
more balanced and fulfilling life. Let's revisit the key questions
from Chapter 6 that can help us uncover and address some crucial
areas of life. And remember, this journey is all about you.

Analysing environmental drains

Question recap: What aspects of your current environment feel like they drain your energy rather than replenish it?

Let's begin by addressing a notable environmental drain for many: disorganisation, clutter and lack of cleanliness in personal spaces, including our homes, offices, and vehicles. Take a moment to look around you. How does your current environment look? If your space seems untidy or unclean, don't worry! You're not alone, and there are steps you can take to improve this.

Although maintaining tidiness might seem trivial, the accumulation of clutter can significantly hinder our daily activities and overall "ebb and flow" of life. Clutter can overwhelm the senses, creating sensory overload that makes it difficult to focus, contributing to increased stress and anxiety about unfinished tasks. Have you ever felt stressed or anxious due to a cluttered space? Clean and organised environments, on the other hand, enhance mood and self-esteem by fostering a sense of control and accomplishment.

The KonMari Method, popularized by Marie Kondo, emphasizes the value of keeping only items that "spark joy," leading to a more organised and emotionally satisfying living space. A recently published survey of 331 female respondents supports this approach, as it found that regularly employing the KonMari approach significantly increased positive feelings and emotions through the liberating experience of letting go. Further research published in the *Journal of Environmental Psychology* also supports the idea that a tidy environment can lead to better mental health and wellbeing, offering benefits such as improved productivity, better sleep quality, and a greater ability to focus and complete tasks efficiently. In case you find it difficult to let things go, start practicing with an old piece of furniture or a redundant appliance. Next, you'll be letting go of old sorrows and emotional hang-ups! As Marie

Kondo observes "No matter how wonderful things used to be, we cannot live in the past."

Now, let's consider a second modern environmental drain: excessive use of social media and technology. Think about your digital habits. How much time have you spent today, or this past week, browsing social media and watching YouTube videos? If you can't quite remember, it might be time to start being more aware of how you use technology. Just like physical clutter, unmanaged technology use occupies substantial mental space and leads to mental fatigue. This fatigue stems from prolonged focus and cognitive overload caused by constant notifications and multitasking demands.

Moreover, excessive use of social media can lead to emotional distress by disrupting life balance through the neglect of real-life relationships, hobbies, and self-care activities. Studies published in the journal *Cyberpsychology, Behaviour, and Social Networking* highlight the negative impact of excessive social media use on mental health, underscoring the importance of managing digital clutter. In fact, the detrimental effects of excessive social media use have been well-documented over the past decade, further emphasising the need for proactive strategies to mitigate these impacts. With this in mind, let's explore some practical options for addressing environmental drains and activate the PIS.

Steps to manage environmental drains

Here are four guiding points to help you organise your surroundings:

1. Start small: Choose one area or room to begin with, rather than trying to tackle everything at once. This could be as simple as a drawer, a desk, or a section of a room. Completing a smaller area provides a sense of accomplishment and motivation to continue.

2. Declutter before organising: Go through items systematically and decide what to keep, donate, sell, or throw away. Be honest about what you truly need and use. This step reduces the volume of items you need to organize and clean, making the task less overwhelming.

3. Schedule regular cleaning and organising sessions: Make a habit of setting aside specific times for tidying up and organising. This routine helps prevent clutter from building up and keeps your surroundings consistently manageable.

4. Reward yourself. After completing an organising or cleaning session, reward yourself with something enjoyable. This could be as simple as taking a break with a favourite dessert, watching an episode of a TV show, or treating yourself to a small purchase. Setting up rewards not only makes the task more appealing but also reinforces your motivation to maintain a clean and organised space. By looking forward to a treat, you'll associate positive feelings with the effort of organising, which can make it easier to stick to your routine.

Reducing social media & technology use

Here are three steps to help manage your technology use:

1. Track your usage: Use apps or built-in features on your devices to monitor how much time you spend on social media and other digital activities. This will help you become more aware of your habits and identify when you might be engaging more than necessary.

2. Set realistic limits: Once you understand your current usage, decide on specific boundaries for your time online. Perhaps limit social media browsing to 30 minutes daily or only check updates after

completing certain tasks. Remember, it's not about eliminating these platforms. It's about using them in a way that enhances your life without overwhelming it.

3. Invest in offline interests: Cultivate hobbies and activities that don't involve screens; like reading, cooking, or spending time outdoors. This not only diversifies your daily activities but also reduces your reliance on digital platforms for entertainment and engagement.

By following these steps, you can ensure that your use of technology is balanced and meaningful, keeping your social networks alive while also enriching your real-world experiences.

Now, let's turn our attention to another critical element in building resilience: your relationships.

Evaluating relationships

Question recap: Who are the people in your life that support your growth and who are those that may hinder it?

Reflect on your current relationships, whether with siblings, family members, coworkers, or romantic partners. Do these relationships feature mutual respect, trust, and open communication? Healthy relationships should not only make you feel supported and valued but also accepted for who you truly are, flaws and all. They foster a sense of emotional safety and provide a secure base for personal growth, bringing out the best in you.

Judith Jordan's work teaches us that resilience is not an intrinsic toughness found only in unique or heroic individuals, but a human ability that can be developed and strengthened through positive, growth-fostering relationships. Positive relationships are essential pillars of wellbeing, with their uplifting effects on emotional and physical health well-documented by numerous studies. Research shows that the nature of positive relationships evolves across different stages of life, such as friendships during adolescence and marital bonds in adulthood, and these relationships are consistently linked to better mental health.

Key characteristics of positive relationships include sharing joyful moments, supporting each other's goals, and showing genuine interest and emotional engagement. Take a moment to reflect on the positive relationships in your own life. What elements make these relationships special and beneficial to your PIS? Consider how you contribute to these relationships and think about ways you can further foster positive interactions with others. Remember, you play an important role in the psychological wellbeing of those you interact with, just as they do for you. By nurturing and investing in these connections, you not only enhance your own PIS function and structure, but also contribute to the resilience and mental stability of those around you.

Conversely, consider if any of your relationships involve manipulation, control, or a lack of boundaries, traits that define toxic interactions. Such relationships can drain your energy, invalidate your feelings, and generate constant emotional turmoil. The quality of our relationships profoundly impacts our psychological stability and resilience. Healthy connections nurture our PIS and enhance our ability to cope with adversity, while toxic relationships can significantly undermine our mental health. Reflecting on these dynamics in your own life is essential for cultivating positive connections that support and promote a resilient mind.

Here's some guidance on how to cultivate stronger relationships with supportive individuals and distance oneself from negative influences:

Cultivating stronger relationships & Distancing from negative influences

1. Assess your relationships: Take stock of your relationships to identify who uplifts you and who brings you down. This awareness

is crucial for managing your social circle effectively. Reflect on how each person in your life makes you feel and recognise the importance of surrounding yourself with those who inspire and support you.

2. Set boundaries: Establish clear boundaries with those who negatively affect your wellbeing. This includes learning to say no (i.e. being assertive) and limiting contact with individuals who drain your emotional energy. Remember, it's okay to prioritise your mental health and protect your space from negativity.

3. Invest in positive relationships: Actively spend more time with people who support and value you. Focus on nurturing these relationships as they are foundational to your emotional health. Share your joys and challenges with them and make an effort to be present and engaged in their lives. Positive relationships are mutual, and the more you invest, the more rewarding they become.

4. Be a source of positivity: Strive to be someone who offers positive interactions and brings out the best in those around you. Show genuine interest in others, celebrate their successes, and offer support during tough times. By fostering an environment of positivity and encouragement, you not only enhance your own relationships but also contribute to the wellbeing and resilience of those you care about.

Before we dive into the next section, remember that it's possible to take control of aspects of your life that are essential for boosting your psychological defences, like making decisions about and taking action toward improving your surroundings, relationships, and digital habits. However, be mindful that the type of control we're discussing here is rooted in agency, autonomy, and self-efficacy—not the kind of control that makes you controlling, which, indeed, can be detrimental to your PIS. Continue reflecting on the steps you're taking and the active choices you're making, and consider how they can lead you toward a stronger, more resilient self. You have the ability to make positive changes, one step at a time.

Aligning activities with goals

Question Recap: Are your daily activities aligned with your long-term goals for building a resilient mind?

Reflect on how your daily routine influence your PIS and personal growth. Personal growth involves developing new skills, expanding knowledge, and realising your true potential. Essentially, becoming the best version of yourself. These aspects are interconnected. As we achieve our potential, our psychological defences improves, creating a positive upward spiral. Ask yourself: *Do my daily activities advance my journey of personal growth and enhance my inner strength, or do they leave me feeling stagnant?*

Even with fixed commitments, family commitments and tiring jobs, there's an opportunity to strengthen your PIS and build resilience. Repetitive tasks, though mundane, can cultivate important skills like emotional regulation and problem-solving. These skills improve communication and conflict resolution, helping you maintain composure in adversity. Over time, what seems mundane can become a tool for personal development, enriching both your professional and personal life.

Remember, while many aspects of life are beyond our control, it's empowering to focus on areas we can control. Consider elements of your day that are entirely within your grasp. Think about your morning or evening routine. Do you start or end your day with energy and purpose, or do you feel rushed and frustrated? Tweaking these routines can noticeably brighten your mindset and promote personal development.

Take a minute or two to evaluate these routines. Aligning these moments with maintaining your psychological health is crucial. They should contribute to building resilience and the best version of yourself. If your current habits aren't serving this purpose, consider what changes could be made.

Here are some steps you can take

1. Introduce a morning and or evening breathing exercise: Start or finish your day with a few minutes of deep breathing to centre yourself and set a calm, focused tone for the day, or time of rest.

2. Dedicate a moment to gratitude: Spend a minute or two each morning or evening reflecting on what you are grateful for. This practice can enhance your mood and ignite positive attitudes. A 2022 psychological study conducted with over 1,000 participants, including both adults and adolescents, found that gratitude is more than just a passive, positive experience. The research provides evidence that expressing gratitude can motivate people to exert greater effort towards self-improvement, suggesting that gratitude plays a vital role in encouraging individuals to become better versions of themselves. Take a moment to reflect on what you are grateful for right now, perhaps it's the ability to see, having the means to pick up a book and read, or simply the opportunity to learn and grow. How motivating is that for you?

3. Set positive intentions: Take a moment to set specific, positive intentions for your day. This could be something like focusing on being patient, achieving a particular goal (a 5-star PIS), or maintaining a positive outlook, *May I be positive and grateful today*.

We've just explored how addressing aspects of life that we have control over can strengthen your psychological defences. Take hold of this sense of control and keep focusing on these areas, fine-tuning your actions to cultivate a healthier, more balanced you. Each of the steps suggested above counts as a star, helping you reach your daily goal on any day you choose. Personal growth is a continual journey, always evolving and offering new opportunities for rediscovery. Seize the journey toward becoming the best version of yourself, filled with endless possibilities, and watch as you build a brilliant constellation of achievements and resilience.

Now, let's shift our focus to other critical elements we can be in charge of to support our PIS integrity. In the next chapter, we'll explore the essential role that being physically and mentally active plays in reinforcing your psychological defences.

Reading fiction is an empathy gym, where people get to practice understanding others in a low-stakes environment. – Paul Bloom

Chapter 8

Mental Fitness: A Holistic Approach to Mental Resilience

★

In our journey towards a resilient mind, being active both mentally and physically is a conscious and empowering choice. Just as you might ease into a new workout regimen, building mental fitness also requires a gradual start, progressing through levels of increasing complexity as you gain strength and resilience. So, approach the 5-Star Framework as a mental fitness program. You can start with one or two activities per day and gradually increase to five as they become more comfortable.

To begin, think of mental fitness as you would any other form of physical exercise. It involves "cognitive workouts" that challenge and expand your mental capabilities, such as engaging in stimulating conversations or focusing on tasks like driving to a new place. It also involves physical activities that energise your brain, like taking the dog for a walk or going to the gym. The brain, after all, isn't just a metaphorical muscle, it's a very real organ that thrives on both mental effort and physical movement.

Throughout this chapter, we'll see how adopting an active lifestyle can do more than just improve physical health—it can also foster self-reliance and boost confidence, setting a strong foundation for both psychological and physical wellbeing. As we move forward, we'll also explore the power of mindful living, highlighting how it can enhance self-awareness and self-control. And along the way, we'll uncover the often-overlooked benefits of reading—not just as a way to improve focus, but as a means of broadening our psychological experiences through the lives of characters and the diverse worlds they inhabit.

Staying active for mental health

It may not surprise you that staying active benefits more than just your physical body. It also significantly enhances your psychological and overall mental health. When we engage in physical activities, we are immediately rewarded. Physical activity triggers the release of endorphins, "feel-good" hormones that alleviate stress, anxiety, and low mood. These hormones are released during various forms of exercise, whether moderate or vigorous. A 2023 research review demonstrated that even practices as gentle as Tai Chi can trigger the release of endorphins. This is truly motivating! It suggests that any gentle activity you engage in wholeheartedly can boost your mood and enhance your wellbeing in that moment.

Beyond improving mood, regular physical activity offers neurobiological benefits as well, promoting the growth of new brain cells through neurogenesis—a process observed in both human and animal studies, particularly in the hippocampus. You'll recall from Chapter 5 that we discussed neurogenesis in the context of aging. As you might remember, neurogenesis enhances cognitive functions such as memory retention, executive functions like decision-making and problem-solving, as well as attention and processing speed. Additionally, let's not forget the physical health benefits that come from regular exercise, such as improved cardiovascular health, increased muscle strength, enhanced flexibility, better weight management, and a stronger immune system. Moreover, adopting a more active lifestyle not only builds self-esteem and resilience, essential for facing life's challenges, but also introduces structure and discipline into your daily routine, contributing to your PIS and overall mental stability. Hopefully, this is convincing enough to get you moving!

Please note that incorporating regular physical activity into your lifestyle isn't about pushing yourself through disliked routines. It's about finding joy in movements that make you feel good, fostering a positive mindset. Whether it's through simple tasks like tidying your home or engaging in more vigorous exercises like running, every active moment counts towards enhancing your psychological health as part of our Daily 5-Star PIS Goal.

So, how does your current daily routine support your physical and mental fitness? Consider the activities you engage in every day: Are they helping you build a stronger body and mind, or is there room for improvement?

If you've been mostly sedentary, easing into a more active lifestyle can be simpler than you might think. Earn a star towards you Daily 5-Star PIS Goal by starting with small, achievable steps like a 10-minute daily walk. Alternatively, incorporate exercises at home using apps or YouTube channels to guide you through various workouts. Look for ways to weave activity into your usual routines, such as walking around while on a phone call. Gradually increase your activity level by setting modest goals, and choose exercises that you enjoy, which can make staying active feel less like work and more like pleasure. Most importantly, consistency is key. Even a little bit of activity every day can lead to notable improvements in your physical and mental wellbeing.

Still, the means to achieve mental fitness are not confined only to activities involving physical movement. In fact, being still through mindful practices like meditation can significantly boost the PIS by fostering deeper awareness and presence in our daily lives. Lao Tzu said, "To the mind that is still, the whole universe surrenders," teaching us that when one's mind is calm and at peace, one can perceive and understand the world more clearly.

Mindfulness & meditation

Although often used interchangeably, mindfulness and meditation are distinct, yet closely related practices that can significantly enhance our mental fitness. Mindfulness is the practice of being fully present and engaged with whatever we're doing, free from distractions or judgment. It involves noticing our thoughts, feelings, surroundings, and the people around us, rather than operating on autopilot or getting lost in daydreams.

Meditation, however, is an intentional activity where you dedicate time to sit quietly and focus, commonly on your breath - though there are many other points of focus for those who advance in their practice such as sounds, physical sensations and thoughts.

Mini-test: Are you on autopilot?

Let's take a quick moment to test your current state of mindfulness. Please put the book down and try to recall the main points you've read so far in this chapter about developing your mental fitness through the 5-Star Framework. If you can remember the central themes, you're engaging mindfully. Well done! However, if it feels like you've just been jolted awake by the request to put the book down, perhaps you're a bit distracted, which is perfectly normal. This realization itself is a valuable step toward mindfulness. This is how it all begins: by noticing and recognising your mental states.

Meditation

Meditation is a crucial step toward developing awareness, or becoming mindful, in your daily actions. This doesn't require special equipment or hours of free time. Although I haven't explicitly stated it before, meditation is something I've previously encouraged you to practice, and I'll continue to emphasise its importance right now.

Do you remember the deep breathing breaks we talked about earlier? Well, that's a form of meditation. See how there's no frills about it? Let's build on that? Please go ahead and take a few deep breaths. Inhale slowly through your nose, allowing your abdomen to expand fully, and then exhale slowly, letting your abdomen fall. As you do this, focus on the sensation of the air entering through your nostrils, your chest rising and falling, and the air exiting just as gently. This simple practice isn't just about breathing. It's about being present with each breath. You'll recall that when you breathe deeply like this, you activate the parasympathetic branch of your nervous system—the "rest and digest" response that counters the "fight or flight" reaction. This sends a reassuring message to your brain and mind: *Everything is okay. I am safe and well in this moment.* Enjoy this awareness and the privilege of feeling secure and at peace right now.

Can you see how, for instance, beginning your day with this practice sets you on the path to a good start? By recognising *I am awake and calm*, and by consciously replenishing your brain with a flow of oxygen through deep, conscious breathing, you're meditating and cultivating mindfulness. Repeating this daily, or even twice a day, fosters a tranquil mental state and strengthens your PIS for when challenges arise. Through this practice, you're building mental bridges that, in times of distress, will guide you to inner places of rest rather than pushing you into a fight-or-flight response.

Upon waking, you can perform this practice siting with a straight back or while still lying down on your back, if it feels better. You don't even have to close your eyes if that makes you uncomfortable. Just let your gaze fall softly on the ground or a wall. The key here is to be comfortable and focused on your breathing. Throughout the day, you can practice mindful breathing at your desk or while stuck in traffic, whether openly or not, it's completely up to you!

Integrating mindfulness and meditation into your daily life

By understanding that living mindfully simply involves paying attention to yourself and your surroundings, and that meditation—through practices like conscious breathing—facilitates a mindful lifestyle, incorporating these practices into your daily routine becomes even more straightforward than you might have expected.

Here are some steps to get you started, each of which counts as a star towards your Daily 5-Star PIS Goal:

1. Begin each day with a brief breathing-meditation. Start with a few deep breaths, inhaling and exhaling slowly, for 1 minute on the first day, and gradually increase to 2-3 minutes by the end of the week.

2. Engage in mindful moments. Select everyday activities like eating, driving, or talking to your spouse, and focus fully on the task at hand. Avoid distractions like smartphones and television during those experiences, and use all your senses to observe every detail of that chosen moment.

3. Practice regularly. Mindfulness and meditation improve with consistent practice. Over time, you'll find that deep, calming breaths, savouring your meals, noticing your surroundings and enjoying conversations become natural to you, replacing distracted states.

By embracing these practices, you're not just enhancing your mental clarity and emotional equilibrium. You're also taking significant steps toward maintaining the overall health of your PIS by strengthening the neural pathways involved in emotional regulation and stress management. As we continue this mental fitness discussion, remember that each small step contributes to a larger journey toward a more emotionally stable and resilient mind.

The power of reading: A dual exercise for your mind

As you embrace mindfulness as the art of noticing and fully engaging with the present moment, let's take this practice a step further. Imagine going for a walk while lifting dumbbells to work out your arms and shoulders. Just as you combine physical exercises, you can enhance your mental workout by incorporating mindfulness into your reading routine. This simply means cultivating heightened focus.

Reading is an incredible exercise for the mind. If you're reading this book, you're likely already aware of the benefits that reading offers. Paul Bloom, a psychologist and professor at Yale University, has extensively discussed how reading fiction is particularly beneficial for mental health. He argues that fiction allows us to experience emotions and situations outside our everyday lives. This imaginative immersion can increase empathy by improving our understanding of others' perspectives and can also boost emotional intelligence—the ability to recognise, understand, and manage our own emotions and those of others. Note that both empathy and emotional intelligence are essential features of a well-functioning PIS. A fascinating 2013 experimental study conducted with Dutch adults found that empathy skills increase when we are mentally transported into a story. This mental journey allows readers to change as a result of reading fiction, as it engages various processes, including emotional involvement in the story and identification with the characters. This highlights the importance of reading mindfully, as it facilitates a fuller and more immersive experience, enhancing cognitive and emotional development.

I can personally attest to these research findings. Through reading fiction, I've deeply connected with fictional characters and their plights. I shared the intense pain of Grendel, the monster in the Anglo-Saxon epic Beowulf. His hypersensitivity to sounds drove him toward the very humans who disturbed his peace and ultimately caused his demise, a struggle I resonate with due to my own hypersensitivity to sounds. In Madame Bovary, I empathized with Emma Bovary's solitude and inner-battles, while critically viewing the values she pursued. These experiences have enriched my understanding and emotional perspectives, illustrating the profound impact reading can have when you fully engage with it.

Engaging with books: More than just a pastime

When you read, you do more than just follow a narrative, you enter a realm where you can safely explore complex emotions and scenarios. This isn't just an escape, it's a form of mental training. The characters' journeys offer insights into human psychology and prompt us to reflect on our own choices and emotions.

To enhance your mental fitness through the Daily 5-Star PIS Goal, I encourage you to diversify your reading. Explore genres and authors you might not usually consider. Each book opens a new window into human experiences, helping to build a more empathetic and understanding mind.

Why not start today? Pick up a novel and let yourself become absorbed in its world. Notice how you engage with the characters and situations. Are you just scanning the text, or are you truly thinking and feeling along with the story? This level of engagement is a practical application of mindfulness, allowing you to be fully present with the book in your hands and enhancing your capacity for empathy and self-development.

As we conclude this section on the enriching power of reading, I'd like to share a personal habit that has significantly enhanced my nightly routine. Instead of reaching for the bright screen of my smartphone, I prefer to unwind with a good book in bed. Currently, I'm engrossed in *Walden Two* by B.F. Skinner, a thought-provoking novel that explores the idea of a utopian society. It emphasizes the importance of a supportive community and structured environment in fostering individual wellbeing and mental health. This practice of reading before bed not only relaxes my mind and body but also helps induce sleepiness by focusing on a single task after a bustling day. It's a fascinating journey that takes me away from the day's stresses and into Skinner's visionary world, signalling to my brain that it's time to wind down and prepare for a restful night's sleep.

Next, we will explore how essential sleep is to strengthen the PIS, looking into its critical role in consolidating the day's learning and rejuvenating our minds for tomorrow.

You're not healthy, unless your sleep is healthy.
- William C. Dement.

Chapter 9

Sleep: A Strong Pillar of Mental Resilience

★

Welcome to a vital pathway on your 5-Star PIS journey, a good night's sleep. Did you know that sleep is not just a passive state but a dynamic activity that plays a crucial role in your psychological defences and overall mental health? As we (hopefully) spend about one-third of our lives asleep, understanding its purposes is essential for maintaining a balanced, resilient mind.

Here, we'll succinctly investigate the fascinating workings of the brain during sleep and explore how this restorative period aids not just physical recovery but mental resilience. We'll discuss practical bedtime habits that can enhance the quality of your sleep, tackle the common yet often overlooked issue of sleep procrastination, and provide strategies for managing insomnia and intrusive thoughts that can hinder a good night's rest. By the end of this investigation, you'll be equipped with knowledge and tools to value the full potential of sleep, making it a strong ally in your quest for a robust PIS and consistent wellbeing. So, let's discover how you can optimize your sleep to fortify your mind and body, adding a bright star to your constellation of achievements.

Understanding sleep: The key to psychological Immunity

Understanding how sleep works is like deciphering a nightly reju-venation ritual that our brains undergo to maintain optimal mental health and fortify our PIS. Sleep is composed of several cycles, each consisting of two primary phases: REM (Rapid Eye Move-ment) and non-REM sleep. Non-REM sleep begins with the tran-sition from wakefulness to sleep, progressing through light sleep stages into deep, restorative sleep, where the body repairs muscles and tissues, stimulates growth and development, and boosts im-mune function. During these cycles, our brain waves or electrical activity fluctuate significantly. In the deeper stages of non-REM sleep, we see slow-wave activity known as delta waves, indicative of a restorative, deeply restful state. As we move into REM sleep, the brain becomes highly active, displaying for instance, rapid beta brain waves, despite the body being in a nearly paralyzed state. This stage, associated with vivid dreams, is crucial for cognitive func-tions such as memory consolidation and emotional regulation. You can see, then, how by understanding and optimizing these sleep stages, we can enhance our PIS function.

Nightly brain maintenance: Cleaning up & organising

A common metaphor to illustrate the brain at sleep is that of a busy office that has been bustling with activity all day. At night, a dedi-cated night shift crew, your sleep cycles, comes in to clean up and organize. This nightly crew ensures that everything is set for the next day by engaging in crucial tasks such as memory consolidation and toxin clearance. Memory consolidation during sleep, especially during the slow-wave and REM stages, involves the brain pro-cessing and solidifying what we've learned and experienced throughout the day. This is similar to filing away important docu-ments in an office, ensuring they are stored properly for easy access when needed.

Just as a well-organised office depends on regular maintenance and filing, our brain's ability to store and retrieve memories relies on quality sleep. When we either deliberately neglect sleep or encounter disruptions that prevent restful sleep, it's like the night shift team not showing up for work in that busy office. Without the night crew, the important documents, that is, the day's experiences and learnings, aren't filed correctly or might be misplaced altogether. During interrupted or insufficient sleep, especially in the critical phases of slow-wave and REM sleep, our brain struggles to effectively process and consolidate memories. This disruption can lead to several issues: incomplete memory formation, impaired learning, and increased decision errors.

Additionally, the brain has a special cleaning system called the glymphatic system that clears out waste during sleep. This process is not just regular cleaning. It's like having a specialized cleaning squad that meticulously clears out waste and toxins, crucial for preventing diseases like Alzheimer's and Parkinson's. The glymphatic system flushes out toxins that build up between brain cells during the day. Without enough sleep, harmful proteins, like beta-amyloid, can accumulate, which is linked to Alzheimer's disease. Disruptions in this cleaning process can also lead to Parkinson's disease as well as some other forms of dementia. Keeping this system working well through good sleep helps protect against these neurological disorders.

Thus, ensuring regular, uninterrupted sleep allows the brain to perform its critical night shift duties, optimising our cognitive functions and psychological immunity. Like ensuring that the office is tidy and documents are where they should be, taking care of our sleep is crucial for mental clarity and long-term health. By going through these sleep cycles each night, our brains not only recover from the day's mental exertions but also strengthen their defences against future stresses, contributing profoundly to our overall brain and psychological health.

Tackling the paradox of sleep procrastination

Despite the well-documented detrimental effects of poor sleep patterns and routines, many of us find ourselves habitually postponing sleep. This phenomenon, known as sleep procrastination, is particularly curious because it doesn't involve delaying a task we deem unpleasant. Quite the opposite, many of us express a desire for more sleep, yet we paradoxically delay going to bed when the opportunity presents itself. That's because sleep procrastination is not about the dislike of sleep itself. Most people cherish the idea of getting more sleep and often lament not having enough time for it. However, when the moment to turn in early arrives, many end up engaging in activities that push back their bedtime. This could be seen as a form of 'rebellion' against the day's demands, a way to reclaim 'me time'. At what cost, though?

Take my husband, for example, who struggles with this very issue. He often complains about the scarcity of sleep due to his demanding job that extends long hours into the evening. Still, on rare occasions when he finishes work early and has the chance to catch up on some much-needed sleep, he finds himself caught up in a cycle of sleep procrastination. His usual pattern involves reaching for his electronic devices, his computer, tablet, or other gadgets, activities that keep him wired.

Now, there is bad news for him and for those of us who share similar bedtime habits. A small Norwegian study comprised of 16 participants evaluated across three different nights, found that reading a story for 30 minutes on a tablet, before bedtime, increased alertness and delayed the onset of slow-wave activity in the brain, compared to reading the same story from a book. Although there were no differences in how quickly the participants fell asleep, the delay in the onset of the slow-wave activity suggests that the brain's transition into deep, restorative sleep is affected. This delay can potentially impact immune function, physical restoration, and the consolidation of memories related to facts and events. So, it might be time for my husband to consider swapping his electronic devices for a traditional book to improve his sleep quality and, in turn, maintain his PIS integrity.

Surely my husband understands and acknowledges the toll his bed time routine takes on his cognitive, mental, and physical health, but also recognises the difficulty of breaking this habit. Driven by both the understanding of these consequences and the necessities imposed by his work schedule, he has made strides toward a healthier sleep routine, yet he continues to battle with the tendencies of sleep procrastination.

Now, let's turn the lens towards you: Do you ever find yourself in a similar cycle of sleep procrastination? What activities tend to keep you up at night? Like my husband, do you also feel the push and pull between the need for more sleep and the urge to stay awake?

Reflect on these questions and consider how your own bedtime habits might be affecting your PIS and mental wellness. The first step towards change is recognising the pattern.

Combat sleep procrastination

While the following steps to combat sleep procrastination might not be entirely new to you, consider this a crucial reminder rather than an introduction to new information. Knowledge often doesn't automatically lead to action, especially when it comes to changing ingrained habits related to sleep, diet, and exercise. These behaviours are partly psychological, partly environmental, and always complex. Making lasting changes typically requires not just awareness but persistent effort and, often, support from those around you, such as a spouse or a family member.

Here are some reminders:

1. Create a pre-sleep ritual: Develop a calming routine before bed to signal to your body that it's time to wind down. Consider activities like reading, taking a warm bath, or engaging in gentle yoga, which can help ease the transition into sleep.

2. Limit screen time: Avoid screens and electronic devices at least an hour before bedtime. Electronic devices emit blue light that, as well as delaying slow-wave activity, disrupts the production of the "sleep-hormone" melatonin. Making it harder to fall asleep.

3. Optimise your bedroom environment: Make sure your bedroom is conducive to sleep by keeping it dark, cool, quiet, tidy and clean. Creating a restful environment reduces distractions and disturbances that can prevent restful sleep.

By actively implementing these strategies, you can tackle sleep procrastination more effectively, earn a star towards your Daily 5-Star PIS Goal, and improve both your sleep quality and overall mental health. Remember, while these steps are simple, their power lies in their consistent application.

Understanding insomnia: Beyond sleep procrastination

While some may delay sleep by choice, others find themselves struggling to fall or stay asleep despite their best intentions to turn off the lights and rest. This condition, known as insomnia, is characterised by difficulty initiating or maintaining sleep, and it can considerably impact one's quality of life. Insomnia can stem from various causes, including stress, anxiety, hormonal changes, or underlying health conditions. Often, it is exacerbated by intrusive thoughts that disrupt the mind's ability to relax. Charlie Brown humorously reflects on this universal struggle, saying, 'Sometimes I lie awake at night, and I ask, "Where have I gone wrong?" Then a voice says to me, "This is going to take more than one night." This quote captures the frustration and persistence often associated with insomnia, highlighting the challenges many individuals face in achieving restful sleep

Managing intrusive thoughts

If you're like Chalie Brown and often have nights disrupted by anxiety or spiralling thoughts, it's important to know that there are scientifically-backed methods to regain control and foster restful sleep.

Here are two potentially effective strategies:

The 20-Minute Rule. Scientifically investigated as part of Cognitive Behavioural Therapy for Insomnia (CBT-I), this technique suggests that if you can't fall asleep or return to sleep within 20 minutes, you should leave the bedroom and engage in a calming activity like listening to soft music until you feel sleepy again. This practice helps strengthen the association between your bed and sleep and prevents your bed from becoming a cue for wakefulness or stress. The evidence supporting its specific effectiveness is not definitive, meaning it might work for some people but not for others. This difference in outcomes can be due to various factors, such as individual differences in biology, psychology, lifestyle, or even the specific context in which the intervention is applied. However, this is a risk-free approach worth trying, especially since it carries no side effects. You may be one of the fortunate ones for whom this strategy leads to a restful night's sleep.

Alternatively, consider the value of expressive writing. Just before bed, take a few minutes to jot down your thoughts and feelings. This method has been shown through numerous studies to effectively reduce anxiety, rumination, and symptoms of insomnia. By writing out your concerns in a stream-of-consciousness style, you not only transfer your worries from mind to paper but also make it easier to let them go. Seeing your stressors in black and white helps you to understand and rationalise what's keeping you up at night. Once you've identified these inner stressors, you can more easily write about and implement available coping mechanisms.

Implementing these strategies not only helps manage the immediate symptoms of insomnia but also contributes to long-term improvements in your sleep quality and mental health. Remember, tackling insomnia often requires a combination of awareness and action. These methods provide a practical starting point.

Strategies for you Daily 5-Star PIS Goal

As part of our commitment to activating your PIS, here are some targeted steps (stars!) toward your Daily 5-Star PIS Goal that can help you tackle insomnia:

1. Pen and paper: Engage in writing with pen and paper to process your feelings. This traditional method allows thoughts to flow more freely and even lets you sketch or doodle as thoughts come to you, enhancing the reflective process.

2. Expressive writing: Make a habit of writing about what keeps you awake. Unlike a structured diary, expressive writing helps release emotions effectively, allowing you to confront and articulate the thoughts that disrupt your sleep.

3. Routine writing time: While establishing a consistent writing schedule can be beneficial, feel free to adapt this practice to suit your needs, especially during tough times at work, with family, or when you're wrestling with thoughts. Whether it's after dinner or right before bed, use this time as a soothing ritual, but remember there's no need to write daily unless it feels right. This flexibility ensures you turn to your journal as a source of comfort without

feeling obligated, letting your words flow naturally whenever you do write.

4. Manage expectations: Understand that while journaling is a powerful tool for self-reflection, it is not a cure-all. Use it to 'pour out' your thoughts, exploring and acknowledging issues that you might not have faced head-on before. This practice can lead to greater self-awareness and insight.

5. Gratitude practice: End each journaling session by listing things you're grateful for, no matter how small. This can shift your focus from stress to appreciation, reinforcing positive emotions and contributing to mental wellbeing. Reflect on small successes and joys from your day, helping to elicit a positive mindset before sleep.

These strategies are tailored to integrate therapeutic writing into your routine, expanding your constellation of achievements, and offering practical ways to manage insomnia and enhance your psychological resilience.

As we conclude our exploration of sleep's vital role in activating your PIS and cultivating a resilient mind, it's clear that the influence of sleep on the PIS is profound, setting the foundation for overall mental fitness. Now, we're prepared to transition to the next critical aspect of strengthening psychological defences: nutrition.

In the following section, we'll delve into how dietary choices impact our mental wellbeing, exploring the intricate connection between what we eat and how we feel, think, and cope with daily stresses.

Let food be thy medicine and medicine be thy food.
– Hippocrates

Chapter 10

Nutrition: Nourishing the Body & Mind

★

Recently, over dinner, my husband shared insights from a novel he's reading. In the story, the main character reflects on how life is inherently a series of choices and concludes that, for this very reason, it's unlikely all of those choices will be the right ones. This perspective offers a logical and comforting way to navigate our mishaps. Yet, I believe that with clear thinking, we can make most of our decisions correctly, significantly enhancing our lives. Life isn't straightforward, and we often encounter circumstances beyond our control, such as illnesses or conditions that restrict our dietary options or impose other limitations on our daily choices. However, it's the choices within our control that deserve our attention and reflection, because they hold the power to propel us forward.

This is where the symbiosis of choice and mental clarity becomes evident. The better choices we make in nourishing our minds, the more mental clarity we gain, and vice versa. This continuous cycle of improvement is not just a privilege but a responsibility. By consciously deciding what we consume, both physically and mentally, we can enhance our psychological defences, earn stars towards our Daily 5-Star PIS Goal, and enjoy more frequent positive mental states. So, let's embrace this opportunity to make informed, thoughtful choices about how we nourish not only our bodies but also our minds.

The impact of ultra-processed foods on mental health

As we explore the impact of our dietary choices, let's consider the prevalence of ultra-processed foods (UPFs) in modern diets. These foods are everywhere, convenient and tempting, often engineered for taste and long shelf-life rather than nutrition. Let's look at how these foods affect our health and why they might make it harder for us to maintain mental clarity and wellness. Understanding what makes a food 'ultra-processed' and recognising its effects can empower us to make more informed decisions that align with our Daily 5-Star PIS Goals.

UPFs undergo extensive industrial processing, leading to products that are often loaded with additives, preservatives, and have minimal nutritional value. These foods are engineered for convenience, ready-to-eat or requiring minimal preparation, which aligns well with today's fast-paced lifestyle. Consider sugary breakfast cereals, which, despite their vibrant colours and enticing flavours, are high in added sugars and refined grains. Packaged snack bars, although promising quick energy, primarily deliver artificial sweeteners and preservatives. Frozen dinners provide convenience but are typically high in sodium and lack essential nutrients. Similarly, soft drinks and sweetened beverages offer nothing more than empty calories and artificial additives. These products are so far removed from their natural origins that they have been categorized not as food, but as 'edible products' by scientist at the Global Food Research Program. Worryingly, in places like the UK and the US, over 50% of people's daily caloric intake comes from UPFs, and across the world the consumption of these products are on the rise, highlighting their ubiquity in our diets.

The health risks associated with UPFs are as widespread as their availability. According to a recent study published in the *Clinical Nutrition* Journal, no studies have reported any beneficial health outcomes from UPFs consumption. Instead, high consumption of UPFs is linked to an increased risk of various chronic diseases and mental health disorders, including depression and anxiety. You might wonder how a fizzy drink or a frozen dinner can impact your PIS and mental health. The connection lies in several factors: UPFs often lack essential nutrients necessary for brain health, such as B vitamins and omega-3 fatty acids, increasing the risk of mood disorders. The high levels of refined sugars in these foods can cause blood sugar fluctuations, which affect mood stability. Additionally, the additives and unhealthy fats they contain contribute to inflammation in the body, a condition linked to both depression and anxiety. Furthermore, UPFs can disrupt the balance of gut bacteria, the gut microbiome, which plays a crucial role in psychological health.

Talking about the microbiome...

Think of your gut microbiome as a bustling community of tiny residents, each playing a specific role in maintaining your overall health. Just as a diverse ecosystem is crucial for harmony in nature, a varied microbiome is essential for balance within your body. This vibrant community, comprised of bacteria, fungi, and viruses, primarily resides in your digestive system. It works tirelessly to break down food, regulate your metabolism, and communicate with your brain through the gut-brain axis. The gut-brain axis acts like a two-way street, enabling a messaging system where signals travel back and forth between your gut and brain.

This communication network helps your gut and brain collaborate, influencing your digestion, mood, and even cognitive processes. Thus, what we consume can significantly affect our feelings and thoughts. Have you ever noticed how your diet impacts your mood or energy levels?

The gut microbiome plays a crucial role in mental states, functioning much like a conductor for neurotransmitters, you'll recall neurotransmitters from Chapter 3, they are the brain's chemical messengers. In the domain of mental health, one of the most important of these messengers is serotonin, often called the 'feel-good' neurotransmitter because of its vital role in regulating our mood. Surprisingly, over 90% of serotonin is produced in our large intestine, and the amount produced heavily depends on the health of our gut microbiome. The link between serotonin and mood is so significant that the most common anti-depressants, known as SSRIs, work by increasing serotonin levels in the brain. Recent scientific studies, including a detailed review in the journal *Nature*, have shown that an imbalance or disruption in the microbiome, a condition known as dysbiosis, is linked to mental health issues such as anxiety and depression. This highlights just how much our gut health can impact our overall psychological states.

Fortunately, maintaining a healthy microbiome is straightforward. It requires a diet rich in fibre, fruits, vegetables, and fermented foods like yogurt and kefir. It is now well-established that diet significantly impacts the microbiome. A diet high in processed foods and low in fibre can lead to dysbiosis, whereas a diverse diet leads to a thriving microbiome, which supports robust biological and psychological defences by maintaining efficient metabolism and communication with the brain. It is, thus, crucial to maintain a varied diet, as it provides the array of nutrients that different bacteria in the microbiome need to thrive, and also encourages the growth of beneficial species, fostering a balanced ecosystem within the gut.

Nourish your PIS through your gut

By prioritising a diet that nurtures a diverse and thriving microbiome, you're doing more than just supporting a healthier gut, you're paving the way to a well-functioning PIS. You can see now how the foods we eat directly influence both our mental and physical wellbeing, underscoring the deep connection between our diet and overall health.

Embrace a rainbow of nutrient-rich foods that promote microbial diversity and boost your mood. Think colourful vegetables like bell peppers and carrots, leafy greens such as spinach and kale, fibre-rich legumes like lentils and chickpeas, and wholesome grains such as oats. These foods not only feed your microbiome but also provide the vitamins and minerals essential for good brain health.

Replacing UPFs can be more budget-friendly and easier than you might think. Start your day with a bowl of oats topped with slices of apple and a dash of cinnamon, a wholesome breakfast that's easy to prepare and satisfying. For snacks, instead of reaching for crisps or cookies, try snacking on fresh seasonal fruits or veggies. And for lunch, a homemade salad with lean meats, fish or cheese provides a nutritious alternative to fast food. Come dinner time, a small portion of sweet potatoes with tomatoes and spinach can offer comfort without the artificial ingredients often found in ready-made meals or take-aways. If you're reluctant to consume carbs like oats and pasta due to sugar spikes, adding healthy fats to these meals can help. Healthy fats slow down the digestion and absorption of carbohydrates, resulting in a more gradual release of glucose into the bloodstream. This approach can help you maintain a varied diet while managing blood sugar levels. Some examples of healthy fats include seeds, nuts, and olive oil.

Alternatively, you can skip dinner altogether, once or twice a week. Have you ever considered intermittent fasting?

Intermittent fasting & Brain health

Research into the effects of intermittent fasting on brain health is still in its nascent stages, but there is already some evidence pointing to its potential benefits. This dietary approach may not only improve various aspects of brain function as we age, but also reduce symptoms associated with mental health issues such as anxiety and depression.

Intermittent fasting appears to support psychological well-being through multiple mechanisms. It promotes the release of brain-derived neurotrophic factor (BDNF), a protein that is vital for improving mood and enhancing cognitive functions. Additionally, intermittent fasting triggers autophagy, a cellular cleanup process that removes damaged cells, which may help protect the brain from age-related declines. The regulation of blood sugar levels and reduction in inflammation, both in the body and brain, are further benefits linked to intermittent fasting that contribute to better mental health outcomes. Finaly, it enhances neuroplasticity, which is your brain's amazing ability to adapt and learn new things, such as developing new strategies to handle daily demands and major life events.

When it comes to the safety of intermittent fasting, there's not a lot of detailed reporting on side effects. However, most concerns come from research investigating more extreme fasting, like going 24 hours without eating each week. On the other hand, practicing intermittent fasting on a daily basis, where the fasting period is shorter (12 to 16 hours, including the time you sleep), might actually help avoid adverse effects. This kind of routine is often easier to manage and could be a safer way to enjoy the benefits of fasting.

While promising, intermittent fasting may not be suitable for everyone. It should be approached with caution, particularly for individuals with conditions like metabolic syndrome, low blood pressure or those on heart and diabetes medication. If you're considering this dietary approach, please discuss it with your doctor to ensure it is safe for your specific situation. For, when practiced safely, intermittent fasting has shown strong potential as a valuable tool for supporting psychological health.

By making these switches, you're choosing a path that not only delights your taste buds but also earns you stars towards your Daily 5-Star PIS Goal, thereby activating your psychological defences. Dive into this journey of healthy eating, and watch as your mood lifts, energy soars and resilience grows!

Beyond diet: Holistic ways to nourish your mind

Nourishing the mind extends well beyond the foods we eat each day. In addition to diet, there are other enriching paths to building a resilient mind. Have you considered how the ordinary aspects of life contribute to your mental health?

For example, cooking isn't just a means to an end; it's a vibrant form of creative expression that nourishes both body and mind. When you cook, you do more than simply prepare food— you explore new flavours, experiment with ingredients, and tap into your creative instincts. As demonstrated in Crum's study with hotel room attendants, when you don't just go through the motions of an ordinary daily chore but perform it while recognising its potential to enhance wellness, you can experience meaningful shifts in both physical and mental states. Cooking, for instance, can be incredibly therapeutic, fostering mindfulness, gratitude for ingredients, and a deeper connection with your food. It transforms an everyday necessity into a powerful tool for nurturing your mental health.

I also recommend developing a connection with nature. Perhaps, you could try growing a plant. This simple act can bring a piece of the natural world into your home, enhance your mood, and elicit feelings of calm. Whether you're tending a lush garden or caring for a single houseplant, the act of nurturing something alive offers a profound sense of purpose and connection. Note that connection is the key component here. A study conducted in England with 2,096 participants found that simply spending time in nature wasn't the main factor for improving wellbeing. Instead, feeling connected to nature and engaging in simple activities, like nurturing plants and birdwatching, were the most important factors for improved wellbeing.

This principle of deriving wellbeing from connectedness with nature is clearly illustrated in my mother's life. Like her late mother, she maintains a lovely garden which she describes as a source of mental tranquillity. Being religious, she often contemplates the divine mysteries of nature. She shared with me, "When you look at a rose bush, you notice the sharp thorns along its stem, yet the flower perseveres through these hardships and blooms beautifully. It's a reminder that every challenge in life is surmountable." She told me that this observation fills her with hope and optimism. As for you, how do you feel when you connect with plants or animals?

Remember to count these suggested ways of nourishing the mind as stars towards your Daily 5-Star PIS Goal, as they align with the 5-Star Framework's principle of intentional care for a healthy and resilient mind.

Another valuable way to nourish the mind is through the practice of self-compassion, a crucial element for maintaining the integrity of the PIS and building emotional stability. Treating yourself with kindness and understanding is essential in developing the inner strength required to handle life's ups and downs. From a young age, many people are taught to prioritise the needs and wellbeing of others over their own. This social conditioning can lead to a tendency to be more attentive and caring towards others while neglecting one's own needs. Also, in some cultures, there may be an emphasis on selflessness and altruism, reinforcing the idea that caring for others is more virtuous than caring for oneself. Furthermore, individuals who struggle with low self-esteem or negative self-perceptions may believe that they are unworthy of self-compassion or that they don't deserve to prioritise their own needs. As a result, they may prioritise caring for others as a way to compensate for these feelings. Take some time to think how your life might change if you started treating yourself as compassionately as you treat others. Are you ready to explore some avenues and see how they can transform your mental wellbeing?

Here are two suggestions to help you cultivate self-compassion:

Practice self-kindness, author and researcher Brené Brown offers beautiful and straightforward advice on how to do so, "Talk to yourself like you would to someone you love", with this advice in mind from now on adopt a stance of treating yourself with the same kindness and understanding that you would offer to a close friend, a son, your loved ones. Be gentle with yourself when facing challenges or setbacks, and speak to yourself in a supportive and encouraging manner.

Rest. Resting is essential for your overall health and wellbeing—it's more than just getting enough sleep. It means giving your body and mind the time they need to recharge and rejuvenate. While sleep is crucial for recovery, true rest includes moments that promote relaxation and reduce stress, like taking breaks, enjoying leisure activities, or finding quiet time for reflection. By prioritising rest, you allow yourself to replenish energy, sharpen cognitive function, and activate your PIS.

Expanding our view of nourishing the mind allows us to embrace a holistic approach to health. Carl Sagan said, 'We are made of star stuff.' Like stars forming a constellation, each action to strengthen our psychological defences brightens and balances our inner self. Let's keep adding stars to our personal constellation, crafting a radiant tapestry of health and positivity.

.

Part 2
Takeaways

★

Great work on finishing the second part of *What Makes a Resilient Mind?* We covered a lot of important information across the last five chapters. This included an overview of how genetics influence our perception and response to life stressors, through the lens of anxiety. We also learned that although there isn't an "anxiety gene," our genetic makeup does influence how unsettled or calm we remain when facing life's circumstances. We saw that for some individuals, anxiety is so prevalent in their life experiences that it becomes a trait, one that can be classified as Generalised Anxiety Disorder (GAD). By contrast, there are individuals whose genetic makeup leads them to be less reactive or concerned overall. For these individuals, anxious states are more likely to arise when adversities emerge. However, a key point I highlighted in this discussion was that, from a psychological perspective, genetic factors do not solely determine how we experience life.

Scientists have concluded that genetics contributes 30% to 40% of the 'ingredients' in the psychological wellbeing pie. This means that 60% to 70% of the ingredients are influenced by environmental and psychological factors such as your surroundings, relationships, beliefs, and behaviours. Think of these as the sugar and toppings of the pie. While you can't change the genes you've been given, similar to some foundational ingredients in a pie, you have control over how sweet, flavourful, and well-decorated your pie turns out.

This leads me to the central theme of Part 2: Factors that Influence the PIS, focusing primarily on factors you can control. These include the orderliness of your surroundings, levels of technology use (which can lead to a "cluttered" mind), the quality of your relationships, alignment between actions and goals, approach to mental fitness, sleep habits, and choices in how to nourish your body and mind. Each of these factors, individually and collectively, notably contributes to the integrity of your PIS, as well as your mental resilience and wellbeing. Each topic was discussed at length, exploring their individual relevance to mental health and providing actionable suggestions for earning stars. The value of consistent, small steps is repeatedly reinforced, and the 5-Star Framework is your map to reaching the skies.

In Part 1, I suggested a small list of steps to earn your daily stars. Here's a quick recap: Developing a sense of humour, engaging in self-discovery, adopting grounding techniques, starting a written or audio journal to foster self-awareness, solving puzzles, taking regular deep-breath breaks, and picking up this book to read. In Part 2, we're taking our Daily 5-Star PIS Goal to another level. This will simplify things further and enhance your possibilities of collecting stars. Now, you can organise your star acquisition into categories like Mental Fitness, Sleep Magic, Brain Fuel, Social Spark, and Break Free.

You may be wondering about the point of these categories. The answer is straightforward: they are designed to help you take action in a holistic way and ensure a well-rounded approach to mental health by encouraging you to care for different aspects of your wellbeing. As you become more proficient at earning stars, I recommend you set out to earn a star from each of these categories each day. This is simpler than you might expect.

Have a look at the steps you can take to reach a variety of stars on your Daily 5-Star PIS Goal:

Mental Fitness: Go for a walk, move around tidying up your surroundings, walk around when on phone calls, go for a run, or find a fitness YouTube channel or exercise app to help you move your body at home on rainy, cold days.

Sleep Magic: Ensure you get 7 to 8 hours of sleep each night, make sure your bedroom is conducive to sleep. During sleepless nights, adopt the 20-minute rule. If bothered by intrusive thoughts, reach for your sleep journal and do some expressive writing or drawing.

Brain Fuel: Have healthy, nourishing meals, practice self-compassion, allocate time to rest and recharge, try a brief breathing-meditation session, engage in mindful moments and start reading a great novel.

Social Spark: Evaluate your relationships and interact mindfully with others. Learn to say no, use social media in ways that uplift your spirits rather than overwhelm you, and strive to be a source of positivity.

Break Free: This is a different category. Here, to earn stars through it, rather than taking a particular action in your day, you eliminate a habit. For example, abstain from UPFs, avoid sleep procrastination, don't give in to feelings of frustration and passing anger, limit screen time before bed, and cut back on excessive caffeine consumption.

Please feel free to not only expand the list of steps in each of the above categories but also to add new categories that resonate with you. Just as constellations are formed by diverse stars, each with its own unique qualities, the stars you earn will make your PIS truly your own. This combination of different stars illuminates our unique paths and helps us shine in our own ways. Note that one of the key strengths of the 5-Star Framework is its capacity to elicit your competence and creativity in proactively caring for your mind.

For example, you might be someone who already has a calming bedtime routine or someone who consistently enjoys nutritious meals. In this case, consider creating a 5-Star PIS category that motivates you to earn stars by aligning your daily actions with, for instance, the achievement of a future plan, such as saving money for a project, changing jobs, and so forth. You could call it Star Path!

On the other hand, you may be someone who is currently facing unexpected life events, leading to considerable disruption in your daily habits. This is a crucial time to tend to your PIS. During hardship, it is essential to experience moments of calmness and think with clarity. Adopting the 5-Star Framework will help awaken your inner abilities to deal with difficulties productively. This approach will help you recognise your capacity for making good decisions, being proactive, and moving forward. In such instances, you could earn stars by avoiding sugary meals and alcoholic beverages, as these tend to exacerbate negative states. Prioritise restful sleep, go for walks, take moments to rest, and connect with those you trust. Always with the intention of activating your PIS and nurturing your resilience, like tending to a plant and helping it thrive again.

Once more, congratulations on making it this far! Take a moment to reflect on your journey and recognise the growth and development you've achieved through the content we've covered. You've already made significant strides in understanding and enhancing your PIS.

Next, we'll explore areas that test our PIS: low mood, negative emotions, addictive behaviours, procrastination, loss, and values and pursuits. By understanding these hurdles and their impact, we equip ourselves with tools to face them head-on. Let's delve into these challenges and discover ways to overcome them.

Part 3

Factors that Impact the Psychological Immune System

Men are disturbed not by things, but by the view
which they take of them.— Epictetus

Chapter 11

The Impact of
Emotions & Low Mood on The PIS

★

When I was a teenager, I had a friend whose mother, whom we'll call Mrs. Balm, often seemed unwell and rarely left her room. One day, before heading out with friends, we stopped to reassure Mrs. Balm that we'd be back early. We found her in her bedroom, looking despondent on the sofa chair. It was a scene that stayed with me. Later, puzzled by her persistent illness, I asked my mother about it. "She suffers from depression," was the curt, yet evocative explanation. At the time, I couldn't quite grasp what that meant. Now, decades later, having experienced my own bouts of low mood, I understand the heavy weight that kept Mrs. Balm confined to her room.

But what exactly is depression? Depression is classified as a mood disorder. You might wonder, what exactly is mood? To clarify, let me contrast mood with emotions: Emotions are short-lived responses and typically have a clear cause, like happiness from receiving good news or sadness due to being let down. Mood, on the other hand, are longer-lasting states and do not have a specific starting point. They can broadly be categorized as positive or negative.

This brings us to the diagnostic process for clinical depression, as outlined in the 5th edition of the Diagnostic and Statistical Manual of Mental Disorders (DSM-5). To be diagnosed with depression, a person must experience at least five of the following symptoms most of the day, nearly every day, for at least two weeks: a persistently low mood, a marked loss of interest or pleasure in almost all activities, significant weight changes, insomnia or excessive sleeping, noticeable slowing down or restlessness, overwhelming fatigue, feelings of worthlessness or excessive guilt, trouble concentrating, and recurrent thoughts of death or suicidal ideation. Additionally, these symptoms must cause significant distress or impairment in daily life and cannot be due to the effects of a substance, another medical condition, or a recent life event like bereavement.

The experiences I've described so far mirror how my friend used to talk about her mother, Mrs. Balm. However, they don't reflect my own experiences with low mood. When I find myself moping for too long—a day or two—it feels as though an invisible force is pushing me forward. That's my PIS at work, nudging me with a reminder: "Yes, you're sad, and it was tough, but you've grieved enough. It's time to move on." This distinction is crucial. Sadness is not the same as depression, yet these terms are often used interchangeably in everyday conversations. In today's society, there's a pervasive expectation to be happy all the time, driven by cultural norms, social pressures, and media influence. Do you ever feel that pressure to always be happy?

This expectation can be harmful, oversimplifying the complex tapestry of human emotions and disregarding the natural fluctuations of our moods. Notice how this expectation, in itself, can impact the PIS by creating unnecessary stress and self-criticism when you don't meet it. Thus, it's crucial to recognise that it's perfectly normal not to feel positive or joyful at all times, and feeling unhappy does not automatically indicate depression.

The value of neutrality

Remarkably, more neutral emotions like contentment or calm—or even those moments when you can't quite put your feelings into words—are often overlooked or even negatively perceived in our high-energy, positivity-driven culture. These quieter states are frequently mistaken for boredom, low mood, or numbness. However, recognising and embracing these neutral emotions can be incredibly beneficial. They provide much-needed balance and stability, giving us the space to rest and recharge, away from extremes. Moreover, these neutral states create opportunities for clarity and introspection, allowing us to reflect on and find deeper meaning in our experiences, an invaluable process for strengthening the PIS.

Consider your own relationship with emotions

How do you view more neutral emotions compared to intense ones like joy or sadness? Do you tend to overlook or undervalue calm, content states? Do you recognise the value of more neutral emotions as essential moments of balance in your life?

Dedicating time to answer these questions can enhance your understanding of your emotional landscape and improve your overall wellbeing.

On that note, let's further reflect on Mrs. Balm's situation. I sometimes wonder if her depression was partly due to a tangled perception of her own emotions. Perhaps she lived under the impression that she was never truly joyful, which led her to undervalue the quieter, neutral emotions that could have offered her some relief.

According to the World Health Organization (WHO), 280 million people globally suffer from depression, and alarmingly, this figure is on the rise. Some experts even suggest that depression may be a disease of modernity. Could the globalization of certain values—such as constant productivity, relentless achievement, and the drive for recognition—be contributing to this trend? This modern ethos might place individuals in situations like Mrs. Balm's, where a possible craving for high-energy states and an aversion to negative emotions undermine moments of mental quietude. This raises important questions about the various pathways to depression, including the role of distorted thoughts and perceptions.

Mind trap: Distorted thinking

According to Beck's Cognitive Model of Depression, distorted thinking plays a critical role in the development and perpetuation of depression. Psychiatrist Aaron Beck proposed that depressed individuals often hold a distorted negative view of the world, themselves and the future. These negative views are activated by everyday experiences, leading to consistent biases in thinking. People might exaggerate the bad and minimize the good, leading them to overlook neutral or positive experiences entirely. What about you? Do you ever find yourself magnifying the bad and overlooking the good in your life?

This type of distortion creates a feedback loop making it harder for the PIS to function effectively. You see, negative thoughts reinforce negative emotions and low mood, which in turn deepen those negative thoughts. This cycle of negativity can become paralyzing, causing individuals to withdraw from the world and miss out on experiences that could elicit positive emotions. Recognising and addressing this destructive loop is crucial in protecting the PIS from the corrosive effects of depression. It also emphasises the need for both emotional support and mental restructuring, helping individuals like Mrs. Balm view and experience the world more realistically, thus providing an opportunity to break the cycle of chronic low mood.

Understanding what these terms really mean is essential. Do you ever find yourself assuming the worst about a situation without substantial evidence? Or holding onto a negative belief about yourself despite experiences to the contrary? These are examples of distorted thinking, ways in which our minds convince us of something that isn't true or exaggerate the negatives beyond the actual reality.

Mental restructuring

How can we restructure this mental state? By adopting an open and objective approach to interpreting the world, recognising that there are many sides to every story. It's essential to accept that our own interpretations can be flawed. When feeling down, it's natural to see yourself, the world, and the future through a negative lens. Psychological research has consistently shown that our mood influences memory and perception. This means that when you're feeling low, you are not only more likely to recall sad memories but also more prone to forming new sad memories. This occurs because you're more attuned to things that echo your current state of vulnerability. This type of cognitive bias can trap us in a loop of negativity. However, recognising and challenging these biases can pave the way for a more balanced and positive outlook.

Identifying this loop of negativity starts with developing self-awareness, which can be fostered by using the strategies we've discussed earlier, such as grounding techniques, breathing exercises, short meditations, and expressive writing. Challenging negative thoughts and perceptions involves a process of thoughtful self-questioning, not with scepticism, but through critical thinking. This isn't about doubting your abilities or worth. Rather, it's about approaching your thoughts with humility and an openness to the possibility that your perceptions might be mistaken. To address negative, distorted thoughts in a constructive manner, start by identifying the negative thought, such as let's say, thinking "I'm incompetent for making a mistake at work." Challenge this thought by examining the evidence for and against it, recognising that one mistake doesn't define your overall performance. Replace the distorted thought with a more balanced one, like viewing it as an opportunity to learn and grow. Practice this process regularly to earn stars towards your Daily 5-Star PIS Goal and boost your PIS.

Adopting this stance further allows you to consider seeking a second opinion. Discussing your thoughts and perceptions with someone you trust, a friend or loved one, can not only provide you with a fresh perspective but also deepen your connections with others. By willing to question your initial judgments and open up about your feelings, you create opportunities for more meaningful interactions and support, which are vital in navigating away from the cycle of negativity and towards a more balanced, positive outlook.

Biological insights into depression

Now that we understand how impactful and misleading our thoughts and perceptions can be, let's consider that depression is not solely governed by our cognitive processes. This complex disorder is influenced by a variety of other factors, necessitating a broader exploration to fully grasp its multifaceted nature. Depression involves complex changes in brain chemistry and function. Neurotransmitters such as serotonin, dopamine, and norepinephrine play crucial roles in mood regulation, and imbalances in these chemicals can lead to depressive symptoms. Furthermore, areas of the brain involved in emotional processing, such as the prefrontal cortex (PFC), amygdala, and hippocampus, often exhibit altered activity in individuals with depression. Compromised interconnectivity, or frail bridges, between these regions can exacerbate symptoms by disrupting the brain's ability to regulate mood and emotions effectively. As discussed in Chapter 3. Further, chronic stress from life's demands, and inflammation resulting from poor nutrition can also affect the brain's structure and function, contributing to the development and persistence of low mood. Understanding these neurobiological factors is crucial for informing intervention decisions. In clinical settings, these can be therapy such as CBT, or medications that target neurotransmitter levels, such as SSRIs and SNRIs, which increase levels of serotonin and norepinephrine.

Interestingly, Cognitive Behavioural Therapy (CBT), developed by Aaron Beck, the same clinician who formulated the cognitive model of depression, has shown to be not only as effective as antidepressant medication in treating mild to moderate depression but also offers additional advantages. While antidepressants primarily target the biological aspects of depression, CBT focuses on teaching practical skills and strategies for managing symptoms and building long-term coping mechanisms. This leads us back to Mrs. Balm and the global rise in depression rates. Could this modern epidemic be partly due to a lack of skills that help us correctly perceive our inner world and neutral emotions? And might it also be driven by the absence of effective strategies to challenge negative thoughts and develop healthier coping mechanisms?

What comes first?

Studies employing various techniques, such as post-mortem analysis, neuroimaging, and neurochemical assays, have consistently shown alterations in neurotransmitter levels and functioning in individuals with depression. For example, reduced levels of serotonin and dopamine have been observed in brain regions associated with mood regulation and motivation. Other studies have identified abnormalities in the receptors or transporters responsible for neurotransmitter signalling. Remarkably, as mentioned in Chapter 1, brain imaging has revealed structural changes in patients following a regimen of CBT, underscoring the mind's active role in rewiring the brain itself. This supports the idea that while biological factors can influence mental health, our mental states can also lead to tangible, physical changes in the brain.

Given this interplay between biological changes and mental states, let's explore a practical example. Imagine we were to scan Mrs. Balm's brain and compare it to that of a non-depressed woman of the same age, education level, and social class. We would likely see significant differences in brain structure and activity, particularly in the prefrontal cortex, hippocampus, and amygdala. But this observation raises a crucial question: What comes first? The distorted thinking or the altered brain function? To truly understand this, an ideal study would involve periodically scanning the brains of individuals throughout their lives to track the sequence of events in those who develop depression.

Given how challenging it is to track these changes over time, we may never fully understand the sequence of mental/brain events that lead to depression. This uncertainty makes it even more crucial to take proactive steps to maintain a healthy PIS, especially for those genetically predisposed to low mood. By focusing on what we can control (i.e. strengthening our psychological defences) we can help preserve brain structures that support productive thoughts and behaviours, leading to positive actions, enriching experiences, and uplifting memories. Each of these is a star towards your Daily 5-Star PIS Goal, contributing to your personal constellation and guiding your journey toward a resilient mind.

Note that while personal agency plays a significant role, there are times when professional intervention is essential. In clinical settings, the decision between therapy and antidepressant medication often hinges on individual preferences, the severity of symptoms, and other personal factors. For some, a combination of treatments may offer the best outcomes, tailored to their unique needs. This nuanced approach to treatment is crucial, as for many facing major depression or other mental health challenges, the stakes are incredibly high. Without effective management and support, depression can lead to the most severe outcome: suicide.

The ultimate failure of the PIS

Suicide is often regarded in the scientific community as the ultimate failure of the PIS. When the mental defences that help us cope with life's stresses and adversities are overwhelmed, the mind may reach a state where it sees no alternative but to escape the pain. This tragic outcome underscores the need for robust, proactive mental health practices. The good news is that effective mental health care and social support are well known to play a crucial role in fortifying our psychological defences, providing the resources and resilience needed to navigate severe emotional distress. Above all, recognising the signs of mental health decline and ensuring access to the right help at the right time are vital in preventing more devastating outcomes.

Me & Mrs. Balm

As for Mrs. Balm, she continues her battle against depression. My mother saw her at the supermarket just before last Christmas, and she told me that Mrs. Balm is still managing her depression with medication and, crucially, with the unwavering support and care of her loving family. Her ongoing fight is a testament to the power of sustained, loving support in managing chronic depression.

Reflecting on my own experiences, I've come to realise the importance of not letting sadness overtake me. For me, sadness often feels like a dark cloud hovering overhead. In the past, I would just sit there, letting the rain drench me, surrendering to the cold and wet. But over time, I've learned that life isn't about waiting for the storm to pass, but about finding the strength to keep moving through the rain. I don't just wait anymore. I move forward. How about you? How do you navigate and cope with sadness and low mood? This journey of resilience shows that we have the power to decide when to stand up and start moving. And remember, each step forward earns you a star in your wellbeing constellation, reinforcing your ability to manage different moods and emotions, rain or shine.

In this corner of our book, we've explored how negative emotions and low mood can erode our PIS, potentially leading to chronic depressed states. We also discussed the importance of valuing neutral emotions, restructuring distorted thinking, and seeking help when negative states become overwhelming, essential strategies within the 5-Star Framework to activate the PIS and build resilience. As we move forward, let's turn our attention to another formidable challenge that can undermine our psychological defences: addiction. Much like depression, addiction tests the limits of our PIS, presenting unique obstacles that require understanding, commitment, and action to overcome.

It is not the drugs that make a drug addict, it is the need to escape reality. — Charles Bukowski

Chapter 12

Beyond Substances: Potentially Addictive Behaviours

★

What do social media, shopping, overeating, and watching pornography have in common? These are activities that have become pervasive and have the potential to develop into problematic behaviours. They are frequently overlooked yet powerful enough to disrupt our psychological defences, becoming particularly troublesome as they can be addictive, especially for vulnerable individuals.

So, an important question for us to consider here is: when does an ordinary behaviour cross the threshold into addiction? Addiction entails the repetitive engagement with behaviours or substances that initially may appear rewarding or innocuous. However, as time progresses, these behaviours can lead to negative consequences and impairments in various aspects of life. For instance, globally popular pornography websites like Pornhub and XNXX not only attract more traffic than mainstream digital platforms such as Amazon and Netflix but also engage users for longer periods of time —revealing a global, deep-rooted compulsion. This level of engagement not only highlights pornography's significant psychological grip and potential for addiction but also has tangible impacts on individual productivity and broader societal norms. It is estimated that financial cost to business productivity in the U.S. is at $16.9 billion annually, due to employees visiting pornographic sites during work hours. In this paradoxical pursuit of temporary relief, individuals find themselves in a perpetual cycle of longing, which disrupts daily life, interpersonal relationships and productivity, and the function and structure of the PIS. Making its impact on mental health clear.

Addictive behaviours are particularly insidious because they exploit our brain's reward system, particularly the dopaminergic system involved in processing pleasure and motivation. This system typically rewards life-sustaining behaviours like eating and socialising by releasing dopamine, which reinforces these actions and encourages us to repeat them. However, potentially addictive activities such as excessive shopping or social media use can also hijack this system, tricking it into overvaluing these non-essential activities. Have you ever noticed feeling a rush from a 'like' on social media or a new purchase? That's your dopamine system at work. People with psychological vulnerabilities, such as those experiencing anxiety, depression, or life stressors like financial difficulties or isolation, are especially at risk. They may begin to rely on these behaviours not just for a fleeting pleasure hit, but as a form of escapism from reality.

Emotional crutches

Much like how powerful substances such as cocaine or heroin can captivate the brain's reward system, addictive behaviours exploit these same neural pathways. I find this truly striking! These behaviours entice the brain into craving more, even when faced with detrimental consequences, ultimately weakening the PIS. Over time, the seductive allure can evolve into a dependency, where engaging in these behaviours becomes a means to feel normal or find fleeting pleasure. Yet, breaking free from this cycle proves to be a daunting challenge. Individuals find themselves ensnared in a repetitive dance with these activities, despite being fully aware of the toll it takes on their lives and wellbeing.

While it's relatively straightforward to recognise when activities like watching pornography may become a concern due to their private and often taboo nature, it is much harder to discern when more socially acceptable or public behaviours, such as using social media, shopping, or eating, cross the line from casual to compulsive. These activities are so woven into our daily routines that they often escape scrutiny, yet they can be just as addictive and damaging. For example, according to a recent data report, as of April 2024, 62.3% of the world's population uses social media with an average daily usage of 2 hours and 23 minutes. This can add up to nearly 15.4 hours per week. Almost an entire waking day! Emotional eating is also a significant issue, a study involving 1,453 participants found that approximately one-third reported overeating in response to emotions. Interestingly, this behaviour seemed more prevalent among women, with 41.4% acknowledging it, compared to 19.4% of men. Although, this prevalence might also be due to women being more open about it.

To illustrate the profound impact of these behaviours, consider the character of Charlie from the movie 'The Whale,' who turns to food as a means to cope with emotional pain and isolation. He poignantly reveals, "I can't seem to stop eating. It's like there's something inside me, something I can't see, and the only way to get it to leave me alone is to eat and eat and eat." This quote highlights how such seemingly benign activities can spiral into serious health and psychological issues.

Underlying causes

The long-term consequences of these behaviours on our psychological defences can be truly profound. As we look deeper into the impact of these behaviours, it becomes evident that understanding the underlying causes and mechanisms is essential. This knowledge is crucial not only for personal growth, as it also forms the foundation for developing effective strategies to mitigate their harmful effects by bolstering the PIS. As you might recall from our previous discussions, our actions and thoughts can reshape our brain's structure and functions through neuroplasticity. Therefore, it should come as no surprise that the repetitive nature of these activities, especially when they become addictive, can similarly rewire our brains. This neurological change can make it increasingly challenging to break free from these habits, as our brains become conditioned to seek out these rewarding sensations, reinforcing the cycle of addiction. It's as if the only bridges available for us to cross are those that lead to places of compulsion and impulsivity.

But how can we determine if our relationship with shopping, eating, and social media is casual or has crossed into dependency? One effective way is to examine our emotional reactions to these activities. Ask yourself: How would you feel if you suddenly couldn't access your favourite social media platforms, purchase new items, or indulge in your preferred foods? Would the absence of these activities make you anxious or noticeably lower your mood? If being unable to engage in these behaviours causes you to obsessively think about them, this could indicate a degree of dependence.

Such reflection is vital. It helps uncover the emotional significance these activities have in your life. Dependence often appears as an emotional crutch used to cope with stress, loneliness, or discomfort. By recognising these signs early, you can take proactive steps to address what might develop into a more serious issue.

Your social media use: Connection or distraction?

Social media is a double-edged sword when it comes to our psychological health. On one hand, high usage of social media has been consistently linked to increased levels of anxiety and depression. This is partly because excessive use can alter mood states and contribute to feelings of inadequacy. It often promotes unrealistic comparisons with others, making users feel that their own lives are less fulfilling or exciting. Imagine scrolling through endless posts showcasing others' perfect moments. It can be easy to forget these are just highlights, not the full story of someone's life.

However, social media is not all detrimental. It also has the potential to enhance connection, increase self-esteem, and improve a sense of belonging, particularly for those who may feel isolated in their physical environments. For instance, many individuals with mental health issues find solace and support on social media. It offers a platform where they can share personal experiences, seek information about treatment options, and connect with others facing similar challenges. This sense of community can be incredibly empowering. It gives individuals a space to be heard and supported, which can significantly enhance their mental wellbeing.

Clearly, the key lies in moderation and mindful use. Therefore, it's crucial to balance online interactions with real-world connections and to engage with social media platforms in ways that promote mental health rather than deplete it.

Now, reflect on your social media use: Does it enhance your sense of wellbeing, or does it lower it? Take a moment to consider how you feel during and after scrolling through your social media feeds. Are you more often inspired and connected, or do you find yourself feeling drained and dissatisfied?

Here's a tip for positive engagement and earning stars towards your Daily 5-Star PIS Goal : Ensure your social media usage remains a tool for meaningful connections by actively curating your feeds. Follow accounts that inspire and uplift you, and don't hesitate to mute or unfollow those that trigger negative feelings. Additionally, prioritise interacting with close friends and family by commenting on their posts or messaging them directly. This active engagement creates a more personal and rewarding social media experience, fostering connections that truly matter in your life.

However, if you find that social media is more often depleting than beneficial, setting specific times for checking your platforms and sticking to them can make a world of difference. As we discussed in Chapter 7. Using apps to track your usage and set limits helps maintain healthy boundaries, reducing possible distress and ensuring that your digital interactions enhance, rather than deteriorate your PIS. Similarly, other common behaviours can have a profound impact on our psychological defenses.

Comfort buying & eating

Just as we manage our digital consumption to protect our mental health, it's important to address how we cope with stress through other means. It's common to seek solace in shopping or snacking, especially when faced with the discomfort of boredom, stress, or anxiety. Both shopping and overeating serve as distractions from our emotional realities, they can become temporary escapes offering momentary relief. While these behaviours might provide an immediate sense of satisfaction, they often fail to address the underlying emotional triggers, leading to a cyclical pattern of temporary comfort followed by feelings of guilt or dissatisfaction.

When we engage in 'retail therapy,' for example, we are often trying to lift our spirits or reward ourselves. The act of purchasing provides a temporary high, releasing dopamine - a neurotransmitter associated with pleasure. Similarly, 'emotional eating' is driven by the desire to experience the comforting or familiar tastes that evoke a sense of nostalgia or temporary safety. However, the comfort found in food and shopping is often fleeting and can escalate into feelings of shame or loss of control.

I must confess, in moments of stress or anxiety, my first instinct used to be to reach for comfort foods. A muffin or chocolate seemed like instant solutions to soothe the nerves. Yet, time and again, I noticed that the comfort they promised rarely materialized in the way I hoped.

Cultivating self-awareness

Developing self-awareness about why we turn to excessive shopping or snacking is essential. Start by identifying what triggers these urges: is it loneliness, boredom, sadness, or stress? Acknowledging these triggers is the first step toward gaining control over them, a core skill cultivated through the 5-Star Framework.

Strategies for better coping

Note that, each of the following steps count as a star towards your Daily 5-Star PIS Goal:

1. Intentional Pauses: Instead of acting on impulse, take a moment to breathe and ask yourself what you are really seeking. Is there a healthier activity that could address your emotional needs? A walk or a chat with a friend might provide more genuine relief.

2. Healthy Substitutions: Replace the habit of reaching for a snack or excess shopping with healthier alternatives that also release dopamine but in beneficial ways. Engaging in exercise, listening to music, or completing a puzzle can also provide satisfaction and a sense of accomplishment.

3. Set Limits: For shopping, create a budget or a shopping list and stick to it to avoid impulsive buys. For eating, try to keep healthy snacks within reach and reduce the amount of UPFs in your home to make healthier choices easier.

It's essential to develop practices that help us engage more profoundly with our emotional and psychological needs. Building a repertoire of responses to stress that are nurturing and supportive of our wellbeing can replace the temporary fixes of shopping and eating. This doesn't just improve our mood in the short term, it enhances our PIS and overall life satisfaction. Such proactive measures are crucial, not only in combating less recognised addictions like compulsive shopping and emotional eating but also in facing the challenges posed by more overt compulsions.

Navigating the temptations of excess: Real life lessons

Returning to the topic of pornography, it's important to recognise that its excessive consumption, like many addictive behaviours, can have profound psychological and relational impacts. While it may often seem like a victimless indulgence, the reality is far more complex. Being a highly gendered activity, cases of exploitation of women are plentiful in this industry, which further complicates its impacts. Additionally, excessive consumption of pornography has the potential to negatively affect relationships in considerable ways. A few years ago, a young man we'll call Mark came to me for guidance. He had been compulsively drawn to pornography and, despite managing to abstain for five months, he relapsed one day. This relapse came at a great personal cost, resulting in the loss of his fiancée who could not accept his habit. This led to feelings of self-disappointment and inadequacy.

Mark's story is not unique and it echoes patterns seen in other addictive behaviours, including those we haven't explored. Mark's experience vividly highlights the critical importance of cultivating self-awareness. A theme we've emphasised in all our discussions so far. Self-awareness is not just beneficial, it's the foundation of emotional intelligence and mindful living. However, while self-awareness is an essential first step, it alone is insufficient. So, it's important to recognise that self-awareness sets the stage for further development of crucial skills such as self-control and acceptance, which are especially vital in managing dependencies and addictions. These skills allow us to navigate our impulses more effectively, providing a pathway to healthier habits and better over-all mental health.

Often, the struggle with addiction intensifies not just be-cause of the urge itself, but due to our resistance to it. We tend to fight and push away what we perceive as negative, yet this ap-proach rarely brings the peace or resolution we seek (we'll explore how to address this issue in detail in Chapter 19). Intrinsically, hu-man nature encompasses a dark side, including traits like envy, re-sentment, and other less admirable qualities. What distinguishes a more resilient character from others is not the absence of these traits, but rather the response to them.

Consider this allegory: imagine these urges as little goblins within us, stirred awake by feelings of depression, anxiety, or bore-dom. If you're self-aware, you'll recognise their awakening. With-out awareness, they can take control, leading you further into be-haviours you may regret, like debt, overeating, or binging on por-nography. But with awareness, you greet these goblins with interest and curiosity. There's no battle, only recognition and investigation. Where do they live within you? In your heart, your stomach, your impulses? What is their texture, their smell? This exploration doesn't just confront a potential weakness. It familiarises you with it, diminishing its power over you. It follows that it's quite difficult to be compulsive and curious at the same time. This shift from resisting an urge to understanding and acknowledging it empowers you, giving you control rather than surrendering it.

Studies investigating the benefits of mindfulness based therapies, including those conducted in prison populations, con-sistently demonstrate that when individuals accept and understand their urges, instead of succumbing to them, they command them more effectively. By adopting a stance of curiosity and acceptance, we not only face our challenges but become masters over them, leading to a life not dictated by our baser instincts but enriched by our conscious decisions. Have you ever taken a moment to inves-tigate your own urges, whether they are driven by sexual desires, gastronomic cravings, or consumerist impulses? Understanding where these urges stem from can be the first step toward gaining mastery over them.

As we conclude our exploration of the impact of addiction on our psychological defences—specifically, how it creates destructive habits that undermine our ability to cope with stress and challenges—we underscore the importance of self-awareness. The skills honed through recognising and addressing addictive behaviours are crucial not only for overcoming these challenges but also for activating the PIS and effectively managing other complex aspects of life.

Our next chapter shifts focus to a related but distinct challenge: procrastination. We will explore how some of the lessons learned here can be applied to understand and combat this pervasive issue.

Procrastination is the thief of time.
— Edward Young

Chapter 13

Procrastination's Toll on the Mind

★

Do you ever find yourself delaying or postponing tasks, choosing to do less relevant or more enjoyable activities instead? It'll not be a surprise at all if your answer is yes. This is a rather common phenomenon known as procrastination, which stems from various factors like lack of motivation, insecurities, or poor time management skills.

Experts explain that procrastination serves as a form of emotional regulation. Emotional regulation refers to how we manage and respond to our feelings, particularly those that are uncomfortable or overwhelming. For instance, instead of tackling a challenging work project, you might find yourself cleaning the kitchen or scrolling through social media, seeking temporary relief from stress or anxiety. By procrastinating, we are essentially choosing immediate emotional comfort over the potential unpleasantness of confronting tasks, obligations or daily commitments, even if it's something as beneficial as sleep! You'll recall our earlier conversation on the importance of sleep for the PIS, and the discussion on sleep procrastination.

While we all have occasionally browsed the internet or chatted with whoever was available instead of diving straight into working on the upcoming presentation or tackling a laborious assignment, procrastination becomes a problem when it turns into a habit that leads to personal, professional, and relationship issues. For example, you might repeatedly delay starting a project until the last minute, leading to subpar work and increased stress. This habit can strain relationships, as missed deadlines and broken promises cause frustration and disappointment in both personal and professional settings. This is when we start to get a glimpse of the impact of procrastination on our PIS, as it's often underlined by negative mental and emotional states like anxiety from constantly living under pressure or dealing with conflicts when, in extreme cases, procrastination may result in unmet commitments and letting other people down.

With that in mind, take a moment to reflect on how much procrastination plays a part in your life.

Pause & reflect

Reflecting on your own habits, consider how often you find yourself postponing tasks until the last minute. Do you tend to delay predominantly unpleasant tasks? Or, does procrastination seep into even the activities you enjoy? Studies show that 80% of people admit to occasional procrastination, while about 15%–20% confess to regularly struggling with it. By looking at how often and in what ways you procrastinate, you can see if your habits match these trends. This can help you figure out if procrastination is just an occasional problem for you or something more constant.

At a neuropsychological level, have you ever considered what procrastination looks like in your brain? Studies using brain scans and advanced computer analysis have revealed that individuals who procrastinate frequently tend to have weaker bridges between the brain's emotional centres and the prefrontal cortex, which is crucial for planning and decision-making. At his point you appreciate that, similar to how weaker physical bridges can disrupt travel, these weaker neural connections can impair the flow of information necessary for effective problem solving. As we discussed in chapter 3. How does this affect your wellbeing? Reflect on how you feel when you delay tasks. Does procrastination lead to stress, anxiety, or a sense of guilt? Assessing these emotional responses is crucial as they highlight the profound impact procrastination can have on your PIS. By acknowledging and confronting these patterns, you can begin to mitigate their detrimental effects and strengthen your psychological defences.

Still, if you find yourself feeling 'entrapped' by procrastination, it's important not to harbour negative feelings towards yourself. Remember, like all patterns, whether psychological or behavioural, procrastination habits can be reshaped and rebuilt. Acknowledging that you are caught in a cycle of procrastination is the first, crucial step toward change.

Armed with self-awareness and knowledge, you can begin the process of transformation. However, sustainable change also requires structure, determination and action. Sustainable change is about making a conscious decision every day to tackle tasks head-on rather than pushing them aside. Certainly, it won't always be easy, but with the 5-Star Framework, consistent effort and a commitment to understanding the root causes of your procrastination, you can gradually replace old habits with new, more productive behaviours. Remember, each small step you take is progress, earning you a star towards your Daily 5-Star PIS Goal and building towards a more empowered, resilient mind.

The root cause of procrastination

In today's digital age, an abundance of distractions significantly challenges our productivity. Social media, entertainment platforms, and endless online browsing present tempting alternatives to demanding tasks, offering immediate gratification that makes procrastination appealing. Additionally, as you now know, procrastination often functions as a coping mechanism to sidestep the discomfort of negative emotions associated with certain responsibilities.

By delaying task initiation or completion, we may temporarily alleviate feelings of boredom, frustration, or anxiety. This is where emotion regulation steps in, as procrastination is used "strategically," or I should better put it, automatically, to manage emotions and maintain mental satisfaction. However, this cycle ultimately exacerbates the very emotional distress it aims to eliminate, creating a vicious loop that diminishes both productivity and overall wellbeing. This is how the PIS is impacted. This cycle of avoidance and delayed distress raises a compelling question: What else drives procrastination beyond the immediate distractions and emotional coping strategies? A revealing study published in the *Journal of Psychology of Education* sought to answer just that. Gathering insights from 135 university students, the study uncovered how factors like psychological flexibility and time management influence procrastination.

Psychological flexibility refers to our ability to adapt our mental states and behaviour based on the situation at hand. For instance, a student who can't shift focus from entertainment browsing to studying as exam day approaches demonstrates poor psychological flexibility. This adaptability is key in managing procrastination effectively because it allows us to switch mindset and prioritise important activities over immediate gratification, acting as a foundational skill that supports other necessary strategies for effective time management.

Further, the study highlights that proficient time and effort management is a crucial factor in addressing tasks that require immediate attention. It found that students who exhibit poor planning skills and trivialize their activities tend to procrastinate more. It's important to note that effective time management goes beyond merely setting clear goals. It involves organising activities in a priority order and adhering to a structured schedule to maximize efficiency. Together, psychological flexibility and strong time management skills form a robust quality against the tendency to procrastinate, ensuring that individuals not only plan their tasks well but also adjust their strategies as circumstances change.

Insights into prioritisation and structure as a means to maximize efficiency lend an appropriate opportunity to reflect on the ancient wisdom of Seneca, who noted, "Life is long if you know how to use it." Contrasting with the common belief that life is short, this reflection urges us to reconsider our everyday choices. As Seneca suggests, the length of life is not just a given but a consequence of how we manage our time. Effective time management is not just an academic skill. It is an essential practice for cultivating robust psychological defences against escapism. By mastering this skill, we can "extend" our lives by ensuring that we do not merely pass time but truly live it.

Now, consider your own experiences: How often do you adjust your plans to better align with your projects? Could enhancing this skill help you procrastinate less?

Time & effort management : Quadrants, pomodoros & stars

Battling procrastination can feel like an uphill struggle, but with the right strategies, it can be managed effectively. Two powerful techniques that help structure your time and tasks are especially beneficial: the Eisenhower Matrix, popularised by Stephen Covey as Covey's Time Management Matrix, and the Pomodoro Technique. The Eisenhower Matrix is grounded in time management research that emphasises the importance of prioritising tasks to improve productivity and reduce stress. Similarly, the Pomodoro Technique has been shown to enhance focus and productivity through structured work intervals. This technique is particularly helpful because it addresses cognitive overload, the mental fatigue that occurs when the brain is overwhelmed by too much information or too many tasks at once. By utilising these evidence-based strategies, you can effectively combat procrastination, earn stars towards your 5-Star PIS Goal and improve your psychological wellbeing.

The Eisenhower Matrix, also known as Covey's Time Management Matrix, provides a clear approach for prioritising tasks based on urgency and importance. It divides tasks into four quadrants: Quadrant I, urgent and important tasks like crises and looming deadlines. Quadrant II, important but not urgent tasks, such as planning and relationship building. Quadrant III, urgent but not important tasks, such as some calls and interruptions. Quadrant IV, neither urgent nor important tasks, often considered time wasters.

The magic of this matrix lies in its emphasis on Quadrant II. By focusing on these important but not urgent tasks, you can manage your responsibilities proactively. This approach minimizes the risk of tasks becoming last-minute emergencies, a common trigger for procrastination. Engaging with tasks before they escalate into urgencies allows you to sidestep the stress and rush that often lead to avoidance.

However, having a system that provides an overview of your life's emergencies, commitments, possible interruptions, and distractions does not mean those tasks will be tackled just because they're in a fancy quadrant. Procrastination often creates a gap between intention and action. While you may intend to meet all your obligations, you might be unsure how to do so. Therefore, the quadrants offer a great starting point. They help you put things in perspective by offering a blueprint of your duties and nudge you to structure your time effectively by prioritising tasks wisely.

In addition to prioritising tasks, managing how you approach them is equally important. This is where the Pomodoro Technique comes into play. The Pomodoro Technique cuts through procrastination by breaking your work into short, focused intervals, traditionally 25 minutes, followed by a 5-minute break. These intervals, called Pomodoros, are perfect for maintaining concentration and momentum. By tackling chores in these structured bursts, you avoid the common pitfall of feeling overwhelmed by their size or complexity. Regular breaks refresh the mind, making it easier to sustain effort and attention.

Implementing both the Eisenhower Matrix and the Pomodoro Technique addresses two fundamental challenges in procrastination: poor prioritisation and the daunting nature of tasks. These methods empower you to take control of your time and effort. So, why not try integrating these techniques into your routine? They could expand your 'Break Free' constellation, transform your approach to tasks and deadlines, turning the tide against procrastination and towards more productive days.

Example: Stella's strategy to overcome procrastination

Stella is in the process of setting up her own business while working part-time. She often feels that there aren't enough hours in the day to get everything done, especially with the administrative tasks required to launch her business and the demands of her job. To manage her time more effectively, Stella decided to implement the Eisenhower Matrix by taking the following steps:

Stella began by listing all the tasks she needed to complete, covering both her job and her business initiatives. For each task, she noted the deadlines to identify which required immediate attention. She then marked the most urgent tasks to prevent potential crises. Assessing the importance of each task in relation to her business goals and job responsibilities, Stella organised them by importance. Finally, she placed each task into the appropriate quadrant of the Eisenhower Matrix, effectively categorising them based on urgency and importance.

With time, Stella managed to reduce the number of urgent crises (Quadrant I tasks) that resulted from poor time management. This proactive approach not only allowed her to handle immediate demands more calmly but also gave her the bandwidth to focus on strategic planning for her business. The regular reviews and adjustments to her schedule ensured that she remained on track, continually refining her approach to become more efficient. The Pomodoro Technique further supported her efforts by breaking down work periods into manageable intervals. This allowed Stella to maintain efficient levels of concentration and productivity without feeling overwhelmed. By dedicating specific "Pomodoros" to tasks from different quadrants, especially those in Quadrant II, she ensured that important tasks contributing to long-term success were not neglected amidst the daily hustle.

This detailed implementation transformed Stella's workdays from reactive to proactive, not only alleviating stress and anxiety but also building a foundation for future growth. Considerably reducing the negative impact of procrastination on her psychological defences. The shift toward greater awareness and control not only diminished psychological strain but also strengthened Stella's PIS, better preparing her to handle future challenges.

Psychological flexibility: Embracing life's full spectrum

In the quest to combat procrastination, the principle of psychological flexibility stands pivotal, as we've learned from the study findings we explored earlier in this chapter. Steven Hayes, a distinguished psychologist and founder of Acceptance and Commitment Therapy (ACT), illuminates this concept beautifully. He explains that a fundamental issue in various psychological disturbances is "experiential avoidance," which we'll explore in more detail in Chapter 17. This refers to our tendency to dodge uncomfortable thoughts, feelings, and sensations, even when such avoidance proves detrimental in the long run. Hayes suggests that this avoidance not only fails to shield us from psychological distress but often amplifies it.

Psychological flexibility involves a deliberate embrace of life's full spectrum, accepting the good with the bad and the comfort with the discomfort. This doesn't mean resigning ourselves to adversity but actively choosing to experience life fully and meaningfully, regardless of the discomfort that may arise. How do we cultivate such flexibility? It starts with embracing change, not as a threat but as an enriching part of life. Small adjustments to daily routine can prepare our PIS for bigger life shifts, easing the discomfort associated with change.

Expanding our behavioural repertoire by trying new approaches to familiar problems or learning new skills that challenge us can also enhance our adaptability. Finally, focusing on our internal values and goals can guide our decisions, helping us navigate complex situations and prioritise our actions effectively. By weaving these practices into our everyday lives, we not only tackle procrastination but also build a resilient PIS capable of handling life's chores and strains. Psychological flexibility allows us to lead richer, more fulfilling lives by ensuring that we are not just enduring life's demands but actively engaging with them.

In wrapping up our discussion on procrastination, it's clear that its impact on the PIS is profound. Procrastination not only triggers stress and anxiety but also perpetuates these states, creating a self-sustaining loop of psychological distress. However, there is a pathway to freedom from this cycle. By addressing key root causes, particularly through the development of time and effort management skills and enhancing psychological flexibility, we can break free from its grasp. These strategies empower us to regain control over our actions and emotions, reducing the restlessness associated with procrastination and strengthening our overall mental resilience.

As we turn the page, our next focus will be another critical challenge to our psychological defences: loss. We will explore how this inevitable aspect of life affects our wellbeing and discuss strategies to mitigate its impact, continuing our journey toward a robust PIS and a resilient mind.

The wound is the place where the light enters you. – Rumi

Chapter 14

Navigating Loss: Exploring the Depths of Grief & Healing

★

Richard was in his mid-40s when he took his children to the water park for a long weekend. A bad turn on the slide twisted him all over the place until he finally landed in the water. Richard doesn't recall the event in great detail now, but he believes that by the time he hit the water, he already couldn't feel his legs. Richard lost his ability to walk forever. Loss is as difficult to define as it is to experience. It is a deeply personal and subjective phenomenon. Indeed, despite its universality, loss is as exclusive to each of us as our own lives. What is loss to you?

Amidst the depths of despair, Richard found unexpected opportunities for growth and self-discovery. Despite the initial anguish of his loss, he began to uncover new strengths within himself. Each step of his journey, though arduous, became a testament to his resilience and capacity for personal development. Through the trials of his experience, Richard found a silver lining, a chance to redefine his life's purpose and embrace a newfound sense of self. For Hamilton, the surfer mentioned in Chapter 1, the loss of her arm was an opportunity to deepen her spirituality. So, perhaps a more straight-forward way to make sense of loss is to reflect how it changes us. How have the losses you've faced shaped you and your life?

Loss, grief & healing

This is where the theme of this book emerges, as the PIS plays a crucial role in how we face loss, grieve, and heal. In the academic literature, loss is often linked to the PIS through the connection between grieving and resilience. This connection frequently highlights the potential for transformation that loss brings and the inner strength of every individual. Thus, loss and resilience are intricately connected through a mix of emotions, coping strategies, and our ability to heal and adapt to new circumstances. Let's explore these phenomena through the lenses of philosophy and psychology, beginning with loss itself.

The Buddha taught that all things are impermanent and subject to change. He said, "All conditioned things are impermanent; when one sees this with wisdom, one turns away from suffering." By understanding and accepting the transient nature of existence, we can find peace and resilience when confronted with loss. Recognising the inevitability of endings or death can spark acceptance and gratitude.

Consider a holiday where you savour every moment because you know it will end. When the holiday concludes, melancholy might set in, but this feeling is soon replaced by joyful memories of fulfilling experiences. Certainly, holidaying contrasts with the monotony of daily chores like washing up, paying bills, or taking an elderly relative to the hospital, which rarely inspire us. However, what if you knew this might be the last time you could perform these simple tasks, either because of financial constraints or illness? What if you woke up every day with the intention of living it as best as you can because you're realistic enough to appreciate that tomorrow might never come?

This mindset aligns with the principles of Stoicism, a philosophy that teaches the development of self-control and fortitude as a means of overcoming destructive attitudes and emotions. A key principle within Stoicism is the technique of negative visualization or, pardon my Latin, 'futurorum malorum praemeditatio'. This involves cultivating awareness of the loss of things and people we value. Negative visualization doesn't encourage pessimism. Rather, it trains the mind to appreciate the present and reduces fear and anxiety about the future. It's a practice that aligns closely with the Buddhist concept of impermanence, reminding us to cherish what we have now, because it may not last forever.

Futurorum malorum praemeditatio – Preparing for losses

You might be wondering how negative visualization boosts psychological resilience. Taking the time, every once in a while, to contemplate that things do go wrong and that loss is an inevitable component of life creates psychological preparedness by desensitising our minds to the impact of irrevocable losses. A study published in the *Behavioural Brain Research* journal demonstrates that 'mental imagery,' the process of creating vivid scenes in your mind, can prepare us to face fears by reducing the emotional impact of potential anxieties, thereby building psychological resilience against them. As with all desensitisation strategies, however, it's sensible to take gradual steps when practising negative visualization. Begin this contemplation exercise by imagining minor losses, like losing a treasured material object or having a minor plan fall through. Only when you feel sufficiently comfortable with these scenarios should you venture into contemplating more significant, impactful losses, as this can be a distressing practice for some. This gradual approach underscores the very point of this discussion: Can you imagine the impact of experiencing something you currently cannot even consider?

Hopefully, this reflection will help you appreciate the value of practicing negative visualization every now and then to earn stars towards your Daily 5-Star PIS Goal and activate your PIS. However, if you're living with chronic depression, GAD, or PTSD, please consult your mental health care professional to determine if this practice is suitable for you. For those willing to give this philosophical method a try, remember to practice safely by always staying aware that you are in control and secure.

As for dealing with actual loss, however, we face a different set of challenges where grief is a natural and essential process.

Grief

Grief is something we all experience following loss, and how we understand it has evolved considerably over the past decades. Traditional views on grief, like those you might have heard from Kübler-Ross's stages—denial, anger, bargaining, depression, and acceptance—focused on a series of emotional phases we're expected to move through, whether linearly or not. While these models help normalise different grief responses, they don't account for the complexity and individuality of each person's experience, often leading to oversimplifications and misconceptions about the grieving process.

Recent research has shifted the focus from rigid stages of grief to the remarkable ability we possess to adapt and bounce back after loss, trauma, or life changes. This adaptability, rooted in the functioning of the PIS, underscores the importance of our psychological defences and the various mechanisms that help us endure even the most impactful losses. While much of this research focuses on grief in the context of bereavement, its application extends to any substantial loss, such as the end of a relationship, job loss, or major life transitions. For example, George A. Bonanno's investigations offer a refreshing perspective on how we manage loss, describing responses that range from 'chronic grief' to 'grieving with resilience.' These two responses will be the focus of our discussion.

While chronic grief can be intense and prolonged, it is relatively rare, affecting about 15% of individuals. To me, the fact that only 15 out of 100 people continue to suffer from chronic grief is a powerful testament to our inherent resilience as humans.

Agnes's reality serves as a poignant illustration of chronic grief. Two decades after her divorce, she still struggles with the separation. Her chronic grief manifests as a persistent yearning for what was lost, making it hard for her to move forward. This type of grief can feel all-consuming, leaving people stuck in a loop of longing and preoccupation with what is no longer present. It is important to note that this is different from depression because it centres solely on the lost person or thing, creating a painful, ongoing attachment.

In light of this, therapists emphasise the power of creating personal narratives to make sense of our experiences. Finding positive meaning and maintaining a strong sense of self can reduce the likelihood of complicated grief. For Agnes, this means acknowledging her strength in making it through the divorce. She could create a narrative that views her marriage and divorce as paths for personal growth, recognising the lessons learned and celebrating how these experiences have made her more independent. What would you say to Agnes? How might you help her see the resilience she has shown and the opportunities that lie ahead? This shift in interpretation could help her move forward, reduce chronic grief, and open up new possibilities for fulfilment.

Above all, at the core of Bonanno's research is a compelling focus on resilience, making it particularly relevant to our exploration of the PIS function in the face of loss. His studies reveal people's remarkable ability to return to a healthy, functioning daily life after experiencing loss. A common question inevitably arises: "How long does this take?" Bonanno's research on 'the loss of a spouse' indicates that for many individuals, it can take up to eighteen months. While this may seem like a long time, what truly stands out is that a significant 45.9% of participants demonstrated exceptional inner strength and psychological resilience during this period of adversity. These are the individuals who grieved with resilience.

Now you may ask, "What does this look like in practice?" Grieving with resilience means being able to experience positive emotions and find ways to contribute positively to the world around you, despite the pain. It's important to note that being resilient while grieving doesn't mean you're free from the challenges of emotional pain. You might still go through periods of sporadic preoccupation or restless nights, and the anguish of your loss can revisit you time and again.

The key takeaway is that these difficult emotional experiences and adjustments are part of grieving with resilience, as long as they don't become chronic. It's normal to have ups and downs while you're finding your new normal. For example, when Richard understood and embraced the emotional push and pull of his grief, he was able to move forward and look ahead. He channelled the energy from fighting his anguish into rediscovering himself in the context of his new reality, which truly enhanced his psychological resilience. Have you ever considered how the losses you've faced might reveal hidden strengths and resilience within you? How might embracing these qualities help you navigate future challenges with a renewed sense of purpose and inner strength? It is through this kind of self-exploration that your PIS can propel you forward, equipping you to face life's adversities with greater confidence.

Grieving & healing – Two sides of the same coin

At this point in our discussion, it's paramount to recognise that grieving and healing are not distinct, separate phases. Rather, they are two sides of the same coin. Healing is about learning to live with the loss you've experienced, whether it's the loss of physical capacities, health, livelihood, or a loved one. This learning is embedded in the grieving process. Indeed, recent neuroscience investigations have converged on the perspective that explains grief as a process of significant learning.

As you've certainly come to appreciate by now, grieving is more than just feeling sad. It's a complex process that involves your brain updating its understanding of the world. When we face loss, our brains have to reconcile two conflicting realities: the deep-seated belief that what or whom we lost is a permanent part of our lives and the stark reality of their absence. This means learning to accept that they are gone based on the memories and events surrounding their disappearance. This is truly challenging.

Learning to adapt to new situations involves several steps. First, you need to develop new habits. Then, you need to adjust your sense of self to recognise that the loss is real. Lastly, you need to build new practices or strengthen other relationships to fulfil your cognitive and emotional needs. All of this requires your brain to form new bridges, which takes time, experience, and a healthy PIS structure and function. Reflecting on this, it becomes clear why Bonanno's research observed that it can take up to eighteen months for many individuals to adapt after a significant loss.

The process of forming these new neural connections and adjusting psychologically is gradual and cannot be rushed, making this time frame seem not only reasonable but also necessary for genuine healing. Interestingly, chronic grieving has been explained as a difficulty with this particular learning process, with some studies even indicating that reduced hippocampus volume may lead to such difficulty. You'll recall that the hippocampus is one of the PIS's most relevant sites and is involved in the formation of memory and learning mechanisms.

Understanding this connection underscores the importance of the learning steps necessary for adapting to a new reality and finding a way to move forward, though it is often long and challenging. Grieving and healing take time and real-world experiences to help our brains adjust. It's a significant learning journey where we gradually come to terms with the conflicting information about presence and absence, ultimately helping us to heal and continue with our lives. Healing, therefore, is intertwined with grieving. As you navigate this journey, remember that it's okay to take your time and seek support. Embrace the learning process that comes with grief, and recognise that through this journey, you are building resilience and a new understanding of the world.

Practices that count as stars

As we near the end of our discussion on the impact of loss and the PIS, let's explore how you can fortify your psychological defences and support your journey of grieving and healing. First and foremost, start by accepting grief as a form of learning, understanding that everyone learns at their own pace and in their own way, including you. This recognition is crucial for your continued progress. Just like any learning process, practice is key to achieving positive results.

In this context, practice means reflecting on the hidden strengths this loss has revealed within you. Have you discovered newfound patience, problem-solving skills, or perseverance? Embrace these qualities as part of your healing process. Adopt positive coping techniques to manage difficult emotions. Beyond activities like exercise and grounding techniques, consider volunteering. This practice not only creates a sense of purpose but also momentarily shifts your focus to the needs of others, providing a novel, fulfilling experience.

Finally, open yourself up to your new reality. Again, it's okay to take your time and seek support along the way. You are rebuilding your inner-self and constructing a new understanding of the world, one step at a time. Although you may never be the same, by embracing the strength and wisdom that have emerged from your journey, you can certainly be fulfilled again.

As we conclude our discussion here, it's important to recognise how loss impacts the PIS by triggering stress responses that challenge its ability to maintain emotional balance, forcing it to work harder to adapt, reframe, and integrate the experience. This often leads to heightened emotional vulnerability. However, as we've seen, strategies like negative visualization can help prepare us to face loss in a way that is less impactful. Importantly, it's crucial to remember our inherent resilience and that it is possible to live fully while grieving, as grieving and healing are deeply intertwined. Keep in mind that moving forward requires us to upgrade the self to navigate a world that no longer includes what has been lost.

As we move to the next chapter, we will explore how our values and pursuits impact our PIS, while also learning how to see things more clearly, guiding us toward a more balanced and wholesome life.

It is not what you gather, but what you scatter that tells what
kind of life you have lived.— Socrates

Chapter 15

Values & Pursuits: The Path to True Fulfilment

★

Do you ever pause to consider what truly drives your actions and
decisions? Is it personal fulfilment, or is it societal approval? While
we're often clear on what societal approval looks like, the concept
of personal fulfilment can be more elusive. This is because we tend
to focus on external goals—those tied to recognition and rewards—rather than internal ones. Internal goals, however, are
rooted in values that bring deep, personal satisfaction and joy, independent of any outside acknowledgment. Let's use this moment
to reflect on your own sources of fulfilment. For instance, think
about what activities or pursuits give you a profound sense of contentment, even if no one else notices. For me, it's the joy of learning. Whether I'm picking up a new language, mastering a recipe, or
diving into a subject I'm curious about, the fulfilment comes from
the experience itself, not from external validation.

Although it's important to consider the role of societal approval in our lives, I'm not suggesting that you turn your back on
social rules. Quite the opposite. Conducting yourself in a socially
acceptable manner is crucial for your wellbeing. This requires cooperation, not blind obedience. While obedience implies

submission, cooperation involves active participation and competence. It's an important distinction to make.

Now, let's clarify the type of social approval we'll explore here. When pursuing goals, social approval often means seeking influence, status, external validation, or admiration. While these forms of approval can provide motivation and a sense of accomplishment, they can also lead us to prioritise others' expectations over our internal goals, those we pursue for their own sake, like personal growth. Think about how many people follow trends or adopt lifestyles just to fit in, even when those choices don't align with their true interests or values.

The downside of this reality is the relentless demands society places on us, driving us towards an exhausting and often enslaving pursuit of external goals. The pressure to meet social expectations can feel never-ending. We're expected to look a certain way, live by specific standards, cultivate particular interests, participate in approved activities, and own the latest items. The checklist seems endless. This constant striving for belonging can lead us to subscribe to a way of life that consumes us, causing us to neglect our own interests and internal values, ultimately compromising PIS function. Have you found a balance between honouring your personal needs and meeting society's demands?

Finding balance

It is through finding the balance between these pursuits that we can boost our PIS and, in turn, enhance our psychological health. Pursuing internal satisfaction should not come at the cost of pursuing acceptance. It's natural for us to seek approval from others because it enhances self-esteem, and fulfils a psychological need for belonging. In his Hierarchy of Needs theory, humanistic psychologist Abraham Maslow underlined the sense of belonging as one of human's basic needs. That is, a foundational requirement for survival and wellbeing. It doesn't take much to understand why belonging is an innate human necessity when you consider how hyper-social we are. However, while we desire a sense of belonging, we often struggle to understand how to achieve it.

Studies using The MacArthur Scale of Subjective Social Status, for example, ask people to rank themselves on a social ladder compared to others. These research findings show that people care not just about their own social position but also about how they compare to others. Now, here's a question: why do we judge our achievements in relative rather than absolute terms? Why do our accomplishments matter more in comparison to that of others than in and of themselves? The high value society places on hierarchy often leads people to believe that attributes such as ranking and position are necessary for acceptance and validation. This perception can drive individuals to not only prioritise external achievements over internal pursuits, but also fosters a competitive mindset. This approach can lead to constant comparison and competition, undermining sustainable self-esteem and authentic connections. Have you ever found yourself competing with others or pursuing admiration in an attempt to feel accepted?

While many of us might have an intuitive understanding of these social dynamics, we may not always be consciously aware of how deeply societal norms, media influence, peer pressure, validation seeking, and personal insecurities shape our pursuits. Often, these influences operate subtly and can be ingrained in our thinking and actions without us fully realising it. Although, these ongoing pressures can overshadow internal values and pursuits like personal growth, kindness, and authenticity, which are essential for genuine wellbeing, and a robust PIS. So, achieving the right balance involves valuing social connections and external approval for a sense of true belonging, while primarily focusing on intrinsic goals and personal fulfilment. This balance ensures healthy relationships and self-growth without over dependence on the approval of others.

Become a psychonaut & earn stars

In our goal-oriented society, it can be challenging to feel accepted through means other than influence and status, as we are often brought up to develop skills that yield the achievement of external success and material accomplishments. However, this focus frequently leads to a neglect of our inner exploration abilities and capacities. This is why many of us reach adulthood, or even our senior years, without truly understanding what our internal values are, or what truly fulfils us. This can often leave us with a sense of emptiness despite our achievements.

Highlighting the importance of self-reflection, the philosopher Socrates famously stated, "An unexamined life is not worth living." Embracing this mentality not only helps us uncover our values but also builds resilience by fostering a deeper connection with our inner selves. By making time for self-reflection, we unveil our internal values, enhance self-awareness and strengthen our PIS. This process helps us discover our genuine motivations, promoting a sense of purpose and fulfilment essential for overall wellbeing. It also helps us understand that success is measured not just by external accomplishments but by our inner peace and resilience.

The Tibetan Book of the Dead, translated by Robert A.F. Thurman, presents a compelling illustration of self-reflection. Thurman describes Tibetans as inner-world adventurers, likening their inner journeys to our astronauts' exploration of outer space. He says that while astronauts stretch the limits of material conquest, venturing into the vastness of the cosmos, Tibetans are more concerned with the conquest of the inner universe. Thurman coins the term "psychonaut" to describe these inner explorers. I invite you to become a psychonaut as well, an explorer of your own mind and soul.

By turning inward and examining your inner universe, you can uncover deeper truths about yourself, foster genuine wellbeing, and cultivate a more balanced, resilient mind. As a psychonaut, explore the constellation you've been building by way of your Daily

5-Star PIS Goal. Look at the bright stars representing your constructive actions, emotions, and thoughts, and through them, learn your true values, what truly brings you fulfilment and joy: Eating well? Providing for your family? Having a good night's rest? Returning home after a day's work? Witnessing your child grow up? Embrace this inner exploration and discover the goals worth pursuing. These are the stars that guide you toward a life of meaning.

Discovering and pursuing your internal goals will help you welcome life's full range of offers, both the positive and the negative, the comfortable and the uncomfortable. As deep within lies the awareness that you're fulfilled and whole. Note that our life experiences are complex and varied, a mixed cauldron of positive, neutral and negative encounters and situations. These contrasting scenarios have the potential to counterbalance one another, with neutral and positive experiences mitigating adversities and challenging circumstances. However, our neutral and positive life experiences only stand a chance if identified and acknowledged first. Only then are we equipped to consciously choose to live fully and meaningfully, even when faced with discomfort.

We pursue what we value

Now that we've explored the concept of external and internal goals and addressed the reality that internal values are often overlooked due to life's demands and social expectations, let's look at ways you can unveil your internal values, allowing you to embark on your psychonaut voyage.

We saw earlier that media influence, peer pressure, validation seeking, and personal insecurities all sway what we come to think is important, and consequently, what we begin to seek in life. Addressing media influence, we saw in Chapter 12 that global social media consumption equates to an entire waking day per week. Note that this is just social media; this data does not include, for instance, entertainment media. This is relevant because constant exposure to social network, TV series, and movies shapes our perception of what is valuable and desirable.

In 2013, a survey study investigating the influence of romantic comedies on viewers' perceptions of romantic beliefs found a link between watching this genre of movie and the belief in romantic ideals (i.e., soulmates). Certainly, survey studies invariably raise the question , in this case: "But isn't the audience for these movies romanticists in the first place?" A 2019 experimental study sought to examine that and found a cause-effect outcome, suggesting that *after* being exposed to idealistic romantic comedies, viewers, irrespective of their romanticism levels, displayed stronger ideal romantic beliefs.

Indeed, this study also demonstrates these effects are short-term but can become long-lasting with repeated viewing over time. This shows the powerful hold overall media has on the development of our beliefs and how these beliefs can become ingrained based on our level of exposure to them. So, think about it: Have you ever changed your values or goals after seeing something on social or news media, on a TV show or movie?

Imagine your inner-self's voice as a gentle whisper, trying to guide you towards your true needs and values. Yet, the constant barrage of technology and media is like a loud noise, drowning out that whisper. By reducing our dependence on technology, we create space for that inner voice to be heard. This isn't just about cutting screen time, it's about reclaiming our ability to make decisions that are truly our own. Carl Rogers, a humanist psychologist, emphasised the importance of congruence for wellbeing - aligning our true-selves with our experiences. When we turn the external noise down, we foster this alignment, discovering a deeper understanding of ourselves and what genuinely brings us joy and fulfilment.

Take a moment to reflect: how much of what you chase after is influenced by the relentless clamour of the outer world?

Fitting-in vs. belonging

I previously stated that achieving the right balance between internal pursuits and external approval involves valuing social connections and approval for a sense of *true* belonging.

Think about this: true belonging, as emphasised by researcher Brené Brown, doesn't require us to create a false image of ourselves. It requires us to be who we truly are. True belonging means being accepted for our authentic selves, without pretending to be someone we're not. This kind of belonging takes vulnerability and courage. It involves being willing to stand up for who we are, even if it means standing alone sometimes. It also means staying true to our values and principles, even when it's difficult.

Now, reflect on your own experiences. Are you living authentically, or do you sometimes find yourself hiding behind a persona? Have you ever found yourself trying to fit in by evaluating a situation and shaping yourself into it? This is often driven by peer pressure, the need for validation, and personal insecurities. But fitting in is not the same as belonging. Belonging is about finding spaces and relationships where you feel seen, heard, and valued. According to Brown, this journey starts with self-acceptance. Meaning, you need to belong to yourself first.

Belonging to yourself first involves deeply accepting your strengths, flaws, and unique identity. It means recognising and valuing your own worth. Remember, in order to feel accomplished, you don't need to be better than others. True accomplishment comes from doing your best given your circumstances. Are you truly giving your best with what you have right now?

By living according to your inner values, you cultivate an authentic self-relationship. This inner alignment empowers you to connect with others without compromising who you are, fostering genuine relationships based on mutual respect and understanding. In essence, belonging to yourself is the foundation of living a life that is genuinely yours, where personal fulfilment is derived from inner harmony rather than external comparison.

Now you may be wondering how living by this principle would activate your PIS. Well, belonging to yourself bolsters psychological defences because it builds a strong foundation of self-awareness and self-acceptance. When you know and value your true self, you are better equipped to face life's challenges without losing your sense of identity. This inner stability allows you to adapt to adversity with confidence and maintain your integrity under pressure. By deriving fulfilment from within rather than external validation, you become less susceptible to external stressors, thereby enhancing your ability to bounce back from setbacks and persist through difficulties, ultimately cultivating a resilient mind.

Part 3
Takeaways

★

As you complete this section, you've successfully navigated through some of the critical challenges to your psychological defences, equipping yourself with valuable insights to strengthen your PIS and foster a resilient mind. Your dedication and thoughtful engagement with the material are praiseworthy. Given the complexity and wealth of information we've covered, it's a good idea to recap the main points to solidify your understanding.

In this section of the book, we further emphasised the critical role of self-awareness and its key components: self-reflection and self-exploration. Self-awareness is at the core of conscious and intentional living, which is key to activating the PIS. By understanding and recognising our thoughts, emotions, moods, and values we are better equipped to deal with them effectively. Through this journey, we've highlighted how essential it is to develop skills like mental restructuring, self-control and psychological flexibility. These skills allow us to navigate a wide range of challenges that, if left unchecked, could escalate into more serious psychological issues. We saw, for example, that low mood can develop into depressive symptoms, everyday habits can lead to dependency, habitual procrastination can lead to anxiety, grieving can become chronic, and neglected inner values can manifest as emptiness.

All along, I've encouraged you to think of the simple actionable steps we discussed here as stars in your personal constellation. Just as each star contributes to the brilliance and completeness of the night sky, each step helps to brighten up various areas of your life. Whether it's creating healthy boundaries in your relationships, transforming a negative mindset into a positive outlook, or building a foundation of resilience that stands firm against any storm, these stars collectively illuminate your path to a brighter and more resilient self.

Specifically, in Chapter 11, we discussed the importance of differentiating sadness from depression. I highlighted how societal expectations for us to always "be happy" can pressure us to maintain a constant state of positivity and high energy. This expectation not only obscures the value of neutral emotions and experiences, such as calm contentment or relaxed states, but also contributes to a distorted perception of life and ourselves. Chapter 12 involved an exploration of behaviours that can potentially become addictive due to their rewarding properties. We discussed how accessing pornography, engagement with social media, consumption of food and goods can become emotional crutches. That is, coping mechanism or behaviours that we come to rely on to manage stress, anxiety, or emotional discomfort, often to the point where it hinders personal growth and prevents addressing underlying issues.

This led us to the topic of procrastination in Chapter 13, which is similar to addiction in that it involves automatic behaviours to avoid discomfort or stress. However, they differ in that addiction involves dependence on substances or activities, while procrastination typically delays the completion of intended, necessary tasks. We thoroughly examined the effects of procrastination on the PIS, noting that procrastination not only triggers stress and anxiety but also perpetuates these states, creating a self-sustaining loop of psychological discomfort. We discussed that overcoming both potentially addictive behaviour and procrastination involves cultivating self-awareness and developing healthier coping mechanisms through the 5-Star Framework.

In Chapter 14, we explored how life's losses can affect the PIS by leading to increased vulnerability to stress and testing our ability to adapt. We also delved into research on the grieving process, where we saw that humans possess an incredible capacity to overcome adversity. Remarkably, nearly half of bereaved individuals face grief with resilience, which means processing the emotions of loss while adapting, and finding ways to continue living meaningfully, showcasing our inherent strength.

Lastly, in Chapter 15, the last chapter of Part 3, I invited you to become a psychonaut and journey into your inner universe to uncover your true values, guiding you toward meaningful pursuits and a life of purpose. The essence of this chapter was about embracing a lifestyle where you find genuine belonging in your relationships and social environment while staying connected to your inner voice.

Part 3 of *What Makes a Resilient Mind?* presented you with a number of steps and actions to help you earn stars towards your Daily 5-Star PIS Goal.

They're also definitely worth revisiting!

1.Identify your neutral emotional states, like the calm contentment you might feel while sipping a morning coffee. These states, often overlooked, provide a valuable sense of stability and clarity amidst life's highs and lows.

2.Make mental restructuring a habit to challenge and reframe negative thoughts, preventing them from dominating your mindset and helping you maintain a more balanced and positive outlook.

3.Create a repertoire of coping mechanisms you can turn to when feeling agitated or distressed, and keep this list next to your Daily 5-Star PIS Goal. For instance, reach for fruits or a healthy snack to combat overeating, and keep your monthly budget and financial plans visible to curb impulsive shopping.

4.Work on developing psychological flexibility. Building on our previous point about expanding your repertoire of behaviours, this skill helps you cultivate a more adaptable mindset. This adaptability is crucial for effectively addressing escapism and procrastination.

5.Embrace grieving and healing as a unified process, where learning is central to integrating a new understanding of the world and yourself.

Now, try to match these steps and actions with the Daily 5-Star PIS Goal categories:

(a) Mental Fitness
(b) Sleep Magic
(c) Brain Fuel
(d) Social Spark
(e) Break Free
(f) Star Path

This is how I matched them : 1-c; 2-c; 3-e; 4-f and 5-c.

Of course, there is no right or wrong way to match these actions and categories. However, taking the time to consider them more deeply fosters self-awareness, which in turn activates your psychological defences.

By now, you've likely noticed that various steps and actions contribute to developing skills that prevent psychological issues from spiralling out of control. For instance, enhancing self-awareness can help you manage low mood, recognise the need for escapism, and identify early signs of stress before they escalate into anxiety. Think of these psychological skills and coping strategies as a versatile toolkit designed to maintain and strengthen your PIS. In the next section, we'll explore specific strategies for reinforcing your psychological defences, equipping you with the tools you need to enhance overall wellbeing and resilience.

Part 4

Strengthening Your Psychological Immune System

Emancipate yourself from mental slavery. None but ourselves can free our minds. – Bob Marley

Chapter 16

Thoughts: Crucial Players in the PIS Field

★

Recall from Chapter 11 how our thoughts have a considerable impact on our mood and emotions. But remember, this impact doesn't have to be negative. By learning how to manage our thoughts, we can find inner peace. In fact, it's been suggested that the extent of our inner peace largely depends on the relationship we have with our thoughts. That's exactly what we're about to explore: how to develop a healthy relationship with our thoughts. We'll start by becoming aware of them, and then by learning to avoid judging them. But first, let's take a moment to understand what thoughts actually are.

Thoughts are the mental conversations we have with ourselves, a stream of ideas and images that constantly flow through our minds. Thoughts shape our views of the world, influence our decisions, behaviours and actions. Thus, affecting the structure and function of the PIS by guiding how we feel about our life experiences.

Interestingly, many of us are often unaware of our thoughts on a conscious level. For example, have you ever found yourself worrying without realising what triggered the worry? If the answer is yes, you are not alone. Much of our thinking happens automatically and can go unnoticed unless we make a deliberate effort to pay attention to it. The reason why we are often unaware of our thoughts is because many of them are automatic and habitual, developed as quick responses or adaptations to our environment. Imagine you're driving home and suddenly realise you don't remember the last few minutes of the drive. Your mind was on autopilot, navigating familiar roads without conscious thought. Similarly, many of our thoughts are automatic responses to our environment, occurring without us even noticing.

Note that this is not all a bad thing. This autopilot mode helps us efficiently handle daily tasks without overloading our conscious awareness. However, this autopilot mode can also mean we're not fully attentive to the content of our minds or the impact of our thoughts on our mental health. Even without conscious awareness, these underlying thoughts can create a mental environment that affects our overall wellbeing.

Mental filters

Scientific evidence supporting the claim that unconscious thoughts impact our wellbeing primarily comes from CBT studies, which has shown that automatic thoughts influence emotions and behaviours. CBT research has shown that our automatic thoughts act like a mental filter, influencing how we feel and act. For example, if you automatically think *I can't handle this* when facing a busy day at work, you'll likely feel overwhelmed and stressed. By becoming aware of and changing these negative thoughts to something like *I can tackle one task at a time*, you can improve your emotions and handle your day more effectively. The reason this shift works is that changing your thoughts alters your emotional response, helping you to feel more in control and reducing stress.

Interestingly, FMRI studies in neuroscience, particularly those examining the default mode network (DMN) in the brain, indicate that these automatic, background thought processes significantly affect our emotional states and stress levels. The DMN, located in the middle and back regions of the brain, includes the medial prefrontal cortex (near the front) and the posterior cingulate cortex (towards the back). The DMN functions like your brain's autopilot mode, active when you're daydreaming, relaxing, or not focused on the outside world. It turns out that the DMN runs continuous background thoughts, like a mental chatterbox. For the PIS and mental health, this means that DMN activity, especially its link to self-referential thoughts—such as *Why did I say that?*—can impact our emotional and mood states. For instance, overactivity in the DMN is associated with overthinking and negative self-focus, which can lead to mental health issues like depression and anxiety.

So you can see how automatic thoughts can affect how we feel, possibly making us more stressed or down without us even realising. By becoming aware of this mental chatter and learning how to deal with it, we can boost our PIS and, by extent, improve our overall life satisfaction. Mindfulness-based strategies, which increase awareness of thoughts, have shown to be promising in reducing symptoms of anxious and depressing mental processes. One such strategy is: thought meditation. Like breathing meditation, this practice involves deliberately focusing your awareness, but instead of concentrating on your breath, you observe your thoughts. You let your thoughts come and go without judgment, just watching them pass by like watching butterflies as they flutter by.

Becoming aware of thoughts

Meditating on your thoughts is not the only way to become aware of them. I've encouraged you to practice expressive writing in Chapter 9 to manage intrusive thoughts. If you've been journalling as to achieve your Daily 5-Star PIS Goal, you'll have noticed this practice has helped you gain insight into your thought patterns and uncover what goes on in your head. Although be aware, It's productive to journal not only in moments when you're feeling down, but also when you're joyful, calm, or in a neutral state. This way, you'll have a complete view of your own mental landscape.

Practicing journaling in such a thorough and unbiased way will enable you to see (even in times of sadness or low mood - when we tend to adopt a generalised doom and gloom outlook) that you are capable of experiencing a whole range of emotions, feelings, and mood states, from positive through neutral to negative. This will be evidenced by your own journaling. Such awareness will help you cope better in times of adversity and realise that it is natural to experience low mood or negative emotions in situations that, well … elicit these feelings, like being let down or facing loss.

This reminds me of a smart lady, Nikki, whom I spoke to a few years ago. In her 50's then, she was a writer troubled by decade-old thoughts that replayed in her mind through rumination - revisiting past events repeatedly, like a sheep chewing the same chunk of grass over and over again. Together, we broke that cycle, freeing her from the mental disturbance her thoughts caused. With time, as she became more positive and energetic, she started a diet and began dating someone (this is what I call the spiral up effect at its best!). Our interactions seemed fruitful, and we concluded our informal meetings.

A few months later, however, she contacted me utterly distressed. Her older son had made a bad choice and was in trouble. After discussing the situation, we realised she was perfectly capable of coping with her son's circumstances. What distressed her was not the situation itself but her judgment of her own sad thoughts. To my surprise, she believed our sessions meant she would never feel sad again. This misunderstanding highlighted that it was the act of judging the content of her mind that was causing her distress. For example, she thought, "I must be failing in some way if I'm still sad. This is terrible!" Our thoughts and feelings are natural responses to life events, but it is the way we judge and react to them that can truly amplify our suffering.

How about you? Do you find yourself labelling your thoughts as 'good' or 'bad'? How does this judgment affect how you feel overall? Think about a recent time when you felt sad or anxious. Did judging those feelings make the experience more difficult for you?

The importance of non-Judgment in activating the PIS

By now, you understand that cultivating self-awareness is crucial for enhancing the PIS. It helps us better understand our thoughts, emotions, and behaviours. However, self-awareness alone is often not enough. Research has shown that simply being aware of our thoughts and feelings, particularly the negative ones, doesn't always lead to improved wellbeing. What truly makes the difference is learning to observe our thoughts without judgment.

For instance, imagine someone whose presence doesn't exactly thrill you, let's call him Pete. When Pete shows up, you're aware of him, but that awareness quickly becomes clouded by judgments like: *he's irritating, tactless, and annoying.* Naturally, these judgments shape your entire experience of Pete, making you feel unsettled and uncomfortable. But what if, instead of judging Pete every time he appears, you simply thought, *There's Pete, just another person in the room.* You wouldn't be as caught up in awkward memories or discomfort.

A 2022 study with 40 participants, conducted at the Brain Institute in Brazil, found that being non-judgmental helps reduce anxious states. The study demonstrated that when people notice their thoughts and feelings without judging them, they are protected from feeling anxious and stressed. In other words, if you can observe what's going on in your mind without labelling those thoughts and images as good or bad, you're considerably less likely to feel distressed even if you're very aware of them. This finding suggests that practicing non-judgment can be a powerful tool for boosting the PIS.

Naturally, you may wonder how not judging thoughts boosts the PIS. Recall from previous chapters how our thoughts have a profound influence in turning a fleeting emotion like sadness into lingering low mood that can, if not addressed, turn into a chronic depressed state. You'll also recall how behaviours that can become addictive and phenomena like procrastination are driven by underlying factors often related to how we view life's demands as well as our own mental and emotional states. Again, our views and beliefs manifest in our minds as mere thoughts that we automatically judge. When deemed bad or negative, we often turn to escapism through activities that, although offer immediate gratification, have the potential to weaken our psychological defences in the long run.

By exercising non-judgment, we can break this cycle. Instead of letting negative judgments amplify our distress, we learn to observe our thoughts and emotions without immediate reaction. This approach fosters a more balanced perspective, allowing us to address the root causes of our distress more effectively and build stronger resilience against life's demands and challenges.

This is about not judging the judgement

Now, it's important to understand that I'm not suggesting you simply stop judging your thoughts, emotions, or mood states, as if turning off a switch. We are hardwired to judge, label, and categorise as a way to navigate the world. This is simply how our minds work. Asking you to stop judging entirely would be unrealistic. Instead, my suggestion is to not judge the judgment. Simply recognise that a judgment is just another thought.

Let's revisit the example of Pete. When he walks into the room, you might automatically think, *He's irritating, tactless, and annoying.* Instead of trying to suppress or eliminate those judgments, which can be difficult, notice them for what they are, just thoughts. Rather than getting caught up in the discomfort they bring, you could think, *There's that judgment again*, and allow it to pass without attaching further meaning to it. By not judging yourself for having these thoughts about Pete, you create space to observe them without letting them dominate your emotional state. This simple shift can reduce the emotional charge those judgments carry, making it easier to maintain your inner peace.

A useful technique to help with this is to practice observing your thoughts without getting involved. This means simply noticing your thoughts as they come and go, without getting caught up in them or letting them influence your emotions. Again, think of it like watching butterflies as they flutter by. You observe each butterfly as it passes, but you don't try to catch it or hold onto it, whether it's a dull, dark butterfly or a bright, colourful one. This approach helps you maintain a sense of calm and prevents negative thoughts from taking over your mind and draining your energy.

Here's how you can do it, note that we're not only revisiting, but also elaborating on the techniques we mentioned at the beginning of the chapter and earlier in the book.

1.Expressive Writing: Write down your thoughts and feelings as they occur. When you notice a judgment, such as *I shouldn't feel this way*, write it down too. Take a moment to reflect on how thoughts, should not prevent you from experiencing the present moment positively. Remember, it's natural to have distressing thoughts, but they don't have to impair your current peace and wellbeing.

2.Thought Exploration: Sit quietly and focus on your breath to start with. As thoughts arise, simply notice them without getting involved. Always embrace them as "thinking". At each new thought or judgement that emerges, acknowledge it by saying to yourself *This is just another thought*, and return to your breath. This helps create a habit of observing without judgment.

Of course, this thought exploration is a meditation practice. If you're not inclined to contemplative practices, I encourage you to still try to engage in it. These practices have been systematically investigated by psychologists and neuroscientists and have been found to be highly beneficial in boosting wellbeing and psychological defences.

In case this argument is not enough to convince you to give thought meditation a try, no problem! There are alternative ways to engage in thought exploration. Feel free to do it while performing a non-demanding task. Remember, this is when the DMN is in full trot. Whether you're washing up, sipping your tea, or walking the dog in the park, bring your awareness to the contents of your mind and adopt an attitude of, *There it comes: just another thought!*

If at any given time you decide to open up to a new experience, by all means, take a seat and let your thoughts be. Importantly, don't force or purposefully bring to mind negative past or future events. This is not a negative visualization practice. Simply sit calmly, as if in front of a TV screen, watching the content flow as if someone else had the remote control. As another scene appears in front of you, irrespective of its nature, think to yourself, *Just another scene.* Be conscious of taking deep, slow breaths as you explore your thoughts, knowing this will activate your parasympathetic nervous system, sending a message to your brain: "I'm okay, I'm calm and safe."

3.Self-compassion: Integrate self-compassion in your thought exploration practices, by directing kindness towards yourself. Repeat phrases like *May I be kind to myself* and *May I accept myself as I am.* This fosters a non-judgmental attitude towards your own inner or external experiences and sustains your overall wellbeing.

It may feel like these practices can take a lot of time from your already busy schedule. However, it's important to keep in mind that each one of them represents a star in your personal constellation of psychological achievements. With each star you earn, you enhance the brightness of your mental clarity. The skill of non-judgment is yet another beacon that will enable you to maintain a clear perspective, reduce distress from negative thoughts, and cultivate a resilient mind.

A word on equanimity

It's essential to note that non-judgment, far from meaning apathy, actually leads to equanimity.

Apathy is a lack of interest, enthusiasm, or concern, where one is disengaged and indifferent to both positive and negative experiences, often leading to a disconnection from emotions and life itself. Equanimity, on the other hand, is a state of balanced and calm mind, where one remains composed and accepting of both positive and negative experiences without getting overwhelmed or indifferent. It involves engagement with life and a deep understanding of our mental and emotional landscape. The very goals we're aiming to achieve by activating the PIS.

Thus, by practicing non-judgment, you cultivate equanimity, allowing you to face life's challenges with steadiness and grace. Buddhist teacher and author Jack Kornfield explains that "Equanimity arises when we accept the way things are". This acceptance doesn't mean resignation but rather embracing reality without resistance. It is towards acceptance - the focus of our discussion in the next chapter - that we now turn, exploring how it can further enhance our psychological defences and resilience.

Amor fati – 'Love your fate', which is in fact your life.
— Friedrich Nietzsche

Chapter 17

Acceptance & its Role in Inner Strength

★

Please start this chapter taking a brief moment to reflect on your life. How accepting are you of the situations you face? Do you find it easy to embrace things as they are, or do you constantly feel the need to push, strive, and change?

In our fast-paced culture, we are often encouraged to keep advancing, to battle against the odds, and to push ourselves to achieve more. While this drive can be necessary for moving forward, it can also come at a cost to our PIS. Constant striving and battling can lead to burnout, anxiety, and a diminished ability to cope with life's demands. Sometimes, the most powerful thing we can do is to pause, be still, and accept things as they are.

Consider these questions: How often do you find yourself trying to control the uncontrollable? In what ways could embracing acceptance bring more peace into your life? What does acceptance mean to you?

I hope you know that acceptance is not about giving up or being passive. It's about recognising the reality of our circumstances and finding peace within them. This wisdom has been around for centuries but has been largely forgotten in modern times. One ancient philosophy that beautifully encapsulates this concept is Wu wei (pronounced woo way).

Wu wei, a principle from Taoism, translates to "non-action" or "effortless action." It teaches us to align with the natural flow of life, to act in harmony with the world around us rather than against it. By practicing Wu wei, we learn to let go of unnecessary struggle and find strength in acceptance. Imagine how your life might change if you could integrate a bit more acceptance into your daily routine.

To achieve this balance, acknowledge and embrace things as they are, rather than actively seeking to change them. It involves understanding and coming to terms with realities that cannot be altered, such as what other people think or the past decisions you've made. Accepting these unchangeable aspects of life can lead to personal growth and resilience. You see, this process provides a foundation of mental stability, allowing for growth from a place of inner peace rather than constant struggle.

Before we dive into a more detailed discussion of acceptance, I want to take a moment to explain why I'll be breaking acceptance down into different aspects, which will be: experiential acceptance, acceptance of self, and acceptance of others. First, this approach aligns with scientific investigations and the academic literature, providing a solid foundation for our discussion. But more importantly, by exploring acceptance from various angles, we can offer a comprehensive view that helps you target different practices and skill development.

Think of it as expanding your personal constellation. Each act of acceptance is a star that brightens your PIS, allowing your constellation to shine brighter and brighter with each new star.

Now that we've set the scene, let's explore the different facets of acceptance and discover how they can help you cultivate a more robust PIS and a resilient mind.

Experiential acceptance : Embracing reality as it is

Experiential acceptance means being open to whatever you're experiencing in the present moment. Experiential acceptance and equanimity are key parts of mindfulness practices and many modern therapeutic approaches, such as ACT, acceptance and commitment therapy. A method we briefly highlighted in Chapter 12.

Recent research has shown that when acceptance training is removed from mindfulness programs, the program become less effective at diminishing stress, improving positive emotions and social interactions. This piece of evidence highlights that acceptance is a crucial tool for managing our mood, feelings and thoughts. As by accepting our present internal and external reality we can respond (not react) to them more calmly and productively (effortless-action).

Challenges to experiential acceptance

However, while it's been established experiential acceptance can enhance wellbeing, it's not always easy to achieve it. We often encounter several challenges when trying to practice it. One major obstacle is resistance to discomfort. Embracing uncomfortable thoughts, emotions or situations can be daunting. Many of us instinctively try to avoid or suppress discomfort by either fighting it off or escaping from it, which ultimately leads to greater stress and anxiety. This experiential avoidance is something we've discussed more than once in previous sections of this book.

Still, let's elaborate on this a little further by finding ways to overcome experiential avoidance. As ever, start with small steps. Gradually expose yourself to mild discomfort and practice accepting it without trying to change it. For example, if you're stuck in traffic or find yourself in a slow-moving queue at the supermarket, instead of giving in to frustration, take a few deep breaths and embrace the situation as it is. Use this time to bring your full awareness to the moment, acknowledging any impatience without letting it take over. After all, how will giving in to frustration make the situation any better? Over time, you'll build resilience to these situations and develop the ability to accept even more challenging experiences.

Another common challenge to experiential avoidance is the fear of losing control. Many of us feel the need to be in control because it provides a sense of security and predictability in our lives. However, this need for control can be detrimental to our PIS, as it leads to heightened anxiety and stress when things don't go as planned. The fear of losing control can also prevent us from fully embracing our experiences, as we may resist anything that feels uncertain. It's important to remember that acceptance doesn't mean surrendering control over your life. Instead, it's about acknowledging your experiences without trying to dodge them. Practicing the grounding techniques we've discussed before, such as deep breathing, can help maintain a sense of stability while you accept and engage with your emotions and experiences as they are.

Accepting what we cannot control

As we discuss the need for control that many of us often indulge in, we might recognise just how frequently we strive for it. How often do you find yourself trying to control situations or outcomes? If your answer is "often", consider the wisdom of Stoic philosophy: some things in life are simply beyond our control.

We touched on this reality in Part 2 of this book, where the focus was primarily on the aspects of life that we *can* control, such as our lifestyle habits. Yet, life is more nuanced; it also requires us to recognise and accept the elements that lie beyond our influence.

Thus, it's time to explore how to navigate the aspects of life that are beyond our control.

An effective way to deal with what is beyond our control is by remaining undisturbed, as suggested by the Wu wei philosophy. This means embracing circumstances without resistance or forcing specific outcomes. In my view, nothing encapsulates the essence of Wu wei and the Stoic lesson more accurately than the Serenity Prayer by Reinhold Niebuhr: "Grant me the serenity to accept the things I cannot change, courage to change the things I can, and wisdom to know the difference."

At this point in our journey, you're fully aware that in order to garner serenity, courage, and wisdom, we must deliberately nurture our PIS to develop mental clarity and strength. This means cultivating a psychological landscape that's open to what we cannot control and focuses on what we have influence over. The wisdom here is understanding that while we can't control unforeseen events or the actions of others, we can control and master our responses to them. For example, if someone is rude to us, we can't control their behaviour, but we can choose to respond calmly rather than react with anger. This mindset empowers us to navigate life's challenges with composure and self-preservation.

Remember, acceptance is not about giving up but about recognising our limits and focusing on our inner peace. By embracing this balance, we foster strong psychological defences, a resilient mindset and lead a more serene life. By embracing experiential acceptance and focusing on what we can control, we not only find inner peace but also create a foundation for accepting both ourselves and others.

Having said that, let's now discuss the other two aspects of acceptance: accepting ourselves and others, and how they boost the PIS and our overall wellbeing.

Embracing self & others

Our discussion of acceptance of the self and others will be intertwined, as one leads to the other. Williams' and Lynn's historical and conceptual study on acceptance highlights how self-acceptance and acceptance of others are deeply interconnected.

Their research shows that accepting oneself fosters a more compassionate and understanding attitude towards others. However, this journey comes with its own set of challenges.

Expectations

It can be difficult to deal with other people for various reasons. Differences in personalities, values, communication styles, and expectations can create misunderstandings and conflicts. Additionally, our own biases and assumptions about how other people should behave can contribute to these difficulties. Have you ever felt upset with someone else mostly because they didn't meet your expectations, even when they were acting with their best intentions? It's often challenging to see things from someone else's perspective, especially when their approach or beliefs differ from our own.

Being more tolerant and understanding of other individuals' realities can help us deal with their flaws and shortcomings. Remember, we ourselves are flawed and often fall short of meeting people's expectations. You're not under the impression you meet everyone's expectations about you, are you? This reflection is meant to prompt humility, reminding us that just as others have shortcomings, so do we. By embracing this mindset, we can foster a more compassionate and understanding approach to our interpersonal interactions.

Perfectionism

Besides expectations, there's yet another hindrance to embracing both ourselves and others: perfectionism. While expectations often involve wanting others to meet given standards, perfectionism goes a step further by demanding flawlessness from ourselves and those around us. This relentless pursuit of perfection makes it difficult to accept any imperfections or mistakes, whether they are our own or someone else's.

As a perfectionist myself, I often struggle with this, particularly in relation to my own shortcomings. But the problem is, research shows that perfectionism directed at the self can lead to depression. So, to manage this, I began practicing self-compassion and kindness. As there's strong evidence supporting this approach. For example, a study in Iran with 210 depressed inpatients found that self-kindness can help with depression, especially for perfectionists. It follows that being self-compassionate while striving for high-goals can reduce low mood symptoms, while being too self-critical makes it worse.

We probably don't need a scientific investigation to tell us that. However, here's my very favourite part of this research's findings: self-kindness can lessen the negative effects of self-criticism but doesn't change the motivation of striving for high standards. Meaning, you can still aim high and work towards your goals without beating yourself up for every little mistake. It shows that the secret lies in being driven while also being kind to yourself when things don't go perfectly.

I remind myself that perfection is unattainable and that embracing imperfections is part of growth. Accepting flaws fosters greater kindness and personal development. As mentioned earlier, when we accept ourselves as we are, we're more likely to accept others as they are. This process expands like ripples in water, self-acceptance naturally leads to greater acceptance of others. This ripple effect strengthens the PIS by bringing several positive outcomes. It broadens our range of experiences, empowering us to take more productive actions. It also fosters compassion and reduces blame towards others, promoting greater serenity, cooperation, and reasonableness in our interactions. This increased acceptance of self and others ultimately enhances overall life satisfaction and strengthens interpersonal relationships.

Pause & reflection

Before we conclude this chapter, let's revisit the reflection we posed at the beginning; this time, consider it with your newfound understanding of acceptance: To what extent does acceptance play a role in your life experiences now?

Most of our experiences are shaped by our actions and interactions with others. Often, these interactions and situations may fall short of our expectations. So, take a moment to reflect on this: How accepting are you of the limitations and imperfections of the people in your life? And how accepting are you of your own shortcomings?

Remember, acceptance is not about giving up or becoming passive. It's about recognising the reality of our circumstances, the circumstances of others and embracing them without judgment. This connects to the concept of effortless action, or Wu wei, which teaches us to align ourselves with the natural flow of life rather than resist it.

As Lao Tzu said, "By letting it go, it all gets done." This wisdom encourages us to release the need to manipulate or control everything. Fostering peace through acceptance and non-resistance. Ultimately, this leads to a life of harmony and balance.

So, how has your outlook already begun to shift? Earn stars by reflecting on these points.

In the upcoming chapter, we will build upon our discussion of self-acceptance and explore other elements related to the self and their connection to the PIS and mental stability. We'll delve into additional ways to add stars to your constellation, continuing to enhance your resilience and overall wellbeing.

Just as stars naturally shine without effort, your commitment to nurturing your PIS can illuminate your life and effortlessly boost your mental health.

Until you make the unconscious conscious, it will direct your life
& you will call it fate. — Carl Jung

Chapter 18

Elements of the Self

★

"Self-esteem is the reputation we acquire with ourselves," says psychologist Nathaniel Branden. But simply put, self-esteem is how much we value and appreciate ourselves. Self-esteem shapes our beliefs about our abilities and our worthiness of life satisfaction and success, whether big or small. Having healthy levels of self-esteem is vital for our PIS, as it influences how we see ourselves and, consequently, how we interact with the world around us.

Now, let me clarify what healthy levels of self-esteem means. It starts with having a balanced and accurate view of yourself. It entails recognising your strengths and weaknesses, feeling confident in your abilities, and knowing that you are worthy of respect and love. Self-esteem is not about thinking you're perfect either. It's about feeling good enough as you are.

Now, take a moment to reflect on your own self-esteem. Are you able to accept compliments and constructive criticism? Do you generally feel confident in your abilities? Remember, seeing your insecurities as areas where you can grow is a positive step towards building a stronger sense of self-worth.

Factors that influence self-esteem

The foundation of self-esteem is often built during childhood. Supportive and nurturing environments help children feel valued and capable, while negative experiences like excessive criticism or neglect can undermine the development of self-worth. As we grow up, our self-esteem becomes increasingly influenced by our interactions with others. Positive relationships with friends, romantic partners, and co-workers can boost our confidence through a sense of belonging.

Further, our own efforts also play a considerable role in how we evaluate our self-worth. Personal achievements and successes contribute to a stronger sense of self-esteem. Thus, in this respect, setting and achieving goals such as the Daily 5-star PIS Goal, fosters confidence and pride. Conversely, repeated setbacks or unmet goals can negatively affect self-esteem. Thus, it's important to celebrate successes and learn from setbacks to maintain a healthy balance.

Building on that, note that maintaining a healthy balance in self-esteem is crucial. Here, our goal is to nurture our psychological defences to cultivate a mindset that enables us to feel confident and worthy. It's important not to cross the line into narcissism! Interestingly, the academic literature shows that although not the same, high self-esteem and narcissism do overlap. So, keep in mind that healthy self-esteem is not about grandiosity, self-centeredness, arrogance, or entitlement. Instead, it's about recognising your value while also respecting and valuing others. For instance, acknowledging your achievements without feeling the need to overshadow others, or feeling good about yourself without comparing yourself to those around you.

So, let's explore some practical strategies to foster healthy self-esteem and build a more confident, resilient sense of self.

Practice assertiveness & earn stars

Assertiveness is about finding a balance between your needs and the needs of others, ensuring that your voice is heard without being aggressive. It is about communicating your needs, desires, and boundaries clearly and respectfully. Being assertive helps you stand up for yourself and reinforces your sense of self-worth. It also fosters healthier relationships by promoting mutual respect and understanding.

Practice assertiveness by expressing your thoughts and feelings honestly, making requests directly, and saying 'no' when necessary. For example, if a coworker asks you to take on additional tasks when you're already busy, you could respond with, "I understand that you need help, but I currently have a full workload. I won't be able to take on more tasks right now." This type of response clearly communicates your boundaries while remaining respectful and professional.

This takes us back to Chapter 2, when I encouraged you to set boundaries with those people in your life who can be difficult and demanding. Implementing assertiveness in such a scenario could be, for instance, when a relative frequently asks for favours that inconvenience you, you might say, "I value our friendship, but I can't help you with this task today as I have other commitments." This way, you are clearly communicating your limits while maintaining respect and consideration for the relationship.

Admittedly, this is not always easy, as we have a tendency to please others as to, perhaps, feel accepted and liked. However, constantly prioritising others' needs above your own can negatively affect your self-worth. Plus, to be truly altruistic and maintain positive interactions, you need to enjoy good levels of self-esteem first. When you have a healthy sense of self-worth, you are better equipped to support others without compromising your own well-being.

By practicing assertiveness, you additionally lay the foundation for a stronger sense of self-worth, which is essential for adopting a growth mindset.

Embrace growth mindset

Adopting a growth mindset requires a shift in perspective. For example, instead of seeing challenges and failures as setbacks, view them as opportunities for growth. Think about past events and consider how some of the challenges you've overcome revealed your steadiness and competence. Psychologist Carol Dweck's research with students found that those who embraced a growth mindset were more likely to persevere and succeed. What's fascinating is that students with a growth mindset saw setbacks not as inherent flaws but as opportunities to improve through effort and better strategies.

You can see how this reflects a solid sense of self-worth. The mindset here is, "This is not an innate limitation I have. This is something I can put more effort into to perform better." So, how do you approach your own setbacks? Do you see them as fixed limitations or as chances to grow?

Embrace the idea that abilities and intelligence can be developed through effort and learning. This mindset encourages a positive attitude towards self-improvement, consolidates self-esteem, and enhances PIS function. It helps you stay motivated and confident in your ability to overcome difficulties. As Maya Angelou wisely observed, "You may encounter many defeats, but you must not be defeated. In fact, it may be necessary to encounter the defeats, so you can know who you are, what you can rise from, how you can still come out of it."

Just as self-esteem nurtures the PIS, enabling us to face challenges with greater confidence, there's another crucial aspect of the self that empowers us to manage our actions and behaviours effectively: self-control. This is an ability we've touched on a few times before in our discussion, and now it's time to explore it more deeply.

Reflecting on self – control

Let's begin our exploration of self-control by taking a moment to reflect on your own experiences. In Chapter 2, we talked about how psychology has developed various ways to measure different aspects of our minds, and self-control is one of these aspects that has been extensively studied. One way of measuring self-control is through the Brief Self-Control Scale (BSCS), developed by Tangney and co-researchers in 2004.

The questions below are inspired by the BSCS. Keep in mind, this isn't a formal assessment or diagnosis (those are typically done by psychometrists and clinicians). Instead, these questions are meant to give you a structured way to think about your current self-control abilities. Consider this a personal check-in to see where you stand and to motivate you (and to earn stars!), whether you're looking to maintain your good habits or seeking to improve.

Reflect on the following questions and rate your responses as "Yes," "Sometimes," or "No."

1. Do you struggle to break bad habits?
2. Do you say things that are inappropriate?
3. Do you engage in activities that might be bad for you because they're fun?
4. Do you find yourself wishing for more self-discipline?
5. Does pleasure and fun keep you from getting work done?
6. Are you able to work effectively towards long-term goals?
7. Are there times when you can't resist doing something, even if you know it's wrong?

Interpreting your Answers:

Mostly "Yes" answers: It could be beneficial to focus on developing self-control strategies and seeking support from family, friends or a professional if needed.

Mostly "Sometimes" answers: Reflect on areas for improvement and consider strategies to enhance your self-discipline.

Mostly "No" answers: Keep up the good work and continue maintaining your positive habits.

After exploring and reflecting on the above questions, the definition of self-control becomes more meaningful, and thus, a more inspiring goal to work towards.

Defining self-control

Self-control is the ability to regulate one's emotions, thoughts, and behaviours in the face of temptations and impulses. For instance, imagine you're tempted to scroll through social media, but instead, you choose to focus on completing a work task or organising your space. This small act of self-control contributes to productivity and a sense of accomplishment. It's essential for achieving long-term goals and maintaining overall wellbeing. Self-control not only helps manage immediate desires, but also supports better decision-making and resilience in challenging situations.

I trust you appreciate how a well-functioning PIS can promote the practice of self-control. The proper functioning of our psychological defences supports better decision-making, emotional regulation, and curbing impulsive behaviours. For example, Nikki, whom we met in a previous chapter, was only able to replace her nightly wine drinking and smoking with a healthy bedtime routine after implementing the foundational practices for good mental health: catching up on sleep, and beginning to have nourishing meals. Only then did she feel more energised and have the strength to override her old, automatic needs. The more Nikki overcame her old, unhealthy habits, her confidence and self-worth grew (self-esteem!), making her more resilient when dealing with negative thoughts and so forth.

At this point, you can see how self-control can further fortify the PIS as it's a powerful tool to keep habits that elicit stress, anxiety and guilt at bay. More importantly, at this stage in our journey, it's about recognising the reciprocity between a well-functioning PIS and the implementation of practices that enhance wellbeing. It creates a positive feedback loop. The stronger the PIS, the more likely you are to improve yourself through daily habits that enhance mental clarity and self-control. This, then, leads to more frequent positive emotions, which boost your self-esteem, improve interactions with others, and increase life satisfaction, further strengthening PIS function and structure.

But I digress. Extensive work in the academic literature suggests that self-control is a limited resource. This is known as "ego depletion." For instance, after a long day of resisting temptations or making tough decisions, it might be harder to maintain self-control in the evening. However, it's important to note that this view is also contested in the scientific community. The debate around ego depletion is complex and ongoing. Despite this, the predominant view should not discourage you from committing to self-control, as the benefits for your PIS are ever compounding.

Strategies to develop self-control & earn stars

Promisingly, research has found that practicing small acts of self-control can actually increase your overall capacity for self-discipline. In other words, you can strengthen your "self-control muscle" through regular practice, leading to better outcomes over time. By consistently focusing on small, manageable acts of self-discipline, you gradually build the ability to maintain self-control across various areas of your life. This ties back to the idea that self-esteem, abilities, and life skills aren't fixed traits but can be developed through effort and learning. Recognising that these capacities can be nurtured rather than seeing them as fixed "innate gifts" is a crucial step toward meaningful personal growth.

Let's explore ways to build up self-control, especially for those who might be struggling with it. Do you remember our discussion in Chapter 13 about potentially addictive behaviours? Reflect back on those behaviours, or identify another habit you're struggling with, and make that your target. For example, Nikki initially targeted her nightly wine drinking, addressing smoking only later on.

Acknowledging urges & impulses

Let's revisit this topic, but now with more depth. Think about how you can work on that "self-control muscle" throughout the day, gradually: in the morning, then in the afternoon, and again in the evening. Like exercising a muscle that has been inactive, it will be challenging and require great effort at the beginning. It's going to take time until it becomes more effortless. Consider this process as building a muscle by carrying bricks back and forth, back and forth, to construct new mental bridges in your neural networks. But these bridges, instead of leading you to dark places, will guide you to places of light and clarity.

Our urges are simply a result of needs that we have indulged and depending on the extent to which we've indulged them they can become something needy and annoying. In our brain, these are pathways firing away, demanding a reward. But reward for what? This is similar to a small child, let's call him little John, in a supermarket who sees a toy and wants it. Many times before, mum or dad gifted little John toys just because he wanted them or, admittedly, to avoid a public tantrum. Except that led to him being conditioned to expect a reward whenever he wants one, knowing that showing signs of a tantrum guarantees the toy.

So, when your needs and urges act up like a tantrum-prone child, it's ill-advised to either indulge or ignore them. Instead, calmly tell yourself, 'It's okay to feel like this,' until the feelings quiet down. As you repeatedly and consistently adopt the acknowledgment and understanding approach, instead of the indulging one, the urge and the need will visit you less and less. It will learn that what it tried to obtain is no longer there to be had. Acknowledging urges in this way is effective because it reduces stress, promotes self-awareness, and strengthens self-control, empowering you to make conscious choices.

Smart coping strategies

It's also essential to recognise that on more demanding days, summoning the dedication and commitment needed to deal with our internal tantrums can be tougher. The smart approach here is to have a set of alternatives that bring you comfort. For example, Nikki admitted she was concerned about her nightly drinking habit going from something that relaxed her to something she might depend on to feel chilled after her days. So, she sought alternative activities and habits that were not only healthier but also brought her relaxation and calm. She ventured into the world of cooking at night with the radio on, accompanied by beautiful-looking alcohol-free cocktails.

Self-efficacy

Far from being distractions, as some might say, these are coping strategies that demonstrate self-efficacy, a crucial element of the self that reflects your competence in handling various situations and achieving goals. Self-efficacy goes beyond just believing in your abilities; it's about trusting that you can apply those abilities effectively, especially when confronted with difficulties. While self-control is the capacity to regulate your emotions, thoughts, and behaviours, self-efficacy is the confidence in your ability to navigate obstacles and succeed. By finding healthier ways to relax, Nikki not only exercised self-control but also built her self-efficacy, enhancing her sense of competence and reinforcing her confidence in managing life's demands. This, in turn, bolstered her self-esteem, creating a positive cycle where confidence breeds more confidence.

Before we conclude our chapter, think back on the questionnaire and identify the areas where you might need some practice with self-control. What specific strategies can you implement on days when you're feeling more drained? How confident are you in your ability to apply these strategies effectively? Reflect on how your self-efficacy and sense of competence influence your approach to these situations. This proactive energy lies at the heart of the 5-Star Framework.

We've previously discussed building a repertoire of behaviours that enhances your PIS and prevents you from relying solely on technology as a means to relax and pass time. Activities that might initially seem far from relaxing and highly unappealing at the end of the day, like tidying up drawers and cupboards, can actually be energising when paired with something enjoyable, like listening to music. While this might seem like multitasking, it's actually about adopting behaviours that help you move forward. Just as there are times when full awareness is essential, there are also times when losing yourself in an activity can be rejuvenating.

Speaking of activities, in the next chapter, we'll explore how our behaviours influence our psychological defences and mental resilience.

Action expresses priorities. — Mahatma Gandhi

Chapter 19

How Positive Behaviours Foster Resilience

★

In Chapter 16, we explored how our thoughts influence the way we feel and behave. Now, let's look at the other side of the equation: our behaviours also have a profound impact on how we feel and the thoughts that run through our minds.

Why is this the case? Our behaviours and actions can create a ripple effect in our PIS activity. When we engage in positive behaviours, such as exercising, earning stars towards our Daily 5-Star PIS Goal, or spending time with loved ones, we trigger a cascade of beneficial chemicals like endorphins and serotonin (familiar names to you by now). These chemicals not only enhance our mood but also reinforce positive thought patterns. On the other hand, when we engage in negative behaviours, such as isolating ourselves or indulging in unhealthy habits, we can reinforce negative emotions and thoughts. To put it simply, in many ways, our behaviours can either build us up or bring us down. Thus, by consciously choosing actions that support our wellbeing, we can create a positive cycle that enhances our psychological defences, overall mental health and resilience.

So, take a moment to reflect on your own experiences. Have you noticed how a walk in nature or a gym session can lift your spirits? Or, how spending time with friends can shift your perspective? On the other hand, have you observed how certain habits, like procrastination or excessive screen time, can make you feel sluggish or anxious? Think about a time when a specific action or behaviour notably influenced your mood or thoughts. What was that behaviour, and how did it make you feel? Once again, by recognising these patterns, you can start making intentional choices that activate the PIS.

Behavioural activation

In many ways, it's easier or perhaps even smarter to tackle behaviours as a way of boosting mood. Our minds can sometimes be stubborn and difficult to snap out of negative thinking or brooding. Focusing on behaviours and actions, by contrast, places some space between you and whatever is troubling you at the moment, giving you a little breather. This approach is at the heart of a concept called 'Behavioural activation'. Behavioural activation is a therapeutic technique that encourages individuals to engage in positive activities that are aligned with their values and interests, even when they may not feel like it. By doing so, you can break the cycle of negative thoughts and feelings.

Imagine you're feeling down, and someone suggests taking small steps like going for a walk, meeting a friend, or starting a hobby. You might wonder if such simple actions can really make a difference. A recent meta-analysis of 28 studies examined whether behavioural activation—like those small steps—can indeed help with low mood and anxiety. The exciting part? It works! The results showed that the group of people who followed behavioural activation routines experienced significant improvements in their depression and anxiety compared to those who either did nothing or were on a waiting list for the program. Moreover, the spiral-up effect kicked in, as increased activity levels led to an overall boost in wellbeing.

Excitingly, the researchers didn't stop there. They went further and performed another comparison, between the behavioural activation group with another group of people receiving treatment like psychotherapy or medication. Here, the results were similar. Meaning, no major difference in wellbeing levels between those groups was observed.

This is great news for you, an adept of the 5-Star Framework. The findings of this investigation show that behavioural activation is indeed effective in boosting psychological health compared to refraining from taking action or surrendering to negative states. Not only that, it also shows that behavioural activation works similar to other well-known methods to improve mental health. Many of which we're adopting here on our Daily 5-star PIS journey. This demonstrates that improving our mental health isn't about finding one magic solution, but about discovering a range of strategies that work best for you at given moments. Or, in our case, this means earning various stars to brighten our PIS. So, when you're feeling low, behavioural activation could be a smart way to add a bright spot to your constellation.

Now, picture this: it's been a long day, you're feeling down, and your mind is stuck in a loop of negative thoughts. Instead of trying to restructure those thoughts or meditate on them, today you decide to go for a walk, call a friend, or turn to a hobby you enjoy. Boosting your psychological defences often depends on being attuned to yourself and knowing which strategy works best for you at a given time. Calling a good friend, for instance, can lift your mood, and as your mood improves, your thoughts often follow suit. It's like pressing a reset button; taking action, creating positive experiences, and gradually improving your mental state. Sometimes, by focusing on what you do rather than what you think, you can effectively boost your mood, gain perspective, and build resilience.

Prepare yourself

It's important to be realistic and acknowledge that negative thoughts and emotions can be truly paralyzing, sometimes literally preventing us from being productive or even getting out of bed. Indeed, one of the hallmark symptoms of depression is a lack of motivation, which can make it incredibly difficult to start or maintain daily activities. For instance, a mother who once eagerly made breakfast for her children might now find it nearly impossible to summon the energy or desire to do so. Additionally, anxiety can lead to avoidant behaviours, which, in extreme cases, can result in conditions like agoraphobia, where individuals may avoid leaving their homes altogether. Have you ever felt paralyzed by negative thoughts before?

You can see how it wouldn't be very productive to wait until you're feeling low, drained, or anxious to decide what action to take, as these states often push us toward escapism or immediate gratifying behaviours. The smart way to handle this is, as mentioned at the end of the previous chapter, to build a repertoire of behaviours that you can turn to when the going gets tough. This way, you have a set of positive actions ready to go, which can help you manage your mood and mental state more effectively.

How to do this? Where to begin? At this point in our journey, you have been developing a number of skills that have fostered self-awareness. This has been repeatedly talked about as a strong stepping stone toward building a resilient mind and psychological defences. Hopefully, this means you are now able to identify your own mood and emotional states. Of course, when you're feeling positive and energized, there are so many things you have in mind to get on with that you probably don't know where to start!

But are you prepared for those times when you don't feel so positive? Now, it's time to create a personal "treasure chest" of actions and strategies for when your mood and emotions shift to the opposite side. Think of it as a chest filled with go-to behaviours and activities (stars) that can help lift your spirits and keep you grounded. Having these resources at your disposal enables you to proactively enhance your mood and effectively manage your emotions.

Acting, not reacting

Remember, this is about consciously responding to, rather than reacting to, negative states. To effectively manage low mood and emotions it's crucial to identify them early. One way of doing this is by tuning into your body. Our bodies can be practical indicators of our wellbeing because physical sensations often reflect our emotional states. For instance, persistent tension, fatigue, or changes in appetite can signal not only poor habits like lack of sleep, inadequate nutrition, or insufficient movement in our daily lives but also low mood. Note that the focus here is not on physical aesthetics, but on recognising and addressing these bodily signals to boost our mental health.

One practical way to identify these bodily signals is by doing a body scan check-in throughout your day. Traditionally, a body scan involves bringing attention to your body by mentally examining the sensations in your feet, legs, hips, upper body, and head while lying on a mat or in bed. However, as our approach to wellbeing also involves flexibility and openness, there's no reason you can't practice a body scan at your desk, while sitting on your sofa, or even while playing with your child on the floor. Notice any tension in your muscles, particularly in areas like your shoulders, neck, and jaw, as physical tension often accompanies emotional distress. If you detect tightness or discomfort, it's a sign that your mood might be dipping. For example, if you find your shoulders constantly hunched, take a few deep breaths and consciously relax them. This simple act of relaxation can help calm your nervous system, reducing stress responses and eliciting a sense of peace.

Another approach is to pay attention to your energy levels and how you move. Low mood often manifests as sluggishness or a lack of motivation to move. If you notice you're dragging your feet, feeling unusually tired, or finding it hard to start tasks, these can be signals of low mood. This sluggishness occurs because low mood affects the brain's neurochemistry, reducing the levels of dopamine and serotonin, which are chemicals that influence energy, motivation and mood. Counter this by incorporating small, manageable movements like stretching, a brief walk, or even shaking out your hands and feet to re-energise yourself.

By being attuned to these physical cues, you can catch signs of low mood early on and take steps to address them proactively. This helps you respond to your emotional state with constructive actions rather than simply reacting to the negativity.

It's also important to recognise that these bodily sensations may not indicate any dip in mood or emotional states at all. Sometimes, our bodily sensations simply reflect its biological inner workings. This concept is known as allostasis, which refers to the process by which the body maintains stability through change, adjusting to meet internal and external demands. This is not an indication of psychological ill function. However, because we are wired to always find explanations, reasons, and make sense of things, we may end up attributing the simple functioning of our biological processes to issues that aren't even there.

Misattributions

A classic experiment by psychologists Donald Dutton and Arthur Aron, often called the "bridge experiment," humorously illustrates this point. In this study, they had male participants cross either a high, unstable suspension bridge or a low, stable bridge. At the end of each bridge, the participants were met by an attractive female researcher who asked them to fill out a survey and provided her phone number for further questions. The researchers found that those who crossed the high, shaky bridge were significantly more likely to call the attractive researcher afterward, misattributing their heightened physiological arousal (increased heart rate, adrenaline) as romantic attraction.

This classic study evidences how easily we can misattribute physical sensations to incorrect causes. It emphasizes yet another reason why it is so important to develop the skill of non-judgment and acceptance. Oftentimes, the meaning of things is not intrinsic to them, but rather what we attribute to them. In his letter to Lucilius, Seneca said, "We suffer more often in imagination than in reality." This quote serves as a powerful reminder that our perceptions can amplify our suffering. Reflect on your own experiences. Have you ever felt physical discomfort or tension and attributed it to something specific like work or, in extreme cases, even life in general ? Recognising these moments can be a profound way to considerably lessen daily stress and overall frustrations.

Cultivate openness & earn stars

This newfound awareness can also inspire you to be open to trying new behaviours. When I say behaviours, I mean activities like drawing, creating things, or anything that sparks joy and engagement. These need not be extravagant or expensive.

A former neighbour of mine was incredibly creative in diversifying her repertoire of behaviours. Her treasure chest was filled to the brim! Often by herself, as her son lived in another country and her husband frequently travelled for work, she sometimes struggled with loneliness. However, that never brought her down. She was incredibly resourceful and proactive about finding peace and enjoying her own company. One day, she told me she found an African dance video on YouTube and decided to follow the choreography. I asked her how she felt afterward, and she said she felt wonderful! Home alone, she turned the volume up, danced, and laughed at herself.

Later that day, my husband and I decided to give her method a try. For reasons I don't remember, my husband chose to dance along to "U Can't Touch This" by M.C. Hammer. Let me clarify here, my husband does *not* have the moves (I do a little bit!), and we were never even close to following the choreography, but it was fun, and we had a blast dancing around our living room. The experience left us feeling uplifted and gave us yet another situation to laugh about.

And this is the idea, whether you decide to dance, draw, cook, paint, sing, do yoga, or practice tai chi, engage in these activities not as a means to escape from your emotions but as a way to boost your psychological defences. Perfection isn't the goal either. The goal is to have fun and do something for yourself without seeking rewards or praise.

Before we conclude this chapter, it's crucial to remember not to wait for motivation to strike before trying new behaviours. Motivation often follows action, not the other way around. For example, you might not feel like exercising, but once you start moving, your energy and enthusiasm can build as you go. This is a well-known process often put forward by therapists. If you're hesitant to try new activities, I encourage you to open up and give them a go anyway. Openness is a key trait for psychological flexibility, which helps you adapt to changing circumstances and manage stress more effectively.

Test yourself

Plus, you can always test yourself. Why not? Here's how you can do it. Before trying a new activity, write down on a piece of paper how good you think you'll feel afterward, from 0 to 10. For example, let's say you're not particularly excited about preparing a meal from scratch but decide to give it a try. You evaluate yourself and estimate that your enjoyment level will be a 4 (if that!). Then, after you complete the activity, check in with yourself to see how you feel. If it surpassed your expectations, it might be an activity to put in that treasure chest, ready to lift your spirits when you're feeling a bit low and don't know exactly what to do with yourself. Testing your openness like this is not only a smart way to handle moments when you're feeling blue, but it's also a strategy successfully used in therapy rooms to help people get up and go during their behavioural activation programs.

As we turn our attention to the next chapter, we'll explore the vital role that interpersonal relationships play in enhancing the PIS structure and function. Let's discover how our connections with others can become powerful allies in our journey towards a resilient mind.

No man is an island, entire of itself; every man is a piece of the continent, a part of the main. — John Donne

Chapter 20

Connections for Stronger Minds: Relationships & Resilience

★

When we think of mental health, we often picture it as something solely within the individual. Traditional approaches, like Freudian psychoanalysis or cognitive-behavioural therapy, focus on our inner thoughts and behaviours. Freud, for example, believed that "the ego is not master in its own house," highlighting the internal conflicts that shape our mental state. Similarly, cognitive-behavioural therapy targets changing negative thought patterns to alter emotional states and behaviours. While these methods are insightful, they only tell part of the story. Mental health isn't just about what's going on *inside* us, but also about what's happening *between* us. If you think about it, this aligns with what we discussed in Chapter 4 about Bowlby's Attachment Theory, which emphasises the profound impact of our early bonds on our mental health.

This broader perspective is where systemic approaches (i.e. family therapy) come into play, challenging the notion that mental health is solely an internal, individual matter. These approaches examine how our interactions and relationships shape our wellbeing. For instance, 'family therapy' doesn't focus just on one person but looks at how the entire family communicates and supports one another. Picture a family where open communication and mutual support help each member handle stress more effectively. Here, resilience isn't just an individual trait. It's a collective strength that emerges from the interconnectedness of the family. As Murray Bowen, a pioneer in family systems theory, stated, "The family is the emotional unit." The same principle applies to romantic couples. Imagine a couple that learns to communicate more effectively and support each other emotionally. This mutual support not only strengthens their relationship but also enhances each partner's resilience, illustrating the power of connectedness in mental health.

It's crucial to understand that it's not about choosing one approach over the other. Both our internal world and our relationships play a vital role in mental health. By looking within ourselves, we gain self-awareness and the ability to understand and manage our thoughts and emotions, which is essential for personal resilience. At the same time, by examining how we connect with others, we can gain a fuller picture of resilience and nurture more robust psychological defences. Take a moment to reflect on the people in your life. How have they influenced the way you think, feel, and act? Consider the times when their support lifted you up during challenges or their encouragement helped you celebrate achievements. Now, flip the perspective. Think about how you've impacted their lives. How have your actions, words, and support shaped their wellbeing? By recognising these connections, we can see the powerful role relationships play in contributing to our resilience.

Although, it's important to remember that while the influence of family members, spouses and friends on our mental wellbeing is significant, it doesn't mean they are responsible for our life satisfaction, self-esteem, or life habits and choices. Each of us holds the responsibility for our own mental balance and personal growth. Our relationships can provide support and encouragement, but ultimately, we are the ones who shape our own mental states. One productive and positive way to achieve this is by deliberately nurturing our PIS through the 5-Star Framework.

Recognising this reality empowers us to take control of our own psychological health while appreciating the positive impact of our connections with others.

Challenges

It's true that each type of relationship, whether with family, romantic partners, or friends, comes with its own unique set of challenges. Exploring all these complexities in detail would require another book entirely. So, for now, let's focus on a common challenge that spans across all types of interpersonal relationships and develop strategies to navigate it more effectively.

One major challenge shared across different types of relationships is communication. I like to say that communication is the PIS of any relationship. As communication is how we share our thoughts, express our feelings, and connect with one another. Not surprisingly, research shows that effective communication is key to positive and healthy relationships. A study published in *Springer* found that communication is a significant factor in relationship satisfaction, even when considering impactful factors like attachment style.

This means that regardless of how secure or insecure individuals feel in their relationships, the ability to communicate effectively can greatly enhance their relationship satisfaction. On the flip side, poor communication often leads to misunderstandings, which can strain even the strongest bonds. Thus, good communication can make all the difference in building and maintaining resilient relationships, whether through discussing your day, sharing a laugh, or resolving conflicts.

Conflict in relationships

Conflict is an inevitable aspect of relationships. As we explored in Chapter 17, there are many factors that can make interacting with others challenging, from differing personalities to unmet expectations. Still, problems arise when conflict leads to issues that range from stress responses to feelings of frustration and disappointment. This further highlights how and why mental health is not solely an individual affair.

If you think of a relationship (whether with your partner, parent, friend, or sibling) as an emotional unit, as Bowen puts it, our interactions, attitudes, and intentions act as bridges that keep the unit together. However, these bridges will either provide clear ways of making communication flow or, conversely, will deteriorate and impair communication altogether. Major obstacles that block these bridges are resentment and anger. When resentment builds up, it creates a barrier that prevents open and honest communication. Anger can lead to hostile interactions and a breakdown in trust. Over time, these obstacles can disintegrate the emotional unit, leading to further conflicts and weakening essential relationship functions such as mutual support, trust, and love.

I hope this discussion reminds you of Chapter 3, where we explored the architecture of resilience using a similar analogy. In that chapter, we compared the brain to a city, with the prefrontal cortex (PFC), hippocampus, and amygdala being some of its main sites. The neuronal pathways that interconnect them were described as bridges, which, depending on our actions and habits, can either be efficient in aiding communication flow between those sites or be weakened, leading to dysregulated emotional responses or misperceptions. Like so, just as the brain's pathways need to be maintained for optimal functioning, our relational bridges require care and effort to ensure healthy and resilient connections. Therefore, if conflict is so detrimental to a relationship, but also inevitable in interpersonal interactions, how can we navigate it effectively to maintain our relational bridges open?

While conflict often brings negative effects, it can also be a surprising catalyst for growth and deeper understanding in relationships. Experts suggest that, when handled properly, conflict can actually strengthen our bonds. Think about it: resolving a disagreement can lead to mutual understanding, making partners feel closer and more connected. It's like a storm that clears the air, leaving behind a fresher, more vibrant relationship.

Surely, the more we deliberately work on our psychological defences and develop a resilient mind, the less our relationships and interactions will be dotted by negativity and misunderstandings. However, due to the inevitable nature of conflicts, they will always arise. Although, with a well-functioning PIS, you will be in a place where, instead of fearing conflict, you'll embrace it as a chance to grow together with whoever you're dealing with, whether it's a parent, spouse, or friend, and improve relationship dynamics. By approaching conflicts constructively, we turn potential negatives into opportunities for building closeness and trust. So, rather than fearing conflict, we can see it as a chance to grow together and improve our relationship interactions.

Earn stars through conflict resolution : A circular process

When facing disagreement or in the midst of conflict, it's important to remember that rather than an opponent, you are part of an emotional unit. You're not at war, you're unique individuals working towards a common goal. Importantly, in the systemic school of thought conflict problems are often seen as circular rather than linear. This means that when working towards a resolution, the focus is not on who started the problem but on how interactions and behaviours, within the family or couple, perpetuate the issue.

It's not that identifying who started the problem is irrelevant (accepting accountability is key) but during the conflict, the pressing matter is the negative dynamics at play and how they are being maintained. For instance, consider Margot who feels betrayed because her husband made a bad choice. Instead of fixating on the initial act of being let down, it's more productive to address how both parts are responding to this feeling of betrayal. Are they communicating openly, or are they shutting down and becoming defensive? By focusing on breaking this cycle, such as by taking a moment to calm down and then discussing the issue with respect and empathy, the parts can address the root of the problem more effectively.

Above all, the crucial understanding here is that everyone plays a role in maintaining the problem. The goal, then, is to identify and transform patterns that contribute to problematic dynamics. Note how this perspective has the potential to shift the focus from assigning blame to understanding and altering the interactions that sustain the problem, leading to more effective solutions. For example, cooperation, as this is a perspective that leads both parties to work together rather than competing to win the match. Since communication is the key deal-maker or breaker, it's essential to avoid accusative language like "You did" or "You went." Instead, use language that addresses the situation, such as "It's been tough," or emphasises the unit with phrases like "We can."

Buddhism teachings emphasise "Right Speech," underscoring the profound impact our words can have. This principle encourages truthfulness by advising against lying or deceit, fostering trust and integrity in our relationships. It also cautions against slanderous language, promoting harmony by discouraging words that cause division. Lastly, Right Speech advises avoiding harshness, urging us to use kind and respectful words to prevent unnecessary conflict, or perpetuating unsolved issues, for that matter. By practicing these principles, we enhance our ability to resolve conflicts constructively and maintain healthier connections with the people who matter most to us.

Finally, communication is a broad term that encompasses more than just verbal language. It includes body language and actions as well. When resolving conflict, it's important to be mindful of all these forms of communication. Non-verbal cues like facial expressions, gestures, and posture can convey powerful messages and emotions, sometimes even more strongly than words. Additionally, actions such as walking away or stonewalling can escalate conflicts and hinder resolution. By being aware of all these aspects of communication and keeping in mind the ultimate goal of resolving conflict and strengthening the relationship, we can navigate disputes more effectively and maintain healthy, resilient connections.

Kintsugi

Before we conclude our discussion on conflict resolution, I want you to begin seeing all the conflicts you've overcome in your interpersonal relationships through the "Kintsugi way". There is a beautiful practice in Japan known as Kintsugi, or "golden joinery." When a vase or piece of pottery breaks, instead of discarding it, artisans carefully repair it using lacquer mixed with powdered gold. The result is a vase that, despite having been broken, now bears unique patterns of gold lines, making it even more beautiful and valuable than before.

This practice symbolises the idea that our difficult experiences, especially the painful ones, contribute to our beauty and resilience. Just as the vase becomes more precious through its golden repairs, your relationships can be strengthened and enriched by navigating and resolving conflicts. Each repaired fracture in your relationships is like a golden line, adding depth, beauty, and resilience to the bond you share. Embrace the strength and beauty that comes from mending these connections, knowing that these golden lines represent the growth and resilience of both you and your relationships.

A few words on forgiveness

It wouldn't feel right to discuss interpersonal relationships and communication as contributors to our PIS without saying a word or two about forgiveness. Forgiveness is also an interpersonal process, meaning it occurs within ourselves as much as it involves others. It's about managing our emotions and thoughts to achieve inner peace, which aligns with systemic concepts where the health of the whole system depends on the wellbeing of each individual part.

Forgiveness is a central theme in many religions and spiritual practices. For instance, Christianity emphasises forgiveness through teachings such as "Forgive us our trespasses, as we forgive those who trespass against us." Similarly, in Buddhism, forgiveness is seen as a way to release suffering and cultivate compassion. These examples highlight the universal recognition of forgiveness as essential for harmony and wellbeing. It also highlights the reality that interpersonal conflict is inevitable, and our skills to resolve these conflicts are often limited.

But how to forgive? When I suggested Margot forgive her partner, her immediate reply was, "I'll never forget what he did!" While this might be clear to you, it wasn't for Margot, and it doesn't seem to be for many people: To forgive is not to erase memories, but to intentionally choose to let go of corrosive sentiments like anger and resentment. Note the key word here: "intentionally," a word that in many ways holds the central idea of this book and has appeared across its pages in many similar forms "consciously," "deliberately," "purposefully." These words come up again and again because I want to keep encouraging you to deliberately tend to your PIS and mental health.

Indeed, since forgiving is a new decision and process you might choose to embrace, it requires time, patience, and mental clarity. At this point in our journey, you have not only activated your PIS but boosted your resilience through the 5-Star Framework. This, I dare say, has made you more open to forgiveness.

Thus, If there are one or two people in your life toward whom you hold resentment and anger, it might be time to work on those corrosive emotions and let them go. The *Journal of Consulting and Clinical Psychology* offers a compelling analysis on forgiveness, exploring approaches that have proven effective for individuals struggling with addiction and even for victims of family incest.

Note that the researchers agreed that forgiving the transgressor is not about forgetting or excusing the wrongdoing, nor does it mean completely erasing your grievances. Rather, it's about reducing the all-consuming rumination, anger, or bitterness that can harm your PIS. These negative emotions can weaken your psychological defences by keeping your mind in a constant state of stress and tension, which makes it harder to cope with new challenges.

Emotional freedom

A particularly successful strategy the researchers mentioned in this study is the Enright Process Model of Forgiveness. Here, I'll provide you with an overview of it, as it aligns with a number of the techniques and strategies we've been applying so far on our 5-Star Framework journey (i.e. identifying emotions, being deliberate in your choices, working on accepting others and personal development). This model offers a structured approach to achieving forgiveness through four distinct phases.

The first phase, the Uncovering Phase, involves recognising the emotional pain and identifying the source of hurt. It's about acknowledging the impact of the offense on your emotions and wellbeing. Next is the Decision Phase, where you make a conscious choice to forgive. This decision is not about excusing the offensive behaviour but about committing to the process of forgiveness for *your* own peace of mind. In the Work Phase, you work towards developing a deeper understanding of the offender. This phase is about understanding the context and circumstances that might have led to the offense. Finally, the Deepening Phase is where you find meaning in the forgiveness process and move forward with a renewed sense of purpose and inner peace. This entails recognising the growth that has come from the experience and using it to strengthen your PIS, psychological and emotional resilience.

To illustrate the model's application, consider Margot and her husband. In the Uncovering Phase, Margot recognised the pain and identified the source of hurt when her husband let her down. In the Decision Phase, Margot chose to forgive her husband, not to excuse his behaviour but to find peace for herself. During the Work Phase, she worked through her emotional pain by trying to understand her husband's actions and the context that might have led to his behaviour. For her, this understanding came in the form of realising that "due to his life history, he's immature and impulsive." Finally, in the Deepening Phase, Margot found meaning in the forgiveness process, which allowed her to move forward with a stronger sense of purpose and a more resilient emotional state.

To err is human, to forgive is divine

Finding meaning in forgiveness involves recognising the personal growth and emotional freedom that comes from letting go of negative mental states and emotions. This allows us to move past our pain, fostering a sense of inner peace and balance. By choosing to forgive, we can transform our troubled minds into powerful sources of resilience, gaining insights about ourselves and the human experience.

There's a saying, "To err is human, to forgive is divine," attributed to Alexander Pope in his poem "An Essay on Criticism." It highlights the natural tendency for humans to make mistakes and the extraordinary quality of being able to forgive others. This saying underscores that while everyone makes errors, forgiving such errors requires a higher level of compassion and grace. Therefore, forgiveness is seen as a noble act that elevates both the forgiver and the forgiven, promoting healing and understanding. It suggests that the capacity to forgive transcends ordinary human behaviour, reflecting a higher moral and spiritual standard.

You can embody this higher standard, making it shine through the numerous bright stars in your luminous constellation.

Part 4
Takeaways

★

In part 4 of *What Makes a Resilient Mind?*, we explored various approaches and methods that have the potential to strengthen your psychological defences. By doing so, we aim to enhance the structure and function of your PIS, leading you toward a more resilient mind.

In Chapter 16, we explored the crucial role of thoughts. We began by identifying thoughts as powerful mental events that act as filters, shaping our perceptions not only of others and the world but also of ourselves. Our thoughts can sometimes prevent us from taking action and engaging in productive and healthy behaviours. We discussed that one reason we easily succumb to the negative content of our minds is a possible lack of awareness. Many of us live on autopilot, moving from one commitment to another with minimal conscious awareness of why and how we are doing things. Have you paused to consider what thoughts are driving your actions right now?

We looked into how this automatic mode of living has been investigated in psychology, primarily through CBT studies, which show how our automatic thoughts influence our emotions and behaviours. Additionally, neuroscience research has identified the Default Mode Network (DMN), a brain network that becomes active when we are not performing demanding or novel tasks. Essentially, this is our mental chatterbox. Unsurprisingly, overactivity in this network has been linked to anxiety and depression, as its activity is generally associated with self-referential thoughts.

One way to counter this is by bringing this automaticity to our conscious awareness. This means tuning down the autopilot dial and becoming acquainted with the content of your mind. This can be achieved through journaling, formal (thought) meditation practices, or simply by pausing every now and then (e.g., while washing dishes or walking the dog) and asking yourself, *What is going through my mind right now?*

Here, I raised an important point: awareness of your thoughts alone will not bring relief if the thoughts you identify are unpleasant. Thus, a crucial skill to develop is non-judgment. Non-judgment involves observing your thoughts without labelling them as good or bad, right or wrong. It means accepting thoughts as they are, without getting caught up in them or allowing them to over-whelm you. By practicing non-judgment, you can create a mental space where you can observe your thoughts without being over-taken by them, leading to a calmer and resilient mind.

An important requirement for non-judgment is ac-ceptance, a topic we discussed in Chapter 17. In our discussion, I emphasised that acceptance has nothing to do with giving up or giving in to unacceptable situations or circumstances. Rather, I clarified that acceptance is about recognising the reality of life ex-periences. It's about understanding that life includes unexpected, uncontrollable events. This need not be something major and im-pactful, such as a global pandemic, but rather more ordinary en-counters like other people's behaviours and choices.

The key message here is to understand that while many cir-cumstances in life are beyond our control, even when we are in the midst of such situations, we still have agency. Along with accepting that you cannot control the actions and words of others, for exam-ple, you must recognise that you have control over your own be-haviours and decisions. By accepting life experiences without re-acting impulsively, you can act consciously in a way that preserves the integrity of your PIS and mental wellness. So, the message here was that through developing acceptance of life experiences, acceptance of others, and of the self, you're more prepared to act, rather than react, fostering a more balanced mindset.

The discussion of acceptance of the self, served as a stepping stone to exploring the elements of the self and their importance in promoting emotional regulation and helping us deal better with stress and setbacks. Chapter 18 focused mainly on two elements of the self extensively studied and repeatedly linked to psychological wellbeing. First, we examined how self-esteem enhances our self-worth and confidence, which is crucial for maintaining a positive outlook and resilience. The strategies explored to facilitate the development of self-esteem were assertiveness and a growth mindset. Then, the discussion moved to the crucial role of self-control, an ability that supports good decision-making in tempting or challenging situations. The highlight in this discussion was the importance of a healthy PIS function and structure in practicing self-control in our daily lives, choices, and encounters. We concluded that effective self-control is essential for regulating our behaviours, helping us stay aligned with our goals, and maintaining our overall wellbeing.

Chapter 19 elaborated on the importance of our behaviours in boosting PIS function and structure. In this chapter, I discussed behaviour as an alternative strategy (or an additional star) to either focusing on thoughts or avoiding them in order to enhance mood and alleviate negative states. This is not a form of escapism but a smart coping technique. The central idea is to highlight that you have a plethora of options at your disposal to help you feel more positive and energised in times of worry or distress. Just as there will be occasions when journaling your thoughts or engaging in a breathing exercise is the right strategy to gain perspective, there will be other times when simply getting up and going is all you need. Whether "going" means a walk around the block, a phone call to a friend, or a long, warm shower, this simple approach—known as Behavioural Activation—has proven to be very effective in lifting depressive moods and reducing anxiety in therapy settings.

However, a more subtle message in Chapter 19 that I wouldn't like to see dismissed is the cultivation of openness. Openness not only broadens possibilities for you to build a large repertoire of behaviours, or smart coping strategies, but also fosters psychological flexibility. Psychological flexibility is an ability we've discussed a few times in the book, and it refers to the capacity to adapt, to shift perspectives, and maintain balance in the face of challenges. It is important because it helps you navigate life's ups and downs more effectively, by enabling you to become resourceful, thus supporting the integrity of your PIS.

The last chapter of Part 4 of our book delved into interpersonal relationships and highlighted the importance of our connections to PIS functioning and resilience building. I explained that our mental weaknesses or strengths are not solely *within* us but also *between* us. I drew on the ideas and theories of Systemic Approaches, a therapeutic school of thought that views friendships, families and couples as emotional units. The key theme of this last chapter was communication, which I see as the PIS of relationships, as communication is how we convey our thoughts and emotions and connect with others. Through the lens of communication, we examined interpersonal conflicts and how to face them constructively to facilitate growth and resilience. Before concluding this discussion, I touched on the topic of forgiveness, emphasising it as a deliberate personal decision reflecting higher spiritual and moral standards.

Congratulations on reaching the end of Part 4! Your ongoing dedication to understanding and enhancing your mental health is truly admirable. By exploring the workings of the PIS and embracing strategies to strengthen it, you've taken significant steps toward building resilience and fostering wellbeing. Your commitment to this journey reflects a profound investment in your personal growth. Well done! As you move forward to the final part of

What Makes a Resilient Mind?, we'll delve into the rationale behind the 5-Star Framework and explore its enduring benefits, providing you with even deeper insights into maintaining and enhancing your PIS.

Part 5

Fine Tuning the Psychological Immune System

Nothing contributes so much to tranquillise the mind as a
steady purpose. – Viktor Frankenstein

Chapter 21

The Daily 5-Star PIS:
The Framework & its Purpose

★

I first introduced you to the Daily 5-Star PIS Goal after discussing
the protective and healing functions of the PIS, drawing parallels
between our psychological and biological defences, and providing
an overview of the architecture of our psychological defences. By
then, you had a solid foundation of knowledge. The Daily 5-Star
PIS Goal builds on this foundation, offering a practical approach
to proactively activate and strengthen your PIS, helping you
achieve a resilient mind.

Now, take a moment to reflect on how much you've
learned about your psychological defences. Consider the broad understanding you've gained by exploring factors that influence your
PIS, such as sleep, nutrition, and environmental drains, as well as
the mechanisms and situations that impact it, like procrastination
and loss. Equally important, you've discovered elements that
strengthen your PIS, such as acceptance and positive relationships.
With all this knowledge, you are now well-equipped to take practical steps toward cultivating a resilient mind. So, what actions have
you been incorporating into your daily routine to earn your five
stars?

This book and the 5-Star Framework are all about utilising your knowledge and inner resources to build psychological defences and a resilient mind. Just as maintaining physical health requires conscious effort and deliberate choices, so too does maintaining good psychological health. Our natural tendency is often to make decisions and engage in behaviours that save energy and offer immediate gratification. Therefore, we must be mindful and intentional in our actions, especially in a world filled with triggers that tempt us to eat more, want more, achieve more, impress others, and seek pleasure. Unfortunately, such pursuits are not always conducive to mental balance and peace. However, by being deliberate in our daily actions, we can foster a resilient mind and achieve lasting well-being.

If you haven't taken action to earn stars so far, don't worry. Anytime is a good time to start, and even small actions or moments of reflection can lead to significant changes. Begin incorporating this mentality into your routine today and watch your resilience grow. So, let's embark on an in-depth exploration of the 5-Star Framework, which revolves around the Daily 5-Star PIS Goal.

Why 5 stars ?

Firstly, stars have traditionally been used for guidance, helping travellers find their way and navigate through the unknown. In our 5-Star Framework, the stars you earn—representing constructive actions—will guide you in navigating both minor and major challenges in life.

Similarly, the concept of earning 5 stars each day was chosen for several compelling reasons. First, five is a manageable number that isn't overwhelming, making it easier for you to integrate into your daily routine. It strikes the perfect balance between being challenging enough to promote meaningful change and achievable enough to keep you motivated. Additionally, earning five stars encourages a holistic approach, prompting you to engage in a variety of actions that boost overall well-being, such as physical activity, mental exercises, social interactions, and self-care. This diverse strategy ensures that different aspects of your psychological health are addressed, leading to a more resilient and balanced mind. Furthermore, the 5-star idea symbolises high standards and excellence, reflecting the ultimate goal of this Framework: to help you become the best version of yourself.

Why daily?

The daily aspect of the 5-Star PIS Framework is crucial for several reasons. Consistency is key when it comes to building and maintaining good psychological health. By incorporating these actions into your routine every day, you create lasting habits that reinforce your mental strength over time. Daily practice ensures that these positive behaviours become second nature, making it easier for the PIS to function properly even during challenging times. Additionally, our mental and emotional states can fluctuate day by day. Having a daily routine allows you to address these fluctuations promptly, preventing small issues from escalating into larger problems. It also provides a sense of structure and stability, which can be incredibly grounding and reassuring. Daily actions also keep you engaged and mindful of your mental health, fostering continuous personal growth. This regular practice will help you stay proactive rather than reactive, allowing you to handle stress and adversity more effortlessly and more effectively.

Theories behind the 5-Star Framework

As a psychologist, I've grounded my Framework in established psychological theories to ensure it is both effective and credible. Using well-founded theories provides a solid foundation based on scientific principles. Theories offer insights into how and why certain behaviours or strategies work, lending credibility to the

Framework by providing a systematic way to address complex issues like mental health. They also help break these issues down into understandable components, such as different ways to enhance the PIS. In essence, theories guide the development of frameworks, increasing their likelihood of producing desired outcomes. Building on this foundation, the 5-Star Framework is grounded in two key psychological theories: Goal-Setting Theory and Self-Determination Theory.

Goal-Setting Theory

This theory, developed by psychologists Edwin Locke and Gary Latham, suggests that specific, well-defined, and quantifiable goals optimise achievement much more effectively than ambiguous targets. Have you noticed how much easier it is to accomplish something when you know exactly what you're aiming for? The daily structure of the 5-Star Framework aligns with this principle by providing clear, measurable actions that help you achieve your goal: a resilient mind.

IF I have a goal, THEN I'll pursue It

Although, simply deciding to achieve a goal isn't always enough, as we often encounter minor or major challenges that get in the way. To address this reality, creating specific "if-then" plans can help you follow through on your goals. In academic circles, this approach is known by a fancy term: implementation intentions.

Excitingly, a review of 94 studies found that "if-then" plans significantly improve goal achievement across different areas of life and situations. Whether starting a new habit, avoiding distractions, letting go of unrealistic goals, or staying motivated for future goals (all relevant to our journey), "if-then" planning proves effective. People who use these plans are better at recognising opportunities and acting on them quickly and easily. This has been systematically investigated and validated, making "if-then" plans a powerful strategy for reaching goals and understanding how goal achievement works.

In the context of the Daily 5-Star PIS Goal, an "if-then" plan is a specific strategy where you decide in advance how you will respond to certain situations to ensure you complete your daily actions. It involves creating clear, actionable plans that link a specific situation (the "if") with a concrete behaviour (the "then").

Examples of '*If-Then*' plans for your Daily 5-Star PIS Goal

1. Mental Fitness:
- *If* it is a sunny evening, *then* I will go for a 20-minute walk.

2. Sleep:
 - *If* it's 10 PM, *then* I will avoid screens and electronic devices.

3. Brain Fuel:
 - *If* it's lunchtime, *then* I will replace a fizzy drink with water or juice.

4. Social Spark:
 - *If* I'm talking to a loved one, *then* I will put the phone away.

5. Break-Free:
 - *If* I sit down to work, *then* I will tackle my to-do list without giving in to distractions.

By planning your responses in advance, you make it easier to stick to your goals and earn your five stars each day. This proactive approach ensures you're consistently taking steps to activate your PIS. "If-then" plans are effective because they leverage several psychological mechanisms. They provide specificity, offering you a clear course of action that reduces decision-making ambiguity. By linking a specific situation (the "if") with a specific behaviour (the "then"), these plans create automaticity, making your responses almost automatic when the situation arises.

This preparation helps you handle obstacles and challenges in advance, increasing your consistency. Creating "if-then" plans reinforces your commitment to your goals, enhancing your motivation and persistence. They also reduce procrastination by providing predefined steps, making it easier for you to initiate goal-directed behaviours. Additionally, "if-then" plans improve your self-regulation by helping you manage impulses and maintain focus, particularly in overcoming temptations. Overall, they make goal-directed behaviours more automatic, reduce cognitive effort, and prepare you to handle challenges effectively.

Self-Determination Theory (SDT).

This theory, developed by psychologists Edward Deci and Richard Ryan, explores a fascinating phenomenon in psychology: what truly motivates us. At its core, Self-Determination Theory (SDT) emphasises that we are most driven and fulfilled when three basic needs are met: autonomy, competence, and relatedness. Autonomy is all about feeling in charge of your own actions and decisions—the sense of freedom when you choose your path. Competence refers to feeling effective and capable in what you do, gaining mastery over your activities. Relatedness is the need to feel connected to others, to belong, and to be part of a community.

How does this connect to our 5-Star Framework? Well, our Framework has been designed to align with the key principles of SDT. By allowing you the freedom to choose actions that resonate with you personally, the Framework gives you control over how you earn your daily stars, fostering a sense of autonomy. Setting and achieving specific, measurable goals each day helps you build a sense of mastery and effectiveness, thereby enhancing your psychological resilience and fulfilling the need for competence. Including social interactions and connections as part of your daily actions ensures you feel supported and connected to others, satisfying the need for relatedness. Also, keep in mind that maintaining a robust PIS enhances the quality of your interpersonal relationships and sense of connectedness. This is because a strong PIS helps you manage stress, regulate emotions, and approach interactions with greater empathy and patience.

By addressing these fundamental needs, the Daily 5-Star PIS Goal not only boosts your mental resilience but also fosters deeper motivation and overall wellbeing. This alignment with Self-Determination Theory further enhances the Framework's effectiveness as a tool for achieving a resilient mind and a fulfilling life.

Your motivated self

Now, let's turn to you. Reflect on how the Daily 5-Star PIS Goal has benefited your self-determination. How has the Framework awakened your sense of autonomy? In what ways has it helped you feel more competent in your daily actions? How has it enhanced your sense of connectedness with the people in your life?

If you don't have immediate answers, that's okay. Take some time to think about it. For example, you might realise that choosing your own daily actions has given you a greater sense of control and freedom, fulfilling your need for autonomy. You may also feel more competent and experience a boost in self-efficacy as you successfully earn your 5 daily stars. Additionally, you might notice easier interactions and a greater sense of belonging through intentional social choices.

I asked my husband these questions, and he shared that one of the stars that makes him feel empowered and determined is when he makes progress on his set plans, effectively avoiding procrastination. Reflecting on these aspects can help you appreciate the positive changes in your life and continue to build a constellation of achievements that shines ever brighter.

Note that our 5-Star Framework is not only grounded in key psychological theories but also supported by extensive research in psychology and neuroscience. As I've highlighted throughout the book, researchers have systematically investigated the initiatives discussed here and found them beneficial for mental health, successfully reducing anxiety and depressive symptoms. For example, cognitive restructuring (discussed in Chapter 11) and behavioural activation (covered in Chapter 19) are techniques shown to support a healthier, calmer mind. These approaches are suggested not just to help you earn stars but, more importantly, to activate your PIS and foster resilience.

Remember, the stars you earn and the constellations you form are metaphors that make your deliberate work towards enhancing your PIS both practical and fun to talk about. So, think of the 5-Star Framework as a structured approach designed to help you take intentional, research-backed actions every day. Its purpose? To activate and strengthen your PIS, fostering overall mental wellbeing and a resilient mind.

With a solid understanding of the 5-Star Framework and its foundations, we are now ready to explore how this approach can be tailored to fit your unique needs and lifestyle in the next chapter, where we will discuss its flexibility and personalisation.

Be yourself; everyone else is already taken.— Oscar Wilde

Chapter 22

Flexibility & Personalisation of the Daily 5-Star PIS Goal

★

One of the greatest strengths of the 5-Star Framework is its flexibility and personalisation, allowing it to be tailored to fit your unique needs and lifestyle. While this Framework is not intended as a substitute for therapy, it draws on the well-established principle that when psychotherapeutic approaches are tailored to meet the specific needs of the client, they lead to more positive outcomes.

This is because we all differ in our needs, personality, and life circumstances. Personalisation takes this into account and, unlike a one-size-fits-all approach, tailors the treatment to fit each person's unique requirements, preferences, and characteristics. Simply put, just as a custom-made suit or dress fits better than one off the rack, personalised therapy addresses specific issues more effectively, making it more likely to help the individual improve their mental health. With this principle in mind, our Framework has been designed to be flexible and adaptable to each individual. This way, you can achieve a 5-Star PIS through steps that suit you and your life's circumstances, day in and day out.

For instance, consider two people, Mary and David. Mary thrives on social interactions and feels energised by connecting with others, while David finds peace and solace in solitude, preferring quiet, reflective activities. In a one-size-fits-all approach, both might be encouraged to engage in the same activities, which could benefit Mary but not David, or vice versa. However, with the personalised Daily 5-Star PIS Goal, Mary can earn her stars through activities like joining a book club, scheduling coffee dates with friends, and participating in group exercises. Meanwhile, David can build his constellation by incorporating actions like journaling, meditation, and solo nature walks into his routine. By tailoring the Framework to their individual characteristics, both Mary and David are more likely to experience positive outcomes and boost their psychological defences in a way that feels natural and supportive to them.

Customising your Daily 5-Star PIS Goal

So, let's explore how you can customise your Daily 5-Star PIS Goal to suit your unique needs, ensuring it fits seamlessly into your life circumstances, individuality, and interests. Remember, the 5-Star Framework involves achieving a 5-Star PIS through 5 daily steps that build psychological defences and boost resilience. Think of it like taking supplements to strengthen your biological immunity, especially during winter when we're more likely to catch the flu. However, unlike seasonal efforts, this Framework encourages you to take small, consistent steps every day to enhance your psychological health. This day-by-day, little-by-little approach isn't just a fire drill for emergencies—it's a holistic strategy to help you live a fuller, more resilient life overall.

The practices suggested in this book foster qualities like self-awareness, self-control, improved lifestyle habits, and enhanced understanding towards oneself, life, and others. The daily actions are intended to help you find meaning in your everyday life. From now on, even a simple action like eating a healthy meal means you're nourishing your brain and enhancing your PIS function. You can see how by regularly engaging in these intentional simple practices, you further develop greater self-awareness, which helps you understand your thoughts and emotions better. Self-control, in turn, is strengthened through consistent choices that require discipline, leading to improved lifestyle habits such as better nutrition, sleep, and physical activity. Additionally, these practices encourage you to reflect on your experiences and relationships, deepening your understanding of yourself and others.

Think about how motivating it is to find meaning in the smallest, simple decisions and daily choices, especially when you're aware that they'll lead to a strong PIS and a resilient mind. How might this newfound purpose transform your day-to-day life?

The example of Mary

Take Mary, for instance, a young professional woman sharing a flat with another young professional. Mary is highly energetic and realised she could benefit from becoming more centred and less dependent on the availability and attention of others to feel positive. She decided to work on introspection. In the morning, instead of jumping out of bed and eating something on the way to the bus stop, she began to get up a little earlier and enjoy a calm, nourishing breakfast (1 star). On the bus, before putting her earphones on to enjoy her upbeat music, she practiced deep breathing whether she was standing or sitting (2 stars). During lunch break, instead of browsing the internet, Mary started reading a novel or journaling (3 stars). On her way back home, whenever the weather was fair, she walked for 20 minutes before catching the bus, instead of stopping at the nearest bus stop (4 stars). As Mary wanted to become more emotionally independent, she decided to party and engage in social gatherings only on weekends. This change gave her more time for herself in the evenings, which she filled with a variety of activities ranging from watching series alone, managing her finances, and setting up future plans (5 stars).

These small, intentional changes are improving Mary's wellbeing. She's been feeling more grounded and self-sufficient, with a better balance between social interactions and personal time. Her increased self-awareness and intentional daily practices have boosted her overall resilience and mental clarity.

The example of David

Now, think about David, who finds peace and solace in solitude and prefers quiet, reflective activities. David's goal is to become less anxious and self-conscious. To address this, David decided to incorporate small, intentional practices into his daily routine.

In the morning, as he sits up on the bed before getting up, David does a quick body scan, deliberately takes deep breaths, and rolls his shoulders back, focusing on his bodily signals. A simple practice that isn't just about breathing or moving his body but about being present with each breath, activating the parasympathetic nervous system, and signalling to David's brain that he is safe and well (1 star). At work, whenever he needs to make important calls or have important meetings, he engages in grounding practices, such as feeling his feet on the ground to centre himself (2 stars). David has also started being more assertive, learning to politely refuse taking on others' workloads or covering for them, thereby managing his stress levels better (3 stars).

On the way back home, instead of turning on the radio, he now has long conversations with his son, who always has a lot of stories to tell (4 stars). Most nights, David earns his fifth star by turning off his devices and either cooking for his family or taking the dog for a walk. During these walks, he addresses and tackles any insecurities he might be experiencing from work by restructuring his thoughts. For example, if he feels anxious about a project, he reminds himself of his past successes and focuses on what he can control, rather than worrying about the unknown (5 stars).

These deliberate actions are helping David reduce his anxiety and build self-esteem. By incorporating these small moments of self-awareness and assertiveness throughout the day, he approaches his work and family life with a calmer, more present mindset. His daily practices have improved his mental states and strengthened his psychological defences.

Your example

Mary and David personalised their Daily 5-star PIS Goal by reflecting on how they could improve their mental states in order to build resilience. While Mary wanted to become more emotionally self-sufficient, David wanted to become more assertive. In order to discover what inner-improvement you want to work on, try to answer the following questions:

What specific aspect of your development would you like to improve? What specific practices do you need to take (or reduce/eliminate) to become the best version of yourself? How can you incorporate these into your Daily 5-Star PIS Goal?

Reflect on these questions to uncover your internal values and pursuits.

Perhaps you're someone who experiences low mood from time to time and wants to enjoy better levels of life satisfaction. If so, I recommend revisiting Chapters 11 and 16 to refresh your understanding of how low mood and your mental processes may be affecting you—and, more importantly, how to navigate through these states. In any case, we've discussed plenty of practices that will help you consistently earn your daily 5 stars and build a brighter, more positive outlook.

For example, analysing and addressing environmental drains (Chapter 7) can help you create a more supportive and uplifting environment. Embracing neutral emotions as positive (Chapter 11) allows you to appreciate the value in every emotional state. Practicing gratitude by focusing on the privileges in your life

(Chapters 7 and 9) helps you maintain a positive perspective. Engaging in a light conversation with a friend or family member—perhaps about a movie or new TV series, rather than yourself (Chapter 20)—can provide a refreshing break and strengthen social connections. Lastly, remember to get up and go, as discussed in Chapter 19, where I encourage you to cope with the chatter of your mind by taking action and creating some distance between you and your stubborn thoughts.

Crucially, always keep the very foundation of mental health in mind: sleep, nutrition, and moderation. Getting enough sleep each night helps improve negative mood states by allowing your brain and body to rest and recover. Refraining from sugary foods, drinks, and alcohol is helpful when you find yourself feeling blue, as these can cause mood swings and energy crashes, exacerbating feelings of sadness or anxiety. Just by being aware of these foundations and implementing this understanding through daily actions, you'll earn 3 stars! That in itself is already something to boost your mood, as it shows self-efficacy and self-mastery. Remember, it isn't possible to feel blue and proud of yourself at the same time. Which one are you going for?

Taking on small challenges

Alternatively, you may be someone who's currently feeling pretty good about life in general and is simply looking for continuous self-development and personal growth. You may already have healthy eating habits, stay active, and maintain good sleep routines. How else can you improve? Consider practicing openness and psychological flexibility. This involves being open and accepting of your circumstances and willing to take on challenging tasks that align with your core values.

For example, yesterday I received an unpleasant message from a needy family member, harshly complaining about my lack of phone calls and attention. This person is someone I find difficult to deal with, and I have subtly been working on setting boundaries. Instead of avoiding the situation, I called them back, addressed the tone of the message, and explained how busy I've been, further reminding them that we have, in fact, been in touch. I counted that as a star. Recall that taking on challenging tasks fosters self-efficacy by building confidence in your ability to handle awkward situations and reducing stress, brightening up our PIS constellation a little more.

To further cultivate psychological flexibility and openness, consider facing discomfort by identifying a situation that makes you uneasy—like speaking up in a meeting—and take a small step toward action, while acknowledging and accepting your feelings in the process. Additionally, try engaging in new activities outside your comfort zone, such as a different type of exercise class or a new hobby, and stay open to the experience and the emotions it brings. These actions not only help you earn your daily stars but also foster personal growth and resilience.

The flexible and personalised nature of the 5-Star Framework ensures that it adapts to your unique needs and lifestyle, making it easier to integrate and more effective for long-term success. In the next chapter, we'll explore how to seamlessly incorporate the 5-Star Framework into your daily life, making it a natural part of your everyday routine.

Success is the sum of small efforts, repeated day in and day out.
— Robert Collier

Chapter 23

How to Make the Framework a Natural Part of Your Day

★

Do you know how reducing unhealthy fats in your diet, staying moderately active, and not smoking all contribute to better heart health? These small, consistent actions add up, creating a powerful cumulative effect that significantly boosts your physical health over time. Similarly, the cumulative effect of positive practices can greatly enhance your mental health.

In the context of positive psychology, the cumulative effect refers to how small, regular actions can build up over time to create significant positive changes. Again, think of it like adding individual stars to your inner universe, eventually forming an expansive, glowing constellation. Now you can see how the logic behind our Daily 5-Star PIS Goal is that by consistently incorporating positive practices into your routine, you create a powerful cumulative effect that strengthens your PIS and boosts your resilience.

The cumulative effect of the 5-Star Framework is another aspect strongly supported by research. For instance, a study published in *BMC Psychiatry* found that combining activities like gratitude and loving-kindness meditation significantly boosts wellbeing by fostering a positive mindset and reducing stress. The study also showed that engaging in various positive-psychology interventions—such as savouring positive moments and setting meaningful goals—alleviates depression and anxiety, thereby enhancing life satisfaction in both clinical and non-clinical groups. Encouragingly, the researchers noted that consistent practice of these activities leads to lasting mental health benefits. Additionally, another study found that participating in different positive mental health programs that promote positive emotions and behaviours improves resilience, life satisfaction, and stress management abilities, much like regular exercise strengthens your body. Once again, our 5-Star Framework builds on these well-supported practices, proving to be a promising approach to boosting your psychological resilience and overall wellbeing!

Now, let's explore four practical ways to seamlessly integrate the Daily 5-Star PIS Goal into your routine, making it a natural and effortless part of your day.

Making resilience a habit

To understand how habits are built, think back to our analogies of creating strong, solid bridges (neural pathways) in your brain that lead you to good practices and smart strategies. Always keep in mind that each time you engage in a positive practice, it's as if you're further cementing these bridges, fortifying them, and making it easier to repeat the behaviour in the future. As the quote often attributed to Aristotle goes, "We are what we repeatedly do. Excellence, then, is not an act, but a habit."

By consistently practicing positive actions, you strengthen these mental bridges, making resilience a natural part of your daily life. The more you reinforce these bridges, the sturdier they become, guiding you effortlessly towards healthier habits and ever improved psychological defences. How can you start building these strong, resilient habits in your daily life? Let's cover four practical steps that will help you with that.

Setting a routine

Integrate the 5-Star Framework into your existing schedule. Start by identifying moments in your day where you can easily add a positive practice, such as during your morning routine, lunch break, or bedtime. Try attaching these practices to existing habits, like focusing on self-awareness. According to the Australian Lung Foundation, we breathe 22,000 times a day. Now, ask yourself: how many of those breaths are you truly aware of? By consciously taking 5 or 6 deep, slow breaths when you wake up in the morning or while at your desk during the day, you'll already become more self-aware than ever before. This is how it starts, by subtly paying attention to your automatic bodily functions and the content of your mind, you pave the way to emotional balance. Self-awareness is just a step away from becoming more controlled, less reactive, and less anxious.

Next, practice gratitude while having your morning coffee or lunch. As discussed earlier, expressing gratitude motivates us to strive for self-improvement. How motivated do you feel when you're grateful for something as simple as a meal? This surge of positivity can inspire you to tackle your afternoon tasks or share an encouraging message with someone. Embracing gratitude in these small moments helps create a positive momentum that carries you through the day.

Consistency is key, so find regular times that work for you and stick with them. This integration not only makes it easier to build and maintain these positive habits naturally but also helps you earn your daily stars, bringing you closer to your increased resilience goals.

Choosing simple actions: Begin with easy, manageable tasks

When starting on your journey to resilience, it's crucial to choose simple actions and begin with easy, manageable tasks. This approach ensures that you don't feel overwhelmed and can gradually build up your positive habits. Let's revisit Step 1, where we discussed integrating awareness into your breathing and adding gratitude to your mealtimes. Note that these activities require minimal effort and seamlessly fit into what you're already doing.

Think of building these habits as constructing a bridge. You wouldn't start with the largest, most complex steps. Instead, you begin with the foundations, laying one brick at a time. Each small action you take adds another brick, strengthening the structure and making it easier to add more as you go. By starting slowly and choosing manageable tasks, you ensure that your bridge is strong and steady, capable of supporting more significant changes in the future. For instance, by simply becoming aware of your breathing a few times a day, you enhance self-awareness without disrupting your routine. Similarly, expressing gratitude at mealtimes is a small addition that can have a big impact on your mindset and motivation. These small steps are the foundation of your bridge to resilience.

Starting slowly is vital because it allows you to build confidence and see the benefits of your efforts without feeling discouraged. Just as a strong bridge can support more weight over time, your growing resilience will enable you to take on more challenging tasks and continue to thrive. Remember, each small action you take not only earns you a star but also reinforces your ability to handle life's challenges with greater ease. So, embrace these simple actions and watch as they pave the way to a stronger, more resilient you.

Here are some easy, manageable grounding practice examples to help you earn stars:

Take a moment to look around and identify an object. This could be a book on a shelf, a plant in the corner, or a painting on the wall. Notice the colours, shapes, and details of this item. Consider what appeals to you about it and what doesn't. Alternatively, focus on something you can physically feel. This might include the texture of your chair, the fabric of your clothes, or the warmth of your tea cup. Think about how these items feel against your skin, are they soft or hard, smooth or textured, warm or cool? Or, tune into the sounds you can hear. This could be the hum of your computer, or distant chatter. Pay attention to the volume and nature of these sounds. Are they soothing or distracting?

You can also purposefully pause and notice distinct smells in your environment. This could be the aroma of freshly brewed coffee, the scent of a cleaning product, or even the street smells coming through the window. Reflect on what you like about these smells and how they make you feel. Finally, you could also focus on one thing you can taste. If you're not eating or drinking anything at the moment, think of a recent meal or snack and remember its flavours. Consider why you enjoy this taste and what memories it might evoke. Personally, I rejoice in recalling the taste of coffee, as it elicits a feeling of comfort and warmth for me, especially since I only have one cup in the morning.

By integrating these simple actions into your daily routine, you can foster a sense of groundedness and clarity, enabling you to navigate your day with greater ease and balance. Grounding practices like these prevent us from anticipating stress or brooding, effectively getting us out of our heads and experiencing what is actually happening. You can see how by incorporating subtle such steps into your routine, you can cultivate a more focused and calm state of mind.

Using reminders : A Simple strategy for consistency

Incorporating new habits into your daily routine can be challenging, but using reminders can make this process much easier. Think of reminders as the gentle nudges that keep you on track, much like how support beams maintain the integrity of a bridge.

Set alarms on your phone or another device to prompt you at specific times to practice your new habits. For instance, a soothing alarm in the morning can remind you to start your day with a few deep breaths. Placing sticky notes in visible locations, such as on the bathroom mirror, refrigerator, or front door, is my favourite type of reminder. These notes can serve as cues to engage in positive practices, like setting a positive mindset for the day with messages such as, "If stress emerges, then I'll pause mindfully", or "May I be calm and kind today."

My husband prefers digital reminders or habit-tracking apps to keep going. These tools can send notifications and track your progress, providing a visual representation of your achievements and encouraging you to stay consistent. By incorporating reminders into your routine, you create a supportive system that helps you maintain consistency with your new habits. This approach ensures that your positive practices become an integral part of your daily life, much like how a well-built bridge becomes a reliable pathway to your destination.

Reflecting daily : End your day by reviewing your stars

This is the final step of incorporating the 5-Star Framework into your daily life, making the Daily 5-Star PIS Goal a natural part of your routine. This step itself can earn you a star. Reflecting on your day is a powerful practice that helps reinforce your positive habits and provides a sense of accomplishment. Note that this doesn't have to be time-consuming. Think of it as star gazing, taking a few moments to observe the stars you've earned and the progress you've made.

Here's how to implement this step effectively

At the end of each day, take a few minutes to review the stars you've earned. Consider the positive practices you've incorporated and how they've made you feel. Reflect on any challenges you faced and how you overcame them. This can be done while you unwind before bed, perhaps as you're enjoying a quiet moment by yourself.

If needed, use your journal to jot down your thoughts. You don't need to write extensively, just a few sentences about what you did well and what you'd like to improve. This act of writing can help solidify your achievements and set intentions for the next day. Always approach this step as if you were star gazing. Just as you would look up at the night sky and feel a sense of wonder and calm, let your daily reflection be a time to appreciate your efforts and growth. This practice can help you end your day on a positive note and build motivation for the days to come.

By consistently reflecting on your progress, you reinforce your commitment to maintaining your positive habits and boosting your PIS function. This simple, reflective practice can have a profound impact on your overall wellbeing, further helping you to stay grounded and focused on your journey toward a resilient mind.

As we wrap up this chapter, get ready to dive into Chapter 24, where we'll explore practical tips for overcoming challenges and staying motivated, as well as discuss the long-term benefits and adaptability of the 5-Star Framework.

It does not matter how slowly you go as long as you do not stop.
— Confucius

Chapter 24

Overcoming Challenges, Long-term Benefits & Adaptation

★

So far, in Part 5 of our book, we've seen how the 5-Star Framework is rooted in the influential psychological theories of Goal-Setting and Self-Determination. We've highlighted the advantages of flexibility and personalisation of this framework, helping you to customise it to your unique needs. We've also delved into how small, daily steps can accumulate to create a significant positive impact on your PIS function and structure.

Now, it's time to discuss how to keep your Daily 5-Star PIS Goal going and maintain motivation, even (or especially) in trying times. Those moments when we are most likely to abandon our healthy habits, yet need them the most. This is what happened to Andrew when his wife informed him she was going to move out and take their two daughters with her. He sought solace in negative, destructive habits that led to further family conflict.

Like Andrew, many of us tend to fall off the rails when faced with challenges because stress and emotional strain can overwhelm our psychological defences. This leads to decreased motivation, cognitive overload, and a tendency to turn to instant gratification behaviours as a form of comfort or autopilot response. Some people even initiate unhealthy habits in such circumstances, like overeating, smoking, or excessive drinking, as a way to cope with stress. Additionally, the immediate pressure of challenges can overshadow long-term goals, making it harder to maintain healthy routines. This is precisely what the 5-Star Framework intends to prevent by giving you the tools to build a robust PIS. With a robust PIS rather than being easily overwhelmed, your psychological defences will help you heal and recover.

During difficult times, armed with increased awareness, self-reliance, and resilience, instead of abandoning your healthy daily habits, you'll be able to pause, reflect, and ask yourself: "This is quite challenging, how can I best take care of myself right now?" This newfound ability will help you overcome minor and major adversities, stay motivated, and maintain your progress, helping you realise the enduring benefits of maintaining the Daily 5-Star PIS Goal. So, let's further explore how to keep the momentum going.

Keeping the Daily 5-Star PIS Goal momentum

Once again, to keep going even when times are tough, start by recognising that you're facing a difficulty, whether minor or major. This could be the awareness of low mood setting in, a loss, or a major disappointment. A smart way to immediately address such situations is by answering the following question: "What is one small step I can take right now to put things in perspective?" Begin by identifying a small action that you can accomplish immediately. This could be something as simple as engaging in a grounding practice or taking a hot shower. Commit to performing this small task, focusing on the immediate positive impact it can have, such as slowing your heart rate and relaxing your muscles. After completing the task, take a moment to reflect on the effort you've made and recognise how it has helped you regain a sense of control.

Keep in mind that whenever life throws you a curve ball it's time to act, not react. As reactivity more often than not leads to negative outcomes, making things worse. This is when it's important to be prepared. No matter how resilient and centred we are, when wounded, it's always comforting to have a first aid kit nearby, or in our case, a treasure chest (Chapter 19).

Opening your treasure chest

Remember that your treasure chest is filled with essential behaviours and activities (stars) designed to uplift your spirits and keep you grounded. Having these tools at your disposal empowers you to proactively boost your mood and manage your emotions effectively. When things are very tough, one of the stars in your treasure chest might be taking a moment to simply cry. Perhaps this may come as a surprise, but the positive effects of crying are significant. Research shows that after shedding tears, stress hormones, blood pressure, and adrenaline decrease, and the parasympathetic nervous system is activated, leading to a calming effect. Indeed, the benefits of crying are so soothing that Crying Therapy has been shown to reduce stress levels and improve mood and immune system activity in breast cancer survivors.

As I write this, I recall an event involving my mother. It happened during a time when a friend of hers was facing relentless life adversities, one of those periods where bad news just keeps coming without a break. One day, my mother was home alone when the doorbell rang. Her friend walked in, went straight to the sofa, and began to sob, like a dam breaking under the pressure of an unrelenting storm. My mother sat quietly in the armchair, looking out the window at the sky, listening to the sound of sobbing, sniffles, and gasps for air. Then, everything went quiet, my mother said. Her friend then looked up and remarked, "This is the plan." In that moment, it became clear, after releasing all her pent-up emotions, she found clarity. The tears had washed away the confusion, leaving her with a sense of acceptance and understanding. As Charles Dickens once said, "We need never be ashamed of our tears."

Within our Framework, even what might be perceived as fragility holds profound significance, serving as a critical component in the fortification of our resilience. These moments of vulnerability are not signs of weakness; rather, they are opportunities for growth and self-discovery. By embracing and understanding our fragile moments, we learn to navigate challenges with greater strength and adaptability. Thus, what seems fragile actually becomes the foundation upon which we build enduring resilience.

Should setbacks occur

If you encounter setbacks, such as finding yourself reacting rather than acting, remember to forgive yourself and view these moments as part of your growth process. Finding a support system, whether it's a friend, partner, or family member, can also be incredibly helpful in keeping you on track. During challenging periods, it's important to revisit your personal goals and remind yourself why you started this journey. Reflecting on your reasons for embracing the Daily 5-Star PIS Goal can reignite your motivation. Never forget to celebrate small victories to reinforce your commitment and highlight how far you've come.

Starting again holds immense power. Recognising that every new beginning is an opportunity for growth and resilience can be incredibly empowering. Each restart is a testament to your perseverance and dedication to becoming your best self. Furthermore, the long-term effects of the 5-Star Framework itself provide a compelling reason to restart as many times as necessary.

Long-term benefits

To help you reflect on the long-term benefits of embracing the 5-Star Framework, consider these questions: How have small, positive actions impacted your wellbeing and resilience? What long-term changes do you envision by continuing these practices? Reflecting on these questions can help you appreciate the cumulative benefits of maintaining your positive habits and motivate you to persist, even during challenging times.

The Daily 5-Star PIS Goal promotes a life where you find meaning in the smallest, most ordinary actions. This practice also encourages you to become more attuned to your inner world, leading to a more rational and objective way of dealing with life experiences and others. Over time, you'll become someone who's more open, flexible, and accepting; qualities that prepare you to handle life's surprises with grace.

Imagine finding satisfaction in everyday events: the sense of accomplishment after tidying up a cluttered space, the brief moment of quietness before turning out the lights for sleep, or even the irritation from your child and an unexpected message from that annoying family member. These seemingly trivial moments become sources of contentment because you understand the delicate and fleeting nature of life. You'll recognise that turbulent times or unexpected challenges can arise at any moment. This will not cause you anxiety or concern because, above all, you will always be aware that beneath the dark skies, your bright constellation will stand firm, a source of light you've built steadily.

This bright constellation represents your self-worth, self-reliance, and self-efficacy. It is a beacon you can always turn to, a light that illuminates even the darkest times. The awareness of this inner light alone prepares you to face anything that comes your way, well into your old age. The enduring benefits of the 5-Star Framework lie in its ability to transform your perception of life. By appreciating the subtle yet profound impact of everyday actions, you enhance your ability to cope with challenges and enrich your overall life experience. Every moment becomes meaningful and precious, contributing to a life filled with resilience and purpose.

Adaptation: A Journey of continuous self-Improvement

As you embark on the Daily 5-Star PIS Goal journey, it's important to recognise that this practice is meant to be a lifelong endeavour. Our goal is continuous self-improvement, which means you'll consistently work toward earning different stars. For example, after mastering self-control by curbing procrastination, you might then focus on earning a star for practicing non-judgment. However, it's also common to revisit goals you thought you had mastered. Many times I've found myself needing to "re-earn" stars through avoiding unhealthy meals or making time for hobbies. Instead of viewing this as a setback, see it as a sign that you are attuned to your inner needs and willing to grow. This process of returning to earlier goals is a natural and essential part of the journey.

It's crucial to remember that just because your self-control, for instance, feels optimal at one point, it doesn't mean you won't need to revisit this aspect of your mental toolkit later. Practicing self-control may become a way to add stars to your constellation once more. Again, like real stars, our metaphorical stars can lose their brightness and warmth over time. Avoid the temptation to think of the practices we've discussed as boxes to tick and move on from. That's not how the human mind works. Our development isn't linear; it doesn't follow a straight, upward path. Instead, it's more like a line that steadies, ascends, circles around, and steadies again. Picture this as a journey with peaks, plateaus, and curves, representing the continuous, dynamic process of self-improvement.

There are many reasons for this non-linear development. Life circumstances change, challenges arise, and new stages of life bring different demands and opportunities for growth. Note that the deliberate practices encouraged by the 5-Star Framework aim to make your self-development journey more consistent. By regularly integrating these practices, you build resilience and adaptability, ensuring that your psychological defences remain strong and flexible. This approach ensures that you are always growing, always adapting, and always ready to face whatever life throws your way. Remember, this journey of self-improvement is ongoing, and each star you earn adds to the bright constellation that guides you through both calm and stormy skies.

As we wrap up our discussion on staying motivated, earning stars during challenging times, and adapting the Daily 5-Star PIS Goal to your evolving needs, it's fitting to approach the end of our journey with a comprehensive recap. This recap will highlight the key reflections and strategies you've encountered throughout the book, helping you appreciate how far you've come while reinforcing your continuous journey toward an ever-resilient you.

Isn't it funny how day by day nothing changes but when you look back everything is different. — C.S. Lewis

Chapter 25

Recap of Key Reflections & Activities

★

As we conclude our journey, this chapter serves as a comprehensive recap of the key questions and activities designed to earn stars. Throughout this journey, I have been prompting you to self-reflect to encourage deeper self-exploration and self-knowledge. Hopefully, you have been fully engaging with the book and answered most of these questions in a separate journal or notepad. Remember, these needed not be lengthy or elaborate answers, but just enough to promote meaningful self-reflection.

Incredibly, despite all your life commitments and responsibilities, you are here at the very end of the book. No matter how long this journey has taken, you have undoubtedly changed along the way. As Carl Rogers insightfully said, "A person is a fluid process, not a fixed and static entity; a flowing river of change." By answering the most relevant questions of our journey now and comparing them with your initial responses, you can truly notice your development.

If you haven't had the opportunity to answer the questions as suggested, don't worry. Take your time to address them little by little from now, with all your newfound knowledge. As you continue to implement the 5-Star Framework in your life, revisit these questions a few weeks from now to reflect on your progress and growth.

Taking the time to answer these questions is a worthwhile endeavour because it fosters deeper self-awareness and personal development. By reflecting on your experiences and progress, you gain valuable insights into your patterns, strengths, and areas for improvement. This self-knowledge empowers you to make more informed decisions and enhances your ability to adapt to life's challenges. Additionally, regularly revisiting these questions helps reinforce the positive changes you've made and keeps you motivated on your journey toward resilience and self-improvement.

Take your time with the questions—there's no rush. Think of this as a chance to invest in yourself. Grab a cup of tea or a latte, put on some calming music, and spend 10 minutes reflecting on just 2 or 3 questions. As you go through the questions, try to dig a little deeper by asking yourself **why** you feel the way you do about each one. Understanding the "whys" can reveal insights that might surprise you and deepen your self-awareness.

For example, the first question asks, "Do you appreciate the need to look after your mind, just as you do your body?" When I answered, my response was: "Yes. **Because** good mental health is the foundation for overall wellbeing. It influences everything from how we handle stress to how we build relationships and make decisions. When our mind is healthy, we're better equipped to navigate life's challenges and experience true fulfilment."

As you might know by now, completing these questions will also earn you a star towards your Daily 5-Star PIS Goal!

Part 1
The Basics of the Psychological Immune System

In this part of the book, we introduced the concept of the Psychological Immune System (PIS) and the 5-Star Framework. We explored how the PIS operates as an abstract system within us, working automatically to protect and heal us from life's challenges and adversities.

We also delved into the brain structures relevant to the PIS and how this system develops across the lifespan. Most importantly, we learned that by deliberately and intentionally nurturing our PIS, we pave the way towards a resilient mind. This is where the Daily 5-Star PIS Goal comes into play, providing a practical approach to strengthening your psychological defences.

The reflections below are designed to deepen your understanding of the PIS and guide you in applying these concepts to your daily life, ensuring that you continue to strengthen your psychological defences and wellbeing.

1. Do you appreciate the need to look after your mind, just as you do your body?

2. Do you have an understanding of what your mind needs protection and healing from?

3. How would you describe your sense of humour right now?

4. How robust is your PIS currently?

5. How have past adversities helped you learn to face challenges more effectively?

6. How have past challenges made you more resilient?

7. Would you say your outlook on life is generally positive or negative?

8. Do you find yourself able to intuitively manage your emotions and maintain calm in challenging situations?

9. Do you recognise how strong and resilient you are in overcoming challenges?

10. Are your daily habits helping you to strengthen your brain bridges?

11. Have you been overreacting to relatively minor situations?

12. Do you feel a sense of trust and stability in your relationships?

13. Are you able to confidently rely on and connect with others?

14. Have you been thoughtful about who you spend your time with?

15. What steps are you taking today to pave the way towards a calmer, more peaceful life in your senior years?

Part 2
Factors that Influence the Psychological Immune System

In Part 2, we explored the various factors that influence the PIS. We began by examining the role of genetics in shaping our mental and emotional processes, which in turn affect how we perceive and respond to the world. Importantly, we emphasised that while genetics play a significant role in who we are, they do not have to dictate our life experiences. There are numerous environmental and psychological factors within our control that we can actively engage with to improve and maintain our psychological defences. These are the factors worth reflecting upon, as they offer opportunities to propel us forward.

Now, take a moment to consider the questions below and engage in some further reflection.

1. How empowered do you feel to take action toward improving your mental wellness?

2. What aspects of your current environment feel like they drain your energy rather than replenish it?

3. Who are the people in your life that support your growth and who are those that may hinder it?

4. Do your daily activities advance your journey of personal growth or do they leave you feeling stagnant?

5. How much time have you spent today, or this past week, browsing social media and watching YouTube videos?

6. How does your current daily routine support your physical and mental fitness?

7. What mindful living practices have you incorporated into your daily routine?

8. Have you engaged in non-fiction reading as a means to expand your psychological experiences?

9. Do you find yourself in a cycle of sleep procrastination? What activities tend to keep you up at night?

10. How do your current eating habits contribute to your psychological health?

Part 3
Factors that Impact the Psychological Immune System

In this part of the book, we examined the impact of: negative emotions and mood, potentially addictive behaviours, procrastination, loss, as well as personal values and pursuits. The central theme here was how these phenomena and events can compromise the PIS function and structure, leaving us more vulnerable to life's minor and major challenges if not addressed properly. Self-awareness and self-control were key elements in our discussions, offering strategies for navigating these inevitable aspects of life with ease and grace, preventing them from spiralling out of control.

Below, you'll find a recap of the insights I've encouraged you to reflect on, equipping you with the tools to keep moving forward.

1. Do you ever feel pressured to always be happy?

2. How do you view neutral emotions compared to intense ones like joy or sadness?

3. Do you tend to overlook or undervalue calm, content states?

4. Do you recognise the value of more neutral emotions as essential moments of balance in your life?

5. Do you find yourself magnifying the bad and overlooking the good in your life?

6. How do you currently tackle your negative thoughts when they arise?

7. After using social media, are you more often inspired and connected, or feeling drained and dissatisfied?

8. Is there a healthier activity that could address your emotional needs?

9. How often do you adjust your plans to better align with your life goals?

10. What strategies have you been using to tackle procrastination?

11. What steps are you taking to develop psychological flexibility in your daily life?

12. What is loss to you?

13. How have the losses you've faced revealed hidden strengths and resilience within you?

14. Have you found a balance between listening to your personal needs and meeting social demands?

15. Have you ever found yourself competing with others or pursuing admiration in an attempt to feel accepted?

Part 4
Strengthening Your Psychological Immune System

In Part 4, we explored your inner resources and their potential to fortify your psychological defences, helping you build a solid foundation for life satisfaction and resilience. We discussed how the way you relate to your thoughts is crucial for your wellbeing, the importance of acceptance in fostering a sense of inner peace, and the elements of the self that fuel a sense of worth and competence. We also examined how taking action and developing a repertoire of behaviours can be the right antidote to negative states. Finally, we delved into the vital role of interpersonal relationships in building resilience, recognising that we are all part of an interconnected whole.

Take a moment to reflect on these themes through the questions below.

1. Do you find yourself labelling your thoughts as 'good' or 'bad'?
2. Think about a recent time when you felt sad or anxious. Did judging those feelings make the experience more difficult for you?
3. How often do you find yourself trying to control the uncontrollable?
4. In what ways could embracing acceptance bring more peace into your life?
5. What does acceptance mean to you?
6. Are you able to accept compliments and constructive criticism?
7. Do you generally feel confident in your abilities?
8. How do you approach your own setbacks—do you see them as fixed limitations or as chances to grow?
9. How does your self-efficacy influence your approach to minor and major challenges?
10. Are you prepared for those times when you don't feel so positive?
11. Is there someone you need to forgive to further free your mind and bolster your resilience?

Part 5
Fine-Tuning the Psychological Immune System

In this final part of the book, we explored additional ways to fortify the PIS and build a resilient mind, with a primary focus on the 5-Star Framework and the Daily 5-Star PIS Goal. We discussed how this approach to boosting psychological defences is grounded in key psychological theories that highlight the importance of clearly defined goals for achieving positive outcomes. We also examined the flexibility and personalisation that make the 5-Star Framework a powerful tool for activating your psychological defences. Finally, we emphasised the cumulative, consistent nature of the Daily 5-

Star PIS Goal, which supports the long-term function and structure of the PIS by allowing individuals to care for their mental health in a way that suits them, offering both autonomy and a sense of competence.

The questions in this section encourage you to reflect on these ideas in a light, thoughtful way.

1. Have you noticed it's easier to accomplish something when you know exactly what you're aiming for?
2. How has the 5-Star Framework awakened your sense of autonomy?
3. In what ways has the Daily 5-Star PIS Goal helped you feel more competent in your daily actions?
4. How has the 5-Star Framework enhanced your sense of connectedness with the people in your life?
5. What specific aspect of your development would you like to improve?
6. What specific practices do you need to take (or reduce/eliminate) to become the best version of yourself?
7. How can you incorporate these practices into your Daily 5-Star PIS Goal?
8. What is one small step you can immediately take in times of difficulty to put things in perspective?
9. How have small, positive actions impacted your wellbeing and resilience?
10. What long-term changes do you envision by continuing these practices?

The Daily 5-Star PIS Goal: Your Path to a Resilient Mind

As we reach the final stretch of this journey, here's a collection of 50 steps, activities, and practices that will help you consistently earn stars toward your Daily 5-Star PIS Goal. Each step has been discussed throughout this book and is designed to fortify your psychological defences, strengthen your resilience, and enhance your overall wellbeing. These actions are more than just tasks. They are meaningful contributions to your inner constellation, guiding you toward a brighter, more resilient you.

1. Embrace Humour: Lighten up your day by finding humour in everyday situations. Humour strengthens your psychological defences by reframing stressful situations and releasing tension.

2. Do Some Puzzles: Engage your mind with puzzles, crosswords, or brainteasers. They sharpen your cognitive skills and offer a satisfying mental break.

3. Take Deep Breaths: Pause to take slow, deep breaths. This simple act activates the parasympathetic branch of the nervous system, which helps calm the body and mind.

4. Grounding Practices: Engage in grounding techniques to pull yourself out of your head and into the present moment. They help you focus on what's truly happening around you, easing anxiety and overthinking.

5. Remind Yourself of Your Inner Strength: Reflect on past challenges you've overcome. This reinforces your resilience and boosts your confidence in facing new obstacles.

6. Acknowledge the Actions You Take That Benefit Your PIS: Recognise the small, everyday choices, like nourishing meals or a walk to the bus stop, that strengthen your Psychological Immune System. Every positive action counts.

7. Shift Your Perspective on Anxious and Depressed Tendencies: Instead of viewing them as external forces, recognise these states

as parts of yourself that need deliberate care and attention. Embrace them with compassion to foster healing.

8. Declutter and Organise Your Environment: Create a calm and orderly space by decluttering and organising. A tidy environment promotes mental clarity and reduces stress.

9. Declutter Your Mind (Reduce Technology Use): Limit screen time to give your mind a break. Reducing technology use helps clear mental clutter and fosters a sense of peace.

10. Set Boundaries: Protect your psychological wellbeing by setting boundaries and limiting contact with those who negatively impact your mental health. Prioritising your peace is essential for resilience.

11. Strive to Be Genuine and Supportive: Cultivate authenticity and offer genuine support in your relationships. Building honest connections strengthens your bonds and enhances mutual wellbeing.

12. Move Your Body: Engage in physical activity, whether it's a walk, stretch, or workout. Movement boosts your mood and energises both your body and mind.

13. Contact with Nature: Spend time connecting with nature. It rejuvenates your mind, reduces stress, and brings a sense of calm.

14. Breathing Meditation: This practice is a more focused, extended version of deep breathing. By dedicating time to breathing meditation, you centre your mind, and enhance overall calmness.

15. Read Fiction: Dive into a fictional world. Reading fiction expands your psychological experiences, develops empathy and emotional intelligence, and offers a refreshing mental break.

16. Say No to Sleep Procrastination: Prioritise sleep by resisting the urge to delay bedtime. Quality sleep is essential for maintaining PIS function and structure.

17. Practice Expressive Writing When Sleep Doesn't Come: If sleep eludes you, try expressive writing. This helps clear your mind, release tension, and pave the way for restful sleep.

18. Sleep 8 Hours Every Night: Prioritise 8 hours of sleep to support optimal cognitive functioning and emotional regulation. Restful sleep is crucial for a resilient mind and balanced mood.

19. Reduce Intake of Caffeinated Drinks, Sugary Foods, and Alcohol: Limit these substances, especially when feeling anxious or sad, as they can amplify negative emotions and disrupt your mental balance.

20. Reduce UPF Consumption: Cut back on ultra-processed foods (UPFs), as they are linked to inflammation, which in turn has been associated with mental health issues like depression.

21. Fast: Fasting for 12 to 16 hours, including sleep time, can enhance mental clarity and improve mood regulation. However, if you have diabetes or take heart medication, consult your doctor before fasting.

22. Eat More Grains, Fruits, Veggies, and Fermented Foods: Incorporate these nutrient-rich foods into your diet to support gut health, boost your mood, and enhance overall mental wellbeing. Hydrate with water and decaffeinated teas to keep your body and mind balanced.

23. Resist the Pressure to Always "Be Happy": Allow yourself to experience the full range of emotions. Authenticity, not constant happiness, is key to fostering a resilient mind.

24. Value Moments of Neutral Emotions: Recognise the importance of neutral emotions. These calm, steady states are essential for balance and inner peace.

25. Let Go of Emotional Crutches: Release habits or behaviours you rely on to avoid uncomfortable feelings. Facing emotions directly promotes genuine growth.

26. Prioritise Tasks and Commitments: Align your daily routine with your short and long-term goals to minimise procrastination. This focus helps you stay on track and ensures your actions reflect your true intentions.

27. Manage Your Time Wisely: Plan and allocate your time thoughtfully to balance responsibilities, rest and the Daily 5-Star PIS Goal. Effective time management reduces stress and enhances productivity.

28. Practice Psychological Flexibility: Adapt to changing circumstances with an open mind. For example, if your plans fall through, pivot to a new activity rather than getting stuck in frustration.

29. Practice Negative Visualization: Imagine potential challenges or losses to mentally prepare yourself. This practice helps build resilience by reducing the shock and impact when difficulties arise.

30. Embrace Recovery During Loss: View your recovery as a time of learning where healing and grieving are intertwined. Allow yourself to experience joy and positivity, even as you navigate the pain.

31. Become a Psychonaut: Cultivate the habit of self-exploration to uncover your inner values and pursuits, those things that truly fulfil you. This deep self-awareness guides your path to genuine satisfaction.

32. Strive to Belong, Not to Fit In: Focus on being your authentic self rather than conforming to others' expectations. True belonging comes from embracing who you are, not moulding yourself to fit in.

33. Mental Restructuring: Challenge and reframe negative or unhelpful thoughts. By shifting your perspective, you can reduce stress and build a more positive, resilient mindset.

34. Refrain from Judging Your Thoughts, Yourself, and Others: Practice non-judgment by observing thoughts and actions without criticism. This approach fosters inner peace and improves your relationships.

35. Become More Accepting: Cultivate wisdom to distinguish between what you can control and what you cannot. Focus on your attitudes, behaviours, and mindset, letting go of what's beyond your reach.

36. Accept Others by Recognising Your Own Shortcomings: Build empathy and acceptance by acknowledging your own imperfections and limitations. This awareness fosters compassion and understanding toward others.

37. Self-Esteem: Be assertive and view your limitations as abilities you can improve, not as unchangeable traits. Embrace growth and work towards becoming the best version of yourself.

38. Self-Control: Regulate your emotions, thoughts, and behaviours in the face of temptations or impulses. Strengthening self-control leads to better decision-making and long-term wellbeing.

39. Self-Efficacy: Believe in your ability to succeed in specific situations. Cultivating self-efficacy empowers you to take on challenges with confidence and resilience.

40. Behavioural Activation: Combat low mood by engaging in positive, goal-directed activities. Taking action, even when you don't feel like it, can lift your spirits and build momentum.

41. Communicate Effectively: Express yourself clearly and actively listen to others. Effective communication strengthens relationships and reduces misunderstandings.

42. Right Speech: Speak with honesty, kindness, and intention. Choose words that build trust, foster understanding, and promote harmony in your relationships.

43. Kintsugi: Embrace the idea that repairing relationships makes them stronger and more beautiful. Like the art of Kintsugi, these "golden" repairs create unique bonds that add value and resilience to your connections.

44. Forgive: Let go of resentment and embrace forgiveness, not as a way to excuse others, but as a path to inner peace and emotional freedom.

45. Commit to Your Daily 5-Star PIS Goal: Dedicate yourself to earning your daily stars as a path to building resilience through strong psychological defences.

46. Be Creative: Personalise your Daily 5-Star PIS Goal to fit your needs, personal development goals, and life circumstances. Cherish the autonomy this flexibility offers you.

47. Recognise the Bigger Picture: Understand that each star you earn contributes to a larger constellation of wellness. By seeing the purpose behind every small step, you find meaning and fulfilment in your daily actions.

48. Don't Be Afraid to Start Again: Embrace the opportunity to reset and begin anew whenever necessary. Every fresh start is a chance to grow, learn, and strengthen your resilience.

49. Adapt and Readapt: As you journey toward a resilient mind, stay flexible and open to exploring new ways of earning your stars. Continuously adjust your approach to keep building your constellation with creativity and purpose.

50. Shine On: Live a life of self-reflection and commitment to self-development. As you build your constellation, let your brightness illuminate the path for others, spreading light and positivity.

Congratulations on completing this insightful journey toward a stronger PIS and, by extension, a resilient mind! Your commitment to understanding and nurturing your Psychological Immune System reflects a deep dedication to personal growth. As you continue to earn your stars each day, remember that every small action adds a bit more light to your inner constellation.

May this constellation guide you through life's challenges with strength and grace, illuminating your journey to resilience and fulfilment.

★ ★ ★ ★ ★

Continue Your Journey of Growth & Resilience

A star for everyday of the month :
30 More simple steps to build a resilient mind and shine brighter.

★

Scan the QR code below to access your free guide and discover additional stars to activate your PIS.

Enjoyed the Book?

Your feedback is invaluable!
If this book resonated with you, I'd love to hear your thoughts.
Sharing your experience helps others on their journey of growth & resilience.
Thank you for being part of this journey!

Suggested Reading

Introduction

Atkinson, P. A., Martin, C. R., & Rankin, J. (2009). Resilience revisited. *Journal of Psychiatric and Mental Health Nursing, 16*(2), 137–145. https://doi.org/10.1111/j.1365-2850.2008.01341.x

This paper revisits the concept of resilience, exploring its relevance and application in psychiatric and mental health nursing. The authors discuss the factors that contribute to resilience and its significance in promoting mental wellbeing.

Part 1
Basics of the
Psychological Immune System

Bao, S., Qiao, M., Lu, Y., & Jiang, Y. (2022). Neuroimaging mechanism of cognitive behavioural therapy in pain management. *Pain Research & Management, 2022*, 6266619. https://doi.org/10.1155/2022/6266619

This article explores the neuroimaging evidence behind the effectiveness of cognitive behavioural therapy (CBT) in managing pain. The study provides insights into how CBT influences brain activity, offering a deeper understanding of its mechanisms and supporting its use in pain management strategies.

Cuijpers, P., Harrer, M., Miguel, C., Ciharova, M., & Karyotaki, E. (2023). Five decades of research on psychological treatments of depression: A historical and meta-analytic overview. *American Psychologist*. Advance online publication. https://doi.org/10.1037/amp0001250

This meta-analytic review provides a comprehensive overview of research on psychological treatments for depression over the past 50 years. It highlights key developments, trends, and effectiveness of various therapeutic approaches, making it a valuable resource for understanding the evolution of mental health treatment.

Crum, A. J., Akinola, M., Martin, A., & Fath, S. (2017). The role of stress mindset in shaping cognitive, emotional, and physiological responses to challenging and threatening stress. *Anxiety, Stress, & Coping, 30*(4), 379–395. https://doi.org/10.1080/10615806.2016.1275585

This study explores how different mindsets about stress (seeing it as enhancing vs. debilitating) affect cognitive, emotional, and physiological responses to stress. The findings suggest that adopting a "stress-is-enhancing" mindset can lead to better coping and improved outcomes in stressful situations.

Crum, A. J., & Langer, E. J. (2007). Mind-set matters: Exercise and the placebo effect. *Psychological Science, 18*(2), 165–171. https://doi.org/10.1111/j.1467-9280.2007.01867.x

This study investigates how the mindset about exercise influences physiological outcomes. Hotel room attendants who were informed that their work was good exercise showed improvements in health indicators like weight and blood pressure, demonstrating that perception alone can affect physical health.

Eisendrath, S. J., Gillung, E., Delucchi, K. L., Segal, Z. V., Nelson, J. C., McInnes, L. A., Mathalon, D. H., & Feldman, M. D.

(2016). A randomized controlled trial of mindfulness-based cognitive therapy for treatment-resistant depression. *Psychotherapy and Psychosomatics, 85*(2), 99–110. https://doi.org/10.1159/000442260

This randomised controlled trial examines the effectiveness of mindfulness-based cognitive therapy (MBCT) for individuals with treatment-resistant depression. The study highlights the potential benefits of MBCT as an alternative treatment option for those who have not responded to traditional therapies.

Flor-García, M., Terreros-Roncal, J., Moreno-Jiménez, E. P., Ávila, J., Rábano, A., & Llorens-Martín, M. (2020). Unravelling human adult hippocampal neurogenesis. *Nature Protocols, 15*(2), 668–693. https://doi.org/10.1038/s41596-019-0267-y

This article provides a detailed protocol for studying neurogenesis in the human adult hippocampus. By offering methodological insights, the study contributes to a better understanding of the brain's capacity for generating new neurons, which has implications for memory, learning, and neurodegenerative diseases.

Freud, S. (1928). *Humour.* In J. Strachey (Ed. & Trans.), *The Standard Edition of the Complete Psychological Works of Sigmund Freud* (Vol. 21, pp. 159-166). Hogarth Press. (Original work published 1927)

Freud observed that humour often involves a surprising shift in perspective, enabling individuals to gain mastery over difficult situations by making light of them. This psychological insight underscores humour's therapeutic potential.

Goldin, P. R., Thurston, M., Allende, S., Moodie, C., Dixon, M. L., Heimberg, R. G., & Gross, J. J. (2021). Evaluation of cognitive behavioural therapy vs mindfulness meditation in brain changes during reappraisal and acceptance among patients with social anxiety disorder: A randomized clinical trial. *JAMA Psychiatry, 78*(10), 1134–1142. https://doi.org/10.1001/jamapsychiatry.2021.1862

This randomised clinical trial compares the effects of cognitive behavioural therapy (CBT) and mindfulness meditation on brain activity during emotional reappraisal and acceptance in patients with social anxiety disorder. The study provides valuable insights into the neural mechanisms underlying these two therapeutic approaches.

Harnett, N. G., Goodman, A. M., & Knight, D. C. (2020). PTSD-related neuroimaging abnormalities in brain function, structure, and biochemistry. *Experimental Neurology, 330,* 113331. https://doi.org/10.1016/j.expneurol.2020.113331

This article reviews neuroimaging studies related to posttraumatic stress disorder (PTSD), focusing on abnormalities in brain function, structure, and biochemistry. The findings provide a comprehensive understanding of the neural mechanisms underlying PTSD, contributing to the development of targeted treatments.

Kalinin, V., & Edguer, N. (2023). The effects of self-control and self-awareness on social media usage, self-esteem, and affect. *Eureka, 8*(1). https://doi.org/10.29173/eureka28781

This study investigates the relationship between self-control, self-awareness, and their impact on social media usage, self-esteem, and emotional wellbeing. The findings highlight how these psychological traits can influence online behaviour and mental health, offering insights for managing digital life more effectively.

Kant, I. (2007). *Critique of judgment* (N. Walker, Trans.). Oxford University Press. (Original work published 1790)

Kant's *Critique of Judgment* includes discussions on the aesthetic value of humour, highlighting its role in providing mental relief. This work underscores how influential thinkers have long recognised humour's importance for mental wellbeing.

Kubzansky, L. D., Kim, E. S., Boehm, J. K., Davidson, R. J., Huffman, J. C., Loucks, E. B., Lyubomirsky, S., Picard, R. W.,

Schueller, S. M., Trudel-Fitzgerald, C., VanderWeele, T. J., Warran, K., Yeager, D. S., Yeh, C. S., & Moskowitz, J. T. (2023). Interventions to modify psychological wellbeing: Progress, promises, and an agenda for future research. *Nature*. https://doi.org/10.1007/s42761-022-00167-w

This article reviews the current progress and challenges in developing interventions aimed at enhancing psychological wellbeing. It discusses various approaches and their potential impact on mental health, offering a roadmap for future research in this growing field.

Krys, K., Kostoula, O., van Tilburg, W. A. P., Mosca, O., Lee, J. H., Maricchiolo, F., Kosiarczyk, A., Kocimska-Bortnowska, A., Torres, C., Hitokoto, H., Liew, K., Bond, M. H., Lun, V. M.-C., Vignoles, V. L., Zelenski, J. M., Haas, B. W., Park, J., Vauclair, C.-M., Kwiatkowska, A., Steinhoff, A., Eisner, M., Hepp, U., Ribeaud, D., Murray, A. L., & Shanahan, L. (2024). Happiness maximization is a WEIRD way of living. *Perspectives on Psychological Science*. https://doi.org/10.1177/17456916231208367

This article explores the cultural underpinnings of happiness maximisation, arguing that the emphasis on pursuing happiness is predominantly a Western, Educated, Industrialized, Rich, and Democratic (WEIRD) phenomenon. It provides a cross-cultural perspective on wellbeing, challenging common assumptions about the universal pursuit of happiness.

Noftle, E. E., & Shaver, P. R. (2006). Attachment dimensions and the big five personality traits: Associations and comparative ability to predict relationship quality. *Journal of Research in Personality, 40*(2), 179–208. https://doi.org/10.1016/j.jrp.2004.11.003

This study explores the associations between attachment dimensions and the Big Five personality traits, examining their relative ability to predict relationship quality. The research provides valuable insights into how personality and attachment styles interact to influence interpersonal relationships.

Polusny, M. A., Erbes, C. R., Thuras, P., Moran, A., Lamberty, G. J., Collins, R. C., Rodman, J. L., & Lim, K. O. (2015). Mindfulness-based stress reduction for posttraumatic stress disorder among veterans: A randomized clinical trial. *JAMA, 314*(5), 456–465. https://doi.org/10.1001/jama.2015.8361

This study examines the effectiveness of Mindfulness-Based Stress Reduction (MBSR) in treating posttraumatic stress disorder (PTSD) among veterans. The randomised clinical trial provides evidence supporting the use of mindfulness practices to reduce PTSD symptoms, making it a significant contribution to mental health treatment literature.

Rachman, S. J. (2016). Invited essay: Cognitive influences on the psychological immune system. *Journal of Behavior Therapy and Experimental Psychiatry, 53*, 2-8. https://doi.org/10.1016/j.jbtep.2016.03.015

This essay explores how cognitive processes contribute to the psychological immune system, focusing on how thoughts and beliefs influence emotional resilience.

Seppälä, E. M., Bradley, C., Moeller, J., Harouni, L., Nandamudi, D., & Brackett, M. A. (2020). Promoting mental health and psychological thriving in university students: A randomized controlled trial of three wellbeing interventions. *Frontiers in Psychiatry*. https://doi.org/10.3389/fpsyt.2020.00590

This study evaluates the effectiveness of three different wellbeing interventions aimed at improving mental health among university students. The randomised controlled trial highlights practical strategies for enhancing psychological thriving in young adults, making it a valuable resource for educational institutions.

Tjernberg, J., & Bökberg, C. (2020). Older persons' thoughts about death and dying and their experiences of care in end-of-life: A qualitative study. *BMC Nursing, 19*(1), 123. https://doi.org/10.1186/s12912-020-00514-x

This qualitative study explores the perspectives of older adults on death, dying, and their experiences with end-of-life care. The findings provide valuable insights into the emotional and psychological needs of elderly individuals in palliative care, highlighting areas for improving compassionate care practices.

Velasquez, L. (2014, January 17). How do you define yourself? [Video]. YouTube. https://www.youtube.com/watch?v=QzPbY9ufnQY

In this inspiring TEDx talk, Lizzie Velasquez shares her personal journey of overcoming adversity and redefining herself in the face of bullying. Her message emphasises the power of self-definition and resilience, making it a powerful resource for discussions on identity and mental wellbeing.

Young, E. S., Simpson, J. A., Griskevicius, V., Huelsnitz, C. O., & Fleck, C. (2017). Childhood attachment and adult personality: A life history perspective. *Self and Identity, 18*(1), 22–38. https://doi.org/10.1080/15298868.2017.1353540

This study examines how early childhood attachment influences adult personality traits from a life history perspective. The research provides insights into how early relational experiences shape long-term personality development, highlighting the lasting impact of childhood attachment on adult behaviour.

Part 2
Factors that Influence the
Psychological Immune System

Aronofsky, D. (Director). (2022). *The Whale* [Film]. A24.
Hunter, S. D. (2012). *The Whale*. Theatre Communications Group.
The Whale originated as a play by Samuel D. Hunter in 2012, exploring themes of isolation, grief, and self-acceptance. The story

was later adapted into a film directed by Darren Aronofsky in 2022, bringing these powerful themes to a wider audience with a compelling cinematic interpretation.

Bal, P. M., & Veltkamp, M. (2013). How does fiction reading influence empathy? An experimental investigation on the role of emotional transportation. *PLOS ONE, 8*(1), e55341. https://doi.org/10.1371/journal.pone.0055341

This experimental study explores how reading fiction can enhance empathy by facilitating emotional transportation. The research highlights the psychological mechanisms that allow readers to connect with fictional characters, leading to increased empathy and understanding in real life.

Brown, A., & Liu, H. (2021). Interaction between intestinal serotonin and the gut microbiome. *International Journal of Anatomy and Applied Physiology, 7*(4), 192-196. https://doi.org/10.19070/2572-7451-2100036

This review article explores the relationship between intestinal serotonin production and the gut microbiome, highlighting how gut bacteria influence serotonin synthesis and how serotonin, in turn, affects gut microbial composition. The findings underscore the complex interaction between the gut and the brain and its implications for health.

Dai, S., Wellens, J., Yang, N., Li, D., Wang, J., Wang, L., Yuan, S., He, Y., Song, P., Munger, R., Kent, M. P., MacFarlane, A. J., Mullie, P., Duthie, S., Little, J., Theodoratou, E., & Li, X. (2024). Ultra-processed foods and human health: An umbrella review and updated meta-analyses of observational evidence. *Clinical Nutrition (Edinburgh, Scotland), 43*(6), 1386–1394. https://doi.org/10.1016/j.clnu.2024.04.016

This umbrella review and meta-analysis investigate the impact of ultra-processed foods on human health. The findings consolidate observational evidence linking ultra-processed food consumption with various adverse health outcomes, offering a comprehensive overview of current research.

Eike, R. J., Burton, M., Hustvedt, G., & Cho, S. (2021). The "joy of letting go": Decluttering and apparel. *Fashion Practice, 14*(2), 225–241. https://doi.org/10.1080/17569370.2021.1987654

This study explores the psychological and emotional aspects of decluttering apparel, highlighting the concept of the "joy of letting go." The research examines how reducing possessions, particularly clothing, can contribute to mental wellbeing and a sense of personal empowerment.

Grønli, J., Byrkjedal, I. K., Bjorvatn, B., Nødtvedt, Ø., Hamre, B., & Pallesen, S. (2016). Reading from an iPad or from a book in bed: The impact on human sleep. A randomized controlled crossover trial. *Sleep Medicine, 21*, 86–92. https://doi.org/10.1016/j.sleep.2016.02.006

This randomised controlled crossover trial investigates the effects of reading from an iPad versus a book before bed on sleep quality. The study provides evidence that reading from an electronic device can negatively affect sleep, offering important insights for sleep hygiene practices.

Horn, J., Mayer, D. E., Chen, S., & Mayer, E. A. (2022). Role of diet and its effects on the gut microbiome in the pathophysiology of mental disorders. *Translational Psychiatry, 12*(1), 164. https://doi.org/10.1038/s41398-022-01922-0

This study explores the relationship between diet, the gut microbiome, and the development of mental disorders. The findings highlight how dietary interventions could potentially influence mental health by altering gut microbiota, offering new insights into the pathophysiology of mental disorders.

Johnson, D. (2023). A good night's sleep: Three strategies to rest, relax and restore energy. *Journal of Interprofessional Education &*

Practice, 30, Article 100612.
https://doi.org/10.1016/j.xjep.2023.100612

This article provides practical strategies for improving sleep quality, focusing on techniques to rest, relax, and restore energy. The research offers evidence-based recommendations that can be integrated into everyday practice to enhance overall wellbeing through better sleep.

Kross, E., Verduyn, P., Demiralp, E., Park, J., Lee, D. S., Lin, N., & Ybarra, O. (2013). Facebook use predicts declines in subjective wellbeing in young adults. *Cyberpsychology, Behavior, and Social Networking, 16*(9), 587-592.
https://doi.org/10.1089/cyber.2012.0301

This study examines the relationship between Facebook use and subjective wellbeing among young adults. The findings suggest that increased Facebook usage is associated with declines in overall wellbeing, highlighting potential negative impacts of social media on mental health.

Rogers, C. J., & Hart, R. (2021). Home and the extended-self: Exploring associations between clutter and wellbeing. *Journal of Environmental Psychology, 73,* Article 101553.
https://doi.org/10.1016/j.jenvp.2021.101553

This study explores the relationship between home environment, particularly clutter, and psychological wellbeing. The research highlights how physical surroundings can impact mental health, offering insights into the role of decluttering in improving overall life satisfaction.

Tang, A., Crawford, H., Morales, S., Degnan, K., Pine, D., & Fox, N. (2020). Infant behavioural inhibition predicts personality and social outcomes three decades later. *Proceedings of the National Academy of Sciences, 117,* 201917376.
https://doi.org/10.1073/pnas.1917376117

This longitudinal study investigates the long-term effects of infant behavioural inhibition on personality and social outcomes in adulthood. The findings suggest that early behavioural tendencies can have significant implications for an individual's social and emotional development over the course of their life.

UNC Global Food Research Program. (2021, May). *Ultra-processed foods: A global threat to public health* [Fact sheet]. University of North Carolina at Chapel Hill. https://globalfoodresearchprogram.web.unc.edu/...

This fact sheet from the UNC Global Food Research Program highlights the growing concern over ultra-processed foods (UPFs) and their impact on public health. It discusses the prevalence of UPFs, their health risks, and the need for policy interventions to curb their consumption globally.

Verreault, M. D., Granger, É., Neveu, X., Delage, J. P., Bastien, C. H., & Vallières, A. (2024). The effectiveness of stimulus control in cognitive behavioural therapy for insomnia in adults: A systematic review and network meta-analysis. *Journal of Sleep Research, 33*(3), e14008. https://doi.org/10.1111/jsr.14008

This systematic review and network meta-analysis evaluates the effectiveness of stimulus control as part of cognitive behavioural therapy for insomnia (CBT-I) in adults. The findings provide evidence-based recommendations for optimising CBT-I protocols to improve sleep outcomes.

Walsh, L. C., Armenta, C. N., Itzchakov, G., Fritz, M. M., & Lyubomirsky, S. (2022). More than merely positive: The immediate affective and motivational consequences of gratitude. *Sustainability, 14*(14), 8679. https://doi.org/10.3390/su14148679

This study examines the immediate emotional and motivational effects of practicing gratitude. The findings suggest that gratitude is more than just a positive emotion; it also has significant motivational benefits, promoting pro-social behaviour and wellbeing.

You, T., Ogawa, E. F., Thapa, S., Cai, Y., Yeh, G. Y., Wayne, P. M., Shi, L., & Leveille, S. G. (2020). Effects of Tai Chi on beta-endorphin and inflammatory markers in older adults with chronic pain: An exploratory study. *Aging Clinical and Experimental Research, 32*(7), 1389–1392. https://doi.org/10.1007/s40520-019-01316-1

This exploratory study examines the effects of Tai Chi on beta-endorphin levels and inflammatory markers in older adults with chronic pain. The findings suggest that Tai Chi may have beneficial effects on pain management and inflammation, offering a potential alternative approach for improving the quality of life in this population.

Part 3
Factors that impact the Psychological Immune System

All-Party Parliamentary Group on Commercial Sexual Exploitation. (n.d.). *Inquiry into online pornography and its impact on society.* https://www.appg-cse.uk/inquiry/

This inquiry report by the All-Party Parliamentary Group on Commercial Sexual Exploitation examines the impact of online pornography on society, focusing on its effects on individuals and communities. It provides recommendations for policy changes and interventions to address the challenges posed by online pornography.

Bonanno, G. A., & Kaltman, S. (2001). The varieties of grief experience. *Clinical Psychology Review, 21*(5), 705–734. https://doi.org/10.1016/S0272-7358(00)00062-3

This review examines the diverse ways in which individuals experience grief, emphasising that there is no single "normal" path through bereavement. The study challenges traditional grief models and highlights the resilience many people display following loss.

Buser, T., & Peter, N. (2012). Focusing the mind: The Pomodoro Technique and its application. *Journal of Personal Productivity, 28*(4), 235-242.

This article explores the Pomodoro Technique, a time management method that involves working in focused intervals, and its effectiveness in enhancing productivity. The study discusses how breaking tasks into timed segments can improve concentration and reduce procrastination.

Brewster, Z. W. (2023, September 18). How much porn do Americans really watch? *Psychology Today.* https://www.psychologytoday.com/us/blog/everyone-on-top/202309/how-much-porn-do-americans-really-watch

This article discusses the prevalence of pornography consumption in the United States, examining data and trends to provide a clearer understanding of how much porn Americans actually watch. The piece also explores the social and psychological implications of these findings.

Chen, Z., Liu, P., Zhang, C., Yu, Z., & Feng, T. (2021). Neural markers of procrastination in white matter microstructures and networks. *Psychophysiology, 58*(e13782). https://doi.org/10.1111/psyp.13782

This study explores the neural correlates of procrastination by examining white matter microstructures and networks in the brain. The research identifies specific neural markers associated with procrastination, providing insights into the biological basis of this behaviour.

Chaffey, D. (2023, January 26). *New global social media research summary 2023.* Smart Insights. https://www.smartinsights.com/social-media-marketing/social-media-strategy/new-global-social-media-research/

This report provides an overview of global social media usage, including the average daily time spent on social platforms. The data highlights trends in social media growth and user behaviour, offering valuable insights for understanding the impact of social media on society.

Faul, L., & LaBar, K. S. (2023). Mood-congruent memory revisited. *Psychological Review, 130*(6), 1421-1456. https://doi.org/10.1037/rev0000394

This article revisits the concept of mood-congruent memory, exploring how current emotional states influence the recall of past experiences. The research provides a comprehensive review of the mechanisms underlying this phenomenon and its implications for understanding memory processes in both clinical and everyday contexts.

Hailikari, T., Katajavuori, N., & Asikainen, H. (2021). Understanding procrastination: A case of a study skills course. *Social Psychology of Education: An International Journal, 24*(2), 589–606. https://doi.org/10.1007/s11218-021-09621-2

This study investigates the underlying factors contributing to procrastination among students enrolled in a study skills course. The findings provide insights into how educational interventions can address procrastination by enhancing time management and motivation.

Häfner, A., Stock, A., & Oberst, V. (2014). Decreasing students' stress through time management training: An intervention study. *European Journal of Psychology of Education, 29*(4), 603-620. https://doi.org/10.1007/s10212-013-0204-4

This intervention study investigates the impact of time management training on reducing stress levels among students. The findings suggest that effective time management strategies can significantly lower stress, improving both academic performance and overall wellbeing.

Hefner, V. (2018). Does love conquer all? An experiment testing the association between types of romantic comedy content and reports of romantic beliefs and life satisfaction. *Psychology of Popular Media Culture, 8*(1), 10-20. https://doi.org/10.1037/ppm0000201

This study examines how different types of romantic comedy content influence viewers' romantic beliefs and overall life satisfaction. The findings highlight the impact of media on shaping perceptions of love and relationships, raising questions about the messages conveyed by popular culture.

Hefner, V., & Wilson, B. J. (2013). From love at first sight to soul mate: The influence of romantic ideals in popular films on young people's beliefs about relationships. *Communication Monographs, 80*(2), 150–175. https://doi.org/10.1080/03637751.2013.776697

This study examines how romantic ideals portrayed in popular films influence young people's beliefs about love and relationships. The research highlights the impact of media on shaping unrealistic expectations, such as the concept of "love at first sight" and finding a "soul mate."

Hidaka, B. H. (2012). Depression as a disease of modernity: Explanations for increasing prevalence. *Journal of Affective Disorders, 140*(3), 205-214. https://doi.org/10.1016/j.jad.2011.12.036

This article explores the concept of depression as a disease linked to modern lifestyles, examining various factors that contribute to its increasing prevalence. The study offers insights into how changes in environment, social structures, and behaviours may be driving the global rise in depression rates.

Hoppe, J. M., Holmes, E. A., & Agren, T. (2022). Imaginal extinction and the vividness of mental imagery: Exploring the reduction of fear within the mind's eye. *Behavioural Brain Research, 418,* 113632. https://doi.org/10.1016/j.bbr.2021.113632

This study investigates the role of imaginal extinction and the vividness of mental imagery in reducing fear responses. The findings suggest that the mental rehearsal of feared situations can effectively diminish fear, highlighting the therapeutic potential of mental imagery techniques.

Irvine, W. B. (2009). *A guide to the good life: The ancient art of Stoic joy.* Oxford University Press.

This book explores the principles of Stoic philosophy and how they can be applied to modern life to achieve lasting happiness and tranquillity. Irvine offers practical advice on embracing Stoicism as a guide to living a fulfilling and meaningful life.

Lazarevich, I., Irigoyen Camacho, M., Alva, M. C., & Zepeda, M. (2016). Relationship among obesity, depression, and emotional eating in young adults. *Appetite, 107*, 639-645. https://doi.org/10.1016/j.appet.2016.09.011

This study explores the interconnections between obesity, depression, and emotional eating in young adults. The findings suggest that emotional eating may mediate the relationship between obesity and depression, highlighting the importance of addressing psychological factors in weight management strategies.

Lakein, A. (1973). *How to get control of your time and your life.* P.H. Wyden.

This book popularised the concept of prioritising tasks based on urgency and importance, a principle that is central to the Eisenhower Matrix. Lakein's approach to time management has influenced countless productivity strategies and remains a foundational resource in the field.

Naslund, J. A., Bondre, A., Torous, J., & Aschbrenner, K. A. (2020). Social media and mental health: Benefits, risks, and opportunities for research and practice. *Journal of Technology in Behavioural Science, 5*(3), 245–257. https://doi.org/10.1007/s41347-020-00134-x

This article explores the complex relationship between social media use and mental health, discussing both the potential benefits and risks. The authors highlight opportunities for future research and practice in understanding how social media can be used to support mental wellbeing while mitigating its negative effects.

O'Connor, M. F., & Seeley, S. H. (2022). Grieving as a form of learning: Insights from neuroscience applied to grief and loss. *Current Opinion in Psychology, 43,* 317–322. https://doi.org/10.1016/j.copsyc.2021.08.019

This article discusses the concept of grieving as a learning process, drawing on insights from neuroscience. The authors explore how the brain adapts to loss, providing a deeper understanding of the cognitive and emotional mechanisms involved in grief.

Richardson, M., Passmore, H.-A., Lumber, R., Thomas, R., & Hunt, A. (2021). Moments, not minutes: The nature-wellbeing relationship. *International Journal of Wellbeing, 11*(1), 8-33. https://doi.org/10.5502/ijw.v11i1.1267

This study examines the relationship between nature exposure and wellbeing, emphasising that brief, meaningful moments in nature can have significant positive effects. The research suggests that quality, rather than quantity, of time spent in nature is key to enhancing mental health.

Stroebe, M., Schut, H., & Boerner, K. (2017). Cautioning health-care professionals: Bereaved persons are misguided through the stages of grief. *Omega, 74*(4), 455–473. https://doi.org/10.1177/0030222817691870

This article critiques the widespread use of the "stages of grief" model in bereavement care, arguing that it can mislead both professionals and the bereaved. The authors caution health-care professionals about the limitations of this model and emphasize the need for a more nuanced and individualized approach to supporting those who are grieving.

Webroot. (n.d.). *Internet pornography by the numbers: A significant threat to society.* https://www.webroot.com/us/en/resources/tips-articles/internet-pornography-by-the-numbers

This article provides statistics on internet pornography usage, highlighting its widespread prevalence and potential impact on individuals and society. The piece discusses the risks associated with pornography consumption and the challenges in addressing its influence on public health and behaviour.

World Health Organization. (2023, June 7). *Depression.* https://www.who.int/news-room/fact-sheets/detail/depression

This fact sheet from the World Health Organization provides an overview of depression, including its prevalence, symptoms, risk factors, and available treatments. It offers valuable insights into the global impact of depression and highlights the importance of early intervention and support.

Wortman, C. B., & Silver, R. C. (1989). The myths of coping with loss. *Journal of Consulting and Clinical Psychology, 57*(3), 349–357. https://doi.org/10.1037//0022-006x.57.3.349

This article challenges common misconceptions about the process of coping with loss, emphasizing that traditional beliefs about grief may not apply universally. The authors explore alternative ways of understanding and supporting individuals who are grieving, providing insights that counter the "stages of grief" model.

Part 4 - Strengthening Your Psychological Immune System

Part 4
Strengthening the
Psychological Immune System

Aurelius, M. (2006). *Meditations* (G. Hays, Trans.). Modern Library. (Original work published ca. 180)

This classic work of Stoic philosophy, written by Roman Emperor Marcus Aurelius, offers insights on self-discipline, resilience, and the nature of life. *Meditations* remains a timeless guide to personal growth and reflection.

Dweck, C. S. (2006). *Mindset: The new psychology of success.* Random House.

Carol Dweck's book introduces the concept of the growth mindset, which emphasises the belief that abilities and intelligence can be developed through dedication and hard work. This mindset is essential for achieving success in various aspects of life, from education to personal development.

Eğeci, İ. S., & Gençöz, T. (2006). Factors associated with relationship satisfaction: Importance of communication skills. *Contemporary Family Therapy: An International Journal, 28*(3), 383–391. https://doi.org/10.1007/s10591-006-9010-2

This study explores the role of communication skills in relationship satisfaction, highlighting how effective communication contributes to healthier and more fulfilling partnerships. The findings emphasize the importance of improving communication to enhance relationship quality.

Inzlicht, M., Schmeichel, B. J., & Macrae, C. N. (2014). Why self-control seems (but may not be) limited. *Trends in Cognitive Sciences, 18*(3), 127–133. https://doi.org/10.1016/j.tics.2013.12.009

This article explores the perception of self-control as a limited resource, challenging the traditional view and offering alternative explanations for why self-control may seem to deplete over time. The authors discuss new perspectives that suggest self-control might be more resilient than previously thought.

Lindsay, E. K., & Creswell, J. D. (2019). Mindfulness, acceptance, and emotion regulation: Perspectives from Monitor and

Acceptance Theory (MAT). *Current Opinion in Psychology, 28,* 120–125. https://doi.org/10.1016/j.copsyc.2018.12.004

This article presents Monitor and Acceptance Theory (MAT), which offers a framework for understanding how mindfulness and acceptance contribute to effective emotion regulation. The authors discuss how these processes can reduce stress and improve mental health outcomes.

Muraven, M. (2010). Building self-control strength: Practicing self-control leads to improved self-control performance. *Journal of Experimental Social Psychology, 46*(2), 465–468. https://doi.org/10.1016/j.jesp.2009.12.011

This study investigates the concept of self-control as a "muscle" that can be strengthened through practice. The findings suggest that regularly practicing self-control can enhance one's ability to manage impulses and maintain self-discipline over time.

Orth, U., & Robins, R. W. (2022). Is high self-esteem beneficial? Revisiting a classic question. *American Psychologist, 77*(1), 5–17. https://doi.org/10.1037/amp0000922

This article revisits the long-standing question of whether high self-esteem is beneficial, examining the positive and negative outcomes associated with self-esteem. The authors provide a comprehensive analysis of recent research, offering nuanced insights into the role of self-esteem in mental health and wellbeing.

Sousa, G., Lima-Araújo, G., de Araujo, D., & Sousa, M. (2022). Non-judgement prevents positive correlation between observing and state anxiety in healthy non-meditators. *Journal of Psychology and Behavioural Science, 8*(1), 121. https://doi.org/10.36648/2471-9854.8.1.121

This study examines how the practice of non-judgment affects the relationship between observational awareness and state anxiety in individuals who do not meditate. The findings suggest that adopting a non-judgmental attitude can mitigate the anxiety typically associated with heightened awareness.

Stein, A. T., Carl, E., Cuijpers, P., Karyotaki, E., & Smits, J. A. J. (2021). Looking beyond depression: A meta-analysis of the effect of behavioural activation on depression, anxiety, and activation. *Psychological Medicine, 51*(9), 1491–1504. https://doi.org/10.1017/S0033291720000239

This meta-analysis examines the effectiveness of behavioural activation therapy not only for treating depression but also for reducing anxiety and enhancing overall activation. The findings support the broader applicability of behavioural activation as a therapeutic intervention across different mental health conditions.

Tangney, J. P., Baumeister, R. F., & Boone, A. L. (2004). High self-control predicts good adjustment, less pathology, better grades, and interpersonal success. *Journal of Personality, 72*(2), 271–324. https://doi.org/10.1111/j.0022-3506.2004.00263.x

This study demonstrates that individuals with high self-control tend to experience better overall life outcomes, including psychological adjustment, academic performance, and interpersonal relationships. The findings highlight the broad benefits of self-control across various domains of life.

Wade, N. G., Hoyt, W. T., Kidwell, J. E. M., & Worthington, E. L., Jr. (2013). Efficacy of psychotherapeutic interventions to promote forgiveness: A meta-analysis. *Journal of Consulting and Clinical Psychology*. Advance online publication. https://doi.org/10.1037/a0035268

This meta-analysis evaluates the effectiveness of various psychotherapeutic interventions aimed at promoting forgiveness. The study highlights the positive impact of these interventions on emotional wellbeing and relationship satisfaction, providing evidence for their use in clinical settings.

Williams, J., & Lynn, S. J. (2010). Acceptance: An historical and conceptual review. *Imagination, Cognition and Personality, 30*(1), 5-56. https://doi.org/10.2190/IC.30.1.c

This review provides a historical and conceptual overview of the concept of acceptance, tracing its development across various psychological theories and practices. The authors explore how acceptance has been integrated into therapeutic approaches and its significance in promoting mental health.

Part 5
Fine Tuning the
Psychological Immune System

Byun, H. S., Hwang, H., & Kim, G. D. (2020). Crying therapy intervention for breast cancer survivors: Development and effects. *International Journal of Environmental Research and Public Health, 17(13)*, 4911. https://doi.org/10.3390/ijerph17134911

This study examines the development and effects of crying therapy as an intervention for breast cancer survivors, focusing on its impact on emotional wellbeing.

Chakhssi, F., Kraiss, J. T., Sommers-Spijkerman, M., & Bohlmeijer, E. T. (2018). The effect of positive psychology interventions on wellbeing and distress in clinical samples with psychiatric or somatic disorders: A systematic review and meta-analysis. *BMC Psychiatry, 18,* 211. https://doi.org/10.1186/s12888-018-1739-2

This systematic review and meta-analysis examines the impact of positive psychology interventions on wellbeing and distress in clinical populations. The findings suggest that these interventions can effectively enhance wellbeing and reduce distress in individuals with psychiatric or somatic disorders.

Deci, E. L. (1971). Effects of externally mediated rewards on intrinsic motivation. *Journal of Personality and Social Psychology, 18*(1), 105–115. https://doi.org/10.1037/h0030644

This classic study by Edward Deci explores how external rewards can undermine intrinsic motivation. The findings have had a significant impact on understanding motivation, particularly in educational and organisational contexts.

Deci, E. L., & Ryan, R. M. (1985). *Intrinsic motivation and self-determination in human behaviour.* Plenum Press.

This book is a comprehensive source that introduces and discusses Self-Determination Theory, focusing on intrinsic motivation, autonomy, competence, and relatedness as key components of human motivation and behaviour.

Gollwitzer, P. M. (1999). Implementation intentions: Strong effects of simple plans. In P. M. Gollwitzer (Ed.), *Intention* (Chapter 21, pp. 493-503). American Psychologist.

This chapter discusses the concept of implementation intentions, which are strategic plans that link specific situations to goal-directed behaviours. The research presented shows how these simple plans can significantly enhance goal achievement by leveraging automatic processes.

Locke, E. A., & Latham, G. P. (1990). *A theory of goal setting and task performance.* Prentice Hall.

This book by Locke and Latham outlines the principles of Goal-Setting Theory, emphasising the importance of setting specific and challenging goals to improve task performance and motivation.

About the Author

★

Dom de Lima holds a BSc (Honours) in Psychology and Counselling , accredited by the British Psychological Society (BPS), and an MSc in the Psychology and Neuroscience of Mental Health from the Institute of Psychiatry, Psychology and Neuroscience at King's College London. She is dedicated to promoting emotional resilience and wellbeing across all ages, drawing from a strong foundation in psychology, neuroscience and mental health.

Printed in Dunstable, United Kingdom